Postwall German Cinema

Film Europa: German Cinema in an International Context
Series Editors: **Hans-Michael Bock** (CineGraph Hamburg);
Tim Bergfelder (University of Southampton); **Sabine Hake**
(University of Texas, Austin)

German cinema is normally seen as a distinct form, but this series emphasizes connections, influences, and exchanges of German cinema across national borders, as well as its links with other media and art forms. Individual titles present traditional historical research (archival work, industry studies) as well as new critical approaches in film and media studies (theories of the transnational), with a special emphasis on the continuities associated with popular traditions and local perspectives.

POSTWALL GERMAN CINEMA

History, Film History, and Cinephilia

Mattias Frey

berghahn
NEW YORK · OXFORD
www.berghahnbooks.com

Published in 2013 by

Berghahn Books

www.berghahnbooks.com

Library of Congress Cataloging-in-Publication Data

Frey, Mattias.
  Postwall German cinema: history, film history and cinephilia / Mattias
Frey. -- First edition.
      pages cm -- (Film Europa: German cinema in an international
context)
  Includes filmography.
  Includes bibliographical references and index.
  ISBN 978-0-85745-947-3 (hardback: alk. paper) -- ISBN 978-0-85745-948-0
(institutional ebook)
 1. Germany--in motion pictures. 2. Germans in motion pictures. 3.
History in motion pictures. 4. Historical films--Germany--History and
criticism. I. Title.
  PN1995.9.G45F89 2013
  791.43'658--dc23
                          2013003081

British Library Cataloguing in Publication Data
A catalogue record for this book is available from the British Library

ISBN: 978-0-85745-947-3 (hardback)
ISBN: 978-0-85745-948-0 (institutional ebook)

For my parents

CONTENTS

LIST OF ILLUSTRATIONS

ACKNOWLEDGEMENTS

I thank series editors Tim Bergfelder, Hans-Michael Bock, and Sabine Hake as well as the anonymous reviewers for their faith in this project; it has been a real pleasure to work with Mark Stanton and the Berghahn staff. The research behind the book would not have come to fruition were it not for the generous support of the Krupp Foundation, the Frederick Sheldon Traveling Fellowship, and the Graduate Society. Käte Caspar, Benjamin Forkner, Ulrich Kriest, Klaus Lemke, and Christopher Roth graciously furnished images, interviews, tips, or rare films. David Bathrick, Peter Keough, Michelle Carey, Giuliana Bruno, Svetlana Boym, and David Rodowick provided key input, advice, or assignments that benefitted the manuscript. I owe the generous, erudite Eric Rentschler my greatest professional debt.

My colleagues at Harvard University and the University of Kent were brilliant throughout the writing process and I am grateful for a number of loyal, true friends: Ben, Björn and Rosanna, Neil, Rita, Stephen and Emma, Steve, Swen and Júlia, Taylor, Tomas, and others.

Most of all, I thank my family, without whom nothing would have been possible: my brother and sisters (who kept me laughing throughout), grandmother, aunts and uncles, and many cousins. Indeed, I dedicate this book to my parents. To my mother, who has always been my most vocal supporter and advocate, through thick and thin. And to my father, my greatest role model in all things professional and personal. He dedicated his working life to the transmission and understanding of German culture in foreign lands and I like to think that—in a small way—this book continues that effort.

Unless otherwise noted, all translations in this book are my own. A substantially different version of chapter 5 appeared as "No(ir) Place to Go: Spatial Anxiety and Sartorial Intertextuality in *Die Unberührbare*," *Cinema Journal* 45(4) (2006): 64-80.

INTRODUCTION

One of the most remarkable features of contemporary German film is the prominence of the historical genre. In 2003, eight of the fifteen highest-grossing German films on the home market were historical films. In international distribution, the situation is even clearer. With the exception of a few romantic comedies (e.g., *Bella Martha* [*Mostly Martha*, 2001]) and auteur-inflected problem films (the "Berlin School"; *Gegen die Wand* [*Head-On*, 2004]), the global presence of German cinema is associated almost exclusively with one genre. German historical films have dominated the Best Foreign Film category at the Academy Awards since the turn of the millennium. *Nirgendwo in Afrika* (*Nowhere in Africa*, 2001), *Das Leben der Anderen* (*The Lives of Others*, 2006), and Austrian co-production *Die Fälscher* (*The Counterfeiters*, 2007) won the Academy Award. In addition, *Der Untergang* (*Downfall*, 2004), *Sophie Scholl – die letzten Tage* (*Sophie Scholl – The Final Days*, 2005), *Der Baader Meinhof Komplex* (*The Baader Meinhof Complex*, 2008), and *Das weiße Band* (*The White Ribbon*, 2009) reached the five-film shortlist of nominees. In Germany, the genre's prestige productions count among the most popular domestic features of the past decade. Abroad, German historical films have become nearly synonymous with German cinema.[1]

In the last decade, German historical films have enjoyed attendance figures unknown in the heyday of the New German Cinema. Gone are the days when, at most, a few thousand cinephiles would watch Jean-Marie Straub and Danièle Huillet's latest historical provocation, whose merits would later be debated on select German arts pages and dissected by academics in Britain and the United States. For all that has been written about the New German Cinema's dramatic historiographical intervention in the 1970s, and for all the successes of Fassbinder, Herzog, Kluge, Schlöndorff, and Wenders at international film festivals and among cineastes, the question of their films' effectiveness in reaching popular audiences remains, at best, uncertain. One commentator reckons that, of the approximately three hundred productions that might be counted as New German Cinema, only six recouped their production costs in commercial release in domestic theaters.[2]

It is useful to compare the 1970s screenings, which were often poorly attended, to the situation today. Productions such as *Der Untergang*,

Good Bye, Lenin! (2003), *Das Wunder von Bern* (2003), *Die Päpstin* (2009), or *Der Baader Meinhof Komplex* each attracted millions of Germans to theaters, not to mention DVD sales and rentals.[3] Even the most accessible and celebrated incarnations of the New German Cinema rarely counted among the year's Top Fifty box-office list. Today, select German historical films successfully challenge the latest Hollywood blockbuster franchises. For instance, *Good Bye, Lenin!*'s opening-week box office surpassed even the contemporaneous *Harry Potter* and *Lord of the Rings* sequels; its third-place ranking in Germany for the year outpaced *Pirates of the Caribbean: The Curse of the Black Pearl* (2003) and *The Matrix Reloaded* (2003).[4]

The resonance of today's historical films goes well beyond fanzines and specialty cinephile publications such as *epd Film* and *film-dienst*. The government's Federal Agency for Civic Education writes pamphlets to use historical films as instruction in domestic schools: pupils learn about the unification by watching *Good Bye, Lenin!*; the biopic *Luther* (2003) accompanies lessons about the Protestant Reformation.[5] Sometimes they function as political or media events. A Bundestag screening of *Good Bye, Lenin!* launched a fierce debate about the status of the Eastern past.[6] Protagonists—and victims—of 1970s left-wing terrorism exchanged heated letters and lawsuits about their depiction in *Der Baader Meinhof Komplex* and directly confronted each other on television programs; the widow of victim Jürgen Ponto gave up her *Bundesverdienstkreuz* (Federal Cross of Merit) on account of the production's "unrealistic" recreation of her husband's murder, and went to court to alter the scene for the television broadcast.[7] The contemporary German Chancellor Gerhard Schröder watched *Das Wunder von Bern* and admitted crying three times during the screening.[8] In the past such reactions were the privilege of "imports" such as *Holocaust* (1978) and *Schindler's List* (1993).[9]

Emerging Paradigms

How are we to understand the new wave of German historical films? As the subtitle of this book implies, I will be arguing that a complex engagement with film history—and various historiographical forms—characterize these new historical films. Before introducing that approach, however, it is vital to summarize briefly on which grounds these productions have been received hitherto. Postwall historical films have received largely negative middlebrow journalistic treatment and scorn from high-profile auteurs. Critics and scholars are contributing to a burgeoning body of work on the trend for period films in Germany, and approaching the historical film from a number of different perspectives. Four major paradigms have emerged.

One approach places identity politics squarely onto discourses of popular cinema, and in particular, transnational genres and production cycles. Instead of arguing for postwall German historical film as a genre, Jaimey Fisher proposes to see the new historical films as a production trend.[10] Noting that scholars often fail to account for the very singularity of these productions—their popular success—he employs, following the work of Tino Balio in the context of Hollywood, the looser grouping of "production trend," which, unlike a genre recognizes the "fashion" of certain subjects, themes, and semantics in patterns of commercial production.[11] In *German Film after Germany: Toward a Transnational Aesthetic*, Randall Halle situates the recent historical film as a "special form of narration that harbors many of the complexities attendant to the rather fraught nature of European transnationalism."[12] Since the cohesion of communities relies on the articulation of a common past, individual national histories threaten "the project of European union."[13] Halle notes the recent proliferation of war movies and attends to how two such films—*Duell* (*Enemy at the Gates*, 2001) and *Der Untergang*—serve to create a common transnational identity by offering a critical history.

A second major viewpoint regards the recent proliferation of historical films in the context of a wider, multimedia "memory boom" and a particular national attitude toward the past: victimhood. Paul Cooke and Marc Silberman's *Screening War: Perspectives on German Suffering*, which traces "the changing ways German film has addressed the legacy of its recent past" and in particular "the place of German wartime and postwar 'suffering' within this legacy," is paradigmatic for this line of thinking.[14] The editors place postwall historical films within the context of a number of other cultural phenomena. This larger "victimhood" discourse was precipitated by a number of media events and public interventions. W.G. Sebald's 1997 lectures, later published as *Luftkrieg und Literatur* (*On the Natural History of Destruction*), asked why there had been so few significant literary descriptions of the Allied bombings of Germany during World War II. Historians began to speak of the media interventions that followed as a shift in the public discourse about the war from the memorial of Nazis' victims to a focus on the suffering of the German collective.[15] These included Jörg Friedrich's books on the Allied bombing raids on German cities, *Der Brand* (*The Fire*) and *Brandstätten* (*Sites of Fire*), as well as the ever-continuing public debate about a memorial about the expulsion of Germans from Eastern Europe in the 1940s by the Bund der Vertriebenen (League of Expellees). On television, over five million watched Guido Knopp's documentary mini-series on the historical event, *Die große Flucht* (*The Great Escape*, 2001); more recently, *Die Flucht* (*March of Millions*, 2007) has told the story of the German refugees.[16] Examining the intellectual and cultural discursive changes from perpetrator to victimhood over the course of the postwar period, Cooke and Silberman look to a number of reasons for the new prominence of the victimhood discourse in the contemporary period. They include the contemporary historical distance to World War II; new media technologies and increased access to archival resources; millennial and 9/11 anxieties; as well as poststructuralist and postmodern intellectual theories.[17]

A third major approach, the "heritage film" critique, expands in many ways on the second; among scholars, it has served perhaps as the dominant paradigm in studies of postwall historical films. Scholars writing in this ideological-symptomatic vein, such as Lutz Koepnick and Kristin Kopp, use the examples of *Aimée & Jaguar* (1999), *Comedian Harmonists* (*The Harmonists*, 1997), and *Nirgendwo in Afrika* to speak of the postwall historical fictions as the "German Heritage Film."[18] Remarkable about these productions, in the words of Koepnick, "is that many of these films discover relevant heritage values in the sphere, not only of material objects, historical décor, and atmospheric textures, but in symbolic expressions and counter-factual models of social accord and multicultural consensus."[19] In this way, *Comedian Harmonists* relocates 1930s Jews from "oppressed outsiders" to "a particular ethnic group within a multicultural nation"; *Aimee & Jaguar* normalizes lesbianism.[20] German heritage cinema, Kristin Kopp writes in her study of *Nirgendwo in Afrika*, "looks back to the Nazi period, and locates spaces, however small or marginal, onto which instances of positive German practice can be projected and positive German identity imagined."[21] Johannes von Moltke, in his study of the *Heimatfilm*, agrees: "As a generic template for historical consciousness, Heimat appears ready-made for the German cinema's postwall revisionist impulses. This is nowhere more obvious than in the ideological remix of Heimat and heritage that has characterized much recent filmmaking in Germany."[22] The "Heritage/Heimat film," maintains von Moltke, provides conciliatory retroscenarios of the Nazi period in which contemporary German spectators behold comforting fantasies of identification with Jewish victims from the 1930s and 1940s. In sum, these scholars problematize the narratives' triumphant images of German-Jewish love, desire, and cooperation as well as their renegotiation and realignment of identification so that contemporary German spectators are sutured into identification with persecuted 1930s and 1940s Jews.

The final major viewpoint, present in both journalistic and scholarly reckonings, bears down on one of the "heritage film" interlocutors' objections and subjects the postwall German historical film to an ideological critique on the basis of the films' naïve historicism. For example, German film critics, who have often called for more films dealing with the national past and contemporary reality, did not welcome the historical turn. In normative appraisals of the genre, commentators identified realism and an emphasis on "authenticity" as the genre's organizing principle and point of critique. In the weekly *Die Zeit*, Katja Nicodemus invoked Walter Benjamin's "Theses on the Philosophy of History" when she described new German historical films such as *Rosenstraße* (2003), *Good Bye, Lenin!*, *Herr Lehmann* (*Berlin Blues*, 2003), and *Das Wunder von Bern* as "whores in historicism's bordello."[23] For reviewer Cristina Nord, the history wave represented a "new naïveté" among filmmakers.[24] Mourning the New German Cinema's self-reflexive, political approach to the past, she ridiculed the "post-ideological, positivistic" attitude toward national history; the productions' measure of success is to "match the license plate number of the historical automobile."[25] Prominent contemporary arthouse directors and documentarists such as Christian Petzold, Romuald Karmakar, and Andres Veiel complained about the new exercises in retrospection as nauseating forms of "historical hyperstylization"; the films, working together with title pages of weekly glossies and talk shows on public TV, attempt to exhaust history.[26] To examine exemplary scholarly iterations of the "historicism critique," we might cite the critical reception of *Der Untergang*. Several studies address the moral and dramaturgical problems of representing Hitler and Bruno Ganz's performance,[27] and object to the film's naïve claims to "objective historicity" in line with the authenticity debate of Nicodemus and Nord.[28]

Scholar Jennifer M. Kapczynski makes a similar argument in her broader characterization of the "historical turn" in German cinema.[29] Despite imagining a diverse group of historical periods in various narrative forms, the films share an aesthetic preoccupation: a desire for authentic representation. "Consumed with reduplicating the bygone moments that they represent," Kapczynski argues, "recent German historical films employ strategies targeted at conjuring past worlds with a maximum of accuracy" and often strive to revive the past by using historical styles.[30] Although Kapczynski acknowledges that this phenomenon is hardly new in German cinema and was a staple of New German visions of the past such as Rainer Werner Fassbinder's *Die Ehe der Maria Braun* (*The Marriage of Maria Braun*, 1979) or Helma Sanders-Brahms's *Deutschland, bleiche Mutter* (*Germany, Pale Mother*, 1980), she critiques today's productions for their lack of "stylistic practices that regularly remind audiences they are witnessing the unfolding of a highly mediated past—one to which they do not have direct access but rather must work to perceive."[31]

These approaches all have their advantages in taking stock of certain sets and types of productions, but they are also not without some limitations, that, to my mind, need to be articulated before I introduce my own approach to the postwall German historical cinema. Although the heritage critics' individual ideological analyses of the work of Caroline Link, Max Färberböck, and Joseph Vilsmaier may be justified, I would question the tendency to apply a "heritage film" model to the postwall German context. One major problem with the notion of the "German Heritage Film" is the status of the national history in question and how the term has been imported. These commentators have appropriated the term from British discussions about UK middle-brow historical productions (and co-productions) produced in the 1980s and 1990s, with Merchant-Ivory E.M. Forster adaptations singled out for particular critique.[32] Ginette Vincendeau characterized heritage films as period costume dramas, literary adaptations, and historical films "shot with big budgets and production values by A-list directors and they use stars, polished lighting and camerawork, many changes of décor and extras, well-researched interior designs, and classical or classical-inspired music."[33] To my mind there is an important difference between *Chariots of Fire* (1981) and *Comedian Harmonists*, or between *A Room with a View* (1985) and *Aimée & Jaguar*. The "German Heritage Films" that Koepnick and others describe are about war, poverty, suffering, exile, or the Holocaust, and they cast German as the *victims*—not victors—of a cruel history. Even the most cynical commentator would not want to imply World War II was a "highlight" of national history or make a facile analogy between British heritage theme parks and the memorials at Sachsenhausen or Dachau.[34] By coupling aesthetic and ideological claims about the entire landscape of German historical fictions, the term "heritage film" conflates many productions that are actually very different. In spite of the implication that recent German films entertain revisionist histories and prove thus aesthetically conservative (or vice versa), in this book we will encounter examples where prospects of history that many would regard as conservative or even reactionary come in very sophisticated forms. But beyond terminology, perhaps the most significant problem with the attempt to apply the heritage (but also "victimhood") label to recent German cinema is that it only accounts for a subset of historical features looking back to the Nazi period and allows for only one way of seeing that past.[35]

In response specifically to the critics of "historicism," they too have made a valid point regarding a selection of films. Nevertheless, recent German historical films interpret "authenticity" in various ways. Besides the dramaturgical authenticity in *Der Untergang*, *Das Leben der Anderen*, and *Das Wunder von Bern* (and the labored paratextual discourses which accompanied their production and reception), a variety of other forms are at work. Although tropes of authenticity abide in *Sonnenallee*, it and other "Ostalgie" pictures constantly foreground their self-consciousness—if not in the Brechtian way of Fassbinder and Sanders-Brahms. How would the "authenticity" argument take account of *23* (1999) or *Die Unberührbare* (*No Place to Go*, 2000) which approach the past through historical styles but do not attempt to appropriate a "faithful" portrait of the past? Both *Baader* (2002) and *Der Baader Meinhof Komplex* use quotation as historical principle—to much different ends. Although "authenticity" is at stake in contemporary historical productions worldwide, the contemporary German historical film is fascinating precisely for its varied approaches. In a way, the critique of "historicism" and "authenticity" simply reverses the traditional public debate over history on film: fidelity to the historical record.[36] For most professional historians and the general public, period films that depart from the record are "bad"; film critics tend to dislike historical productions that do not "stylize" their representation of the past. Although there are surely specific examples that deserve analysis along these lines (e.g., *Good Bye, Lenin!*, *Das Leben der Anderen*), we should remember that such critique cannot be extended to all recent German historical films, nor deny that, in practice, this is an ideological argument couched in a formal one. In crucial ways, the task of this book seeks to interrogate and complicate the "historicism" critique, by revealing the sophisticated and multifarious ways in which recent German historical films imagine the postwar past.

This very brief resumé of the recent work on this subject is meant not only to telegraph how postwall German historical cinema has been written about hitherto, but also to imagine the potentially productive different ways to deal with phenomenon. The films might be analyzed as indices of new paradigms of history and memory in unified Germany or as economic products that respond to international popular tastes for the dark German past. One might reassess the function of nostalgia and heritage by comparing Germany's historical films with recent developments in other national cinemas, or entertain a symptomatic-ideological analysis of a new national subconscious in the age of Schröder and Merkel.

The scope of my study is more limited, however; my intervention is not to account for the whole phenomenon of postwall historical film. Rather, this book shows how recent German historical film deploys constellations of *film history* to recreate the past. By taking stock of the way that recent German historical films channel—compellingly and uniquely—past styles, cycles, genres, stars, and other filmic elements and forms, this book elucidates the postwall German film historical imaginary.

The Film Historical Imaginary: Intertextuality, Allusion, and Cinephilia in the Digital Age

In order to understand the postwall German film historical imaginary, it is necessary to contexualize my discussion within theoretical debates on intertexuality, allusion, pastiche, and cinephilia—the very concepts at stake in genealogies of cinematic production and consumption.

In their book on the transformation of cinephilia—an "act of memory" which "interpenetrates" with the past[37]—in the age of new technologies, social networks, and economic structures, Marijke de Valck and Malte Hagener observe that contemporary films themselves evince a visibly different representation of the past: "Arguably the most eye-catching characteristic of contemporary cinephilia is its cultural-aesthetic fusions of time and space, its radically different way of employing the historical signifier."[38] With a "media time" increasingly unhinged from "traditional historical time," they write, the new cinephilia "engages in popular reworkings" of the film-historical imaginary.[39]

Of course, the attention toward reworkings of film history in film is not new; scholars have long examined notions of "intertextuality." The term was introduced into the academy by Julia Kristeva's reading of Mikhail Bakhtin's concept of dialogism, or "the necessary relation of any utterance to other utterances."[40] Bakhtin's analysis of linguistic and literary production suggests that "all texts are tissues of anonymous formulae, conscious and unconscious quotations, conflations and inversions of other texts."[41] In Kristeva's structuralist study of the novel, she explores the way in which literature articulates "a complex, composite system, a montage of heterogeneous discourses within a single text";[42] she defines the "three dimensions of textual space": the writing subject, the addressee, and exterior texts. "The word's status," Kristeva writes, "is thus defined *horizontally* (the word in the text belongs to both the writing subject and addressee) as well as *vertically* (the word in the text is oriented toward an anterior or synchronic corpus)."[43] In this sense, history and cultural history become "a mosaic of texts drawn upon by the writer or the reader to produce or interpret any particular word, sentence, or story."[44] Following Kristeva, other literary theorists modified or refined the terms of intertextuality, including Gérard Genette's formulation of intertextuality as the "effective co-presence of two texts," whether this constitutes allusion, quotation, plagiarism, or another more specific relation.[45]

Scholars in the 1980s and 1990s imported literary discourses of intertextuality in order to understand various aspects of film culture— from oeuvres of particular auteurs to cycles in particular national cinemas[46]—as open-ended discursive practices whose matrix of communicative utterances are reached "not only via recognizable influences but also through a subtle process of dissemination."[47] Although, theoretically, the "concept of intertextuality is not reducible to matters of influence or sources of a text in the old philological sense,"[48] in practice and in the course of challenges to structuralist and poststructuralist vocabularies, accounts of intertextuality often include more or less conscious allusionism and homage. Indeed, notions of intertexuality or its romantic conceptual predecessor, "influence," have been explored in film studies under the rubric of other more specific terms which have often been laden with pejorative associations that suggest a sentimental or excessive preoccupation with the past (i.e., "nostalgia") or a loss of aesthetic invention (i.e., "pastiche").

One famous example is Fredric Jameson's comments on the "nostalgia film" as a manifestation of the "postmodern" cultural logic of late capitalism.[49] Committing an "insensible colonization of the present," films such as *Body Heat* (1981) contain—as "constitutive and essential" parts of their structure—an "awareness of the pre-existence of other versions, previous films of the novel as well as the novel itself"; intertexuality is a "deliberate, built-in feature of the aesthetic effect."[50] Exemplars such as *American Graffiti* (1973) "restructure the whole issue of pastiche and project it onto a collective and social level, where the desperate attempt to appropriate a missing past is now refracted through the iron law of fashion change and the emergent ideology of the 'generation.'"[51] Incompatible with "genuine historicity," these projects subject the past to "aesthetic colonization" and "set out to recapture … the henceforth mesmerizing lost reality of the Eisenhower era."[52] Jameson deems this proliferation and visibility of film history in contemporary (Hollywood) cinema as an "elaborated symptom of the waning of our historicity, of our lived possibility of experiencing history in some active way."[53]

Another example is Noël Carroll's landmark 1982 essay on the role of film history in 1970s and early 1980s film—much the same body of work that Jameson treats, albeit with much different conclusions. In "The Future of Allusion," Noël Carroll claims that "allusion, specifically allusion to film history, has become a major expressive device, that is, a means that directors use to make comments on the fictional worlds of their films."[54] In Carroll's idiom, the term includes "quotations, the memorialization of past genres, *homages*, and the recreation of 'classic' scenes, shots, plot motifs, lines of dialogue, themes, gestures, and so forth from film history, especially as that history was crystallized and codified in the sixties and early seventies"; strategies include "imitation of film-historical referents; the insertion of classic clips into new films; the mention of illustrious and coyly non-illustrious films and filmmakers in dialogue; the arch play of titles on marquees," and so forth.[55]

Similar to Jameson, Carroll also notes the way that contemporary filmmaking prompts and sometimes requires knowledge of film history: "informed viewers are meant to recall past films (filmmakers, genres, shots, and so on)" as part of their consumption, but, crucially, "are not supposed to think of this as plagiarism" or derivative "but as part of the expressive design."[56] Nevertheless, unlike Jameson, who sees the "nostalgia film" as a historical symptom, Carroll locates the new prominence of film history in film as a result of institutional, critical, and popular transformations in American film culture. The "boom for allusionism is a legacy of American auteurism,"[57] pertaining to the first generation of American film-school graduates and the enterprise of

Andrew Sarris and other auteurist critics who praised a "demonstrative expressiveness through markedly deliberate style"; indeed, according to Carroll, an auteurist/film-school "concern with style leads to the study of examples and thereby opens the possibility of both learning from the examples and quoting them outright."[58] At the same time, "an unprecedented awareness of film history developed in a segment of the American film audience" during the 1960s and 1970s.[59] The result of these institutional transformations means that "explicit film-historical consciousness [has become] a hallmark of ambitious filmmaking and film going."[60]

Indeed, whereas Jameson sees allusionism as a symptomatic longing for a return to the conservative 1950s, Carroll sees the trend as the legacy of 1968. The baby-boom generation participated in a singular project: "the attempt to create a common cultural heritage."[61] For Carroll, allusionism is initially an expression of utopian urgency; the generation that rediscovered film rediscovered radical politics.

Jameson's culturally pessimistic notions of "nostalgia" and pastiche, and Carroll's (more ambivalent) "allusionism," imply an ethical position toward a perceived historicism. Indeed, much writing from the 1980s and 1990s on film historical genealogy—much like discussions of film adaptations of literature—partake of moralistic discourses that judge films for their (lack of) authenticity, fidelity, or originality.[62] Nevertheless, recent scholarship has tried to come to a more differentiated view of intertextuality and allusionism, locating the film historical imaginary within discourses of new media and the increased access to a more plural film history. Scholars have explored cinephilia—long derided as a type of fandom anathema to serious academic inquiry—as a productive form of nostalgia that innervated much of the film writing (by Bazin, Kracauer, and others) that makes up the canon of film theory.[63] At the same time, Elena Gorfinkel and others have pointed to a new "film historical imaginary" at work in the "retro" stylistic tendencies of contemporary filmmaking.[64] Examining the recent period films *Far From Heaven* (2002) and *Boogie Nights* (1997), Gorfinkel argues that Todd Haynes and Paul Thomas Anderson use "allusion to bridge the gap between past and present through the act of reworking and restaging film history."[65] Citing literary scholar Thomas Green's understanding of anachronism, Gorfinkel interprets "anachronism as a concept and mode of aesthetic recognition [that] becomes a direct means of dialoguing with popular cultural memories of the historical past."[66] Thus, in these films, "reference to 'outdated' historical periods and objects invites spectators to engage affectively, though not necessarily uncritically, with history";[67] "the intense artificiality of [*Far From Heaven*'s] mise en scène and the heightened constrictions on content in effect engine an earnestly emotional response, from an audience that reorganizes the limits and myopias of the cultural past as seen through the fractured mirror of film history."[68]

Indeed, Gorfinkel's notion of "film historical imaginary" encompasses not only academically trained directors' cinephiliac engagement with historical periods and film history, but also pertains to the simultaneous "broadening of cine-literate audiences through the spread and popularity of festivals, multiplexes, discussion forums on the internet, and DVDs," a type of film consumption that transcends the "small and elitist communities of the 1950s–1970s."[69] As Jenna Ng has further argued, the "movie-mad" generation of 1968 that Carroll diagnosed as a constituent part of the proliferation of allusionism in 1970s cinema has yielded to a "similar movie-mania" today, "albeit with two differences: (i) it operates primarily on unprecedented technological development; and (ii) it is marked by an extraordinary diversity of cross-cultural film experience."[70]

In the conclusion to this book I will more closely examine these historical forces at work, in Germany and internationally, that make film historical referencing evident in the production and legible in the reception of film. Today—also in the German example—film connoisseurship is certainly not limited to Hollywood and select West European art cinemas, but a much wider range of international popular and art cinemas. To be sure, an active film historical imaginary was certainly a major constituent element of the 1970s' new waves; in his essay on allusionism, Carroll explicitly extends the phenomenon beyond American filmmaking to the example of the New German Cinema.[71] Thomas Elsaesser has also elaborated on historicity in Fassbinder's period films in a similar manner: *Die Ehe der Maria Braun* "functions as a trigger of memories but at one remove: not so much recalling a reality, as setting up a chain of associations, stories remembered from one's parents, pictures seen in the family album, in short, the standard version of the 1950s as present in the culture at large of the 1970s."[72] Even if the New German Cinema—cited as one of the art cinema movements most associated with reflexive and intertextual filmmaking[73]—has been described as primarily in film historical dialogue with domestic traditions, Hollywood and American popular culture, and French cinema,[74] there is no doubt that German filmmaking today partakes of a globalized industry and international traditions. And even if it emits from the art cinema new waves,[75] the intertextual film historical imaginary has gone mainstream: popular German cinema indulges in this referencing extensively and often consciously; concomitantly, it has become a constituent element of the postwall historical cinema. Tracing the sources and implications of these borrowings will be a major task of this book.

The Cinema of Retro-flection:
History Through, Over, and Against

In her study of memory within treatments of sexuality in postwar West Germany, Dagmar Herzog addresses the function of a "layering of memory" in retrospective assessments:

> That is, with the ways each cohort of postwar West Germans evidently approached the past only through, over, and against the interpretations of their historical predecessors (with New Leftists contradicting the representations of the past offered them by many of their parents, and feminists offering yet a third description of Nazism's purported sexual lessons)….For what is going on in these memory-texts is an attempt to reconstruct the fifties' interpretations of the thirties and forties within the context of the seventies' and eighties' struggle with the meaning ofthe sixties.[76]

Herzog elaborates how Holocaust memory has been instrumentalized as a *"lingua franca* of postwar West German political culture": antinuclear activists warned that atomic war would entail a burning far worse than Auschwitz and Treblinka; leftists in the late 1970s described contemporary global economic injustice as a murderous conspiracy that made "the consequences of Hitler's 'final solution' seem positively charming."[77] Herzog characterizes this broader phenomenon, employed both by conservatives and leftists alike, as a specific feature of the national political culture.

My study builds on Herzog's comments on the often complex twistings of memory, and applies them to film history. It examines how postwall German historical films incorporate, respond to, and rework film history, whether these references pertain to certain directors, stars, genres, traditions, or individual films from Germany or abroad. It investigates how film historiography might probe three other layers of memory: (1) the works' historical interpretation of the period, event, and figures in question; (2) previous interpretations of this event, era, or figure; and (3) the contemporary moment in which the film itself was made and screened. How, for example, does *Das Wunder von Bern* look to the 1954 German soccer World Cup victory *through* a Nazi sports film and *against* the interpretation of this event in the classic New German Cinema historical film, *Die Ehe der Maria Braun*? How does Oskar Roehler assume the mantle of Fassbinder, both literally and figuratively, in the portrait of his mother in *Die Unberührbare*? How does 23 borrow on the conventions of the 1970s American paranoid thriller to represent 1980s West Germany and, at the same time, comment on the late 1990s "end of history"?

These films constitute what one might call a "cinema of retro-flection": a highly ambivalent negotiation of German history and film history which looks back to the recent past through, over, and/or against film history and prior interpretations of national history, and above all those of the New German Cinema. The term "retro-flection" emphasizes how processes of *retro*spection in the German history film wave are functions of *reflection* on film history. This is a group of films in search of a usable past.

The chapters that follow are arranged chronologically by period; proceeding to focus on one or two case studies, each surveys a major sector of the past and provides examples of the major ways of seeing in the postwall historical cinema.

Chapter 1 examines the most antagonistic position toward the traditions of the New German Cinema to be found in the postwall historical cinema: the revisionist impulse toward the war, Adenauerism, and the postwar in *Das Wunder von Bern*. Directed by Sönke Wortmann, an outspoken opponent of left-wing auteurist cinema, the film mythologizes the postwar rebirth of a nation at the same time that it celebrates the restoration of a family. Examining depictions of "emotional masculinity," I demonstrate how the story mobilizes the soccer film in a way reminiscent of the Nazi production *Das große Spiel* (*The Big Game*, 1942). Considering the vital role of color and sound in the formation of memory and the coordinated marketing strategy, I show how the film's sophisticated visual representations of the past work on two levels. It delivers the missing "prosthetic memory" of the 1954 West German World Cup victory and counters the critical memory of the event from the late 1970s, namely Rainer Werner Fassbinder's *Die Ehe der Maria Braun*.

Film critics have taken some recent historical films to task for their "gilded memory," that is, their rosy treatment of terrible episodes in the national narrative. Chapter 2 inspects a group of films often subjected to such critique: those which look back to the political unrest of 1968 and the "leaden years" of left-wing terrorism through a "pop" vision of the past. This chapter probes the new wave of RAF films through their engagement with the terrorist films of the New German Cinema. Besides providing an inventory of the recent incarnations' basic features, the chapter investigates closely the most radical film, *Baader*, a biopic of terrorist leader Andreas Baader, which received a critical excoriation from audiences, journalists, and academics alike. It depicts Baader dying not—as in reality—by suicide in 1977 after five years in maximum-security prison. Rather, it shows him perishing in a showdown with police in 1972, rendered in a scene worthy of Sergio Leone's spaghetti westerns. *Baader*'s pop historiography allows a highly complex engagement with the RAF and its afterlife. Christopher Roth's project eschews the New German Cinema's more analytical approaches to the disastrous history of left-wing terrorism and instead concentrates on its less certain beginnings. *Baader* represents the Baader-Meinhof Group as a *bande à part*, driven and sustained by the cinephiliac dreams of *Pierrot le fou* (1965), Jean-Pierre Melville's ironic gangster pictures, *Bonnie and Clyde* (1967), and *Butch Cassidy and the Sundance Kid* (1969)—in sum, the films that the real Baader and his band watched while on the run.

Chapter 3 investigates the beginnings of the postwall historical cinema and the ambivalent post-68er re-appropriation of the New German Cinema. Although in this book I speak broadly of a "postwall" historical cinema for the sake of simplicity, the critical volume of these films began in the late 1990s. In particular, Hans-Christian Schmid's *23*, released in early 1999, was praised by critics as unique. Suddenly, a German film was exploring the recent past, rather than eighteenth-century authors or World War II.[78] Paradoxically, *23* was so new because it partakes of past ways of seeing. In a close analysis of the film, which serves as an archetype of one strand of retrospection, I show how the story of an errant hacker from 1980s Hannover creates a subject position that criticizes the generation of 1968 at the same time that it draws on that generation's films, in particular Nixon-era paranoid thrillers and the New German "case studies," to enact that critique.

Chapters 4 and 5 focus on projects that employ material culture in order to interpret the last years of the GDR and unification. Chapter 4 examines the so-called *Ostalgie* (nostalgia for the Eastern past) wave that gave rise to multiple features, TV series, a musical, and countless commercial tie-ins. Studying *Good Bye, Lenin!* in the context of the broader "comic" retrospection of the Eastern past reveals how the film satisfied a broader cultural desire to relive the GDR in the safe space of materiality. Gaining insights into the voice-over and nostalgia, I show how the film merges national history with the fictional story of the Kerner family, from a Western viewpoint. Its multilayered temporalities offer an approach to history that is subject to human and media manipulation, only in the end to retreat from the implications of this self-reflexivity. This historical project echoes that of *Forrest Gump* (1994), another exercise in intranational harmony; it smoothes over the historical trauma of the unification and defines nation as a cabinet of mass cultural curiosities. Examining *Das Leben der Anderen* and the other fairy-tale treatments of the Eastern past unveils the paradox of *Ostalgie* and its obsession for historical fidelity.

Chapter 5 reveals the alternative genealogy of productions which engage the problems of unification in gritty, dark, or weird forms, focusing on Oskar Roehler's *Die Unberührbare*. Based loosely on the events of Roehler's mother's life, the film tracks a West German novelist from the fall of the Berlin Wall to her suicide in early 1990. This chapter analyzes the film's constrictive mise en scène, its recourse to film noir, and its careful negotiation of architecture and space. Drawing on Edward Dimendberg's analysis of the centrifugal and centripetal American film noir,[79] I examine how Roehler's film renegotiates the classic noir's preoccupation with the natural and built environment. This portrait dramatizes millennial German spatial anxiety about Berlin, which city planners and architecture critics deemed a city without a center.[80] Furthermore, I demonstrate how the film's many allusions to material objects and fashion, and the works of Billy Wilder, Sam Fuller, Franz Kafka, Orson Welles, and Rainer Werner Fassbinder complement the story of exile and displacement. Returning to the major features of the new regard of the past, Chapter 6 surveys the contributions that institutional and media developments have had on the development of the postwall historical cinema.

Notes

1. Besides the foreign box-office figures and the Oscar nominations, see, for example, the prominent place of the German historical films *Good Bye, Lenin!* (2003) and *Der Untergang* (*Downfall,* 2004) in articles on the renewed foreign interest in German cinema such as Lars-Olav Beier and Wieland Wagner, "Das deutsche Kinowunder," *Der Spiegel*, 11 July 2005, 82–83.
2. Olga Gruber, "Armer deutscher Film," *Transatlantik*, January 1981, 66. Quoted in Thomas Elsaesser, *New German Cinema: A History* (London: British Film Institute, 1989), 37.
3. See the market data of the Filmförderungsanstalt (German Federal Film Board) at http://www.ffa.de.
4. See the German Federal Film Board statistics (http://www.ffa.de) as well as Nicole Dolif, "Lenin lässt die Kinokassen klingeln," *Die Welt*, 18 February 2003.
5. See http://www.bpb.de.
6. See Volcker Eckert, "Good bye, Ahnungslosigkeit: Kino als Geschichtsstunde," *Tagesspiegel*, 6 March 2003; Constance Frey, "Die DDR ist längst Kult," *Tagesspiegel*, 5 June 2003; André Mielke, "Der Bundestag ist auch nur ein Mensch," *Die Welt*, 4 April 2003; Jan Thomsen, "Ein Kino-Besuch voller Missverständnisse," *Berliner Zeitung*, 3 April 2003; and "Betriebsausflug: Bundestag nimmt Abschied von Lenin," *Spiegel Online*, 3 April 2003, http://www.spiegel.de/kultur/gesellschaft/0,1518,243206,00.html.
7. "Nicht realistisch," *Süddeutsche Zeitung*, 2 December 2008: http://www.sueddeutsche.de/kultur/prozess-um-baader-meinhof-komplex-nicht-realistisch-1.365677.
8. See Fritz Göttler, "Hallo Helmut!," *Süddeutsche Zeitung*, 16 October 2003; Richard Bernstein, "Germany's Grief and Glory, Wrapped Up in a Soccer Ball," *New York Times*, 10 November 2003; and Hans-Joachim Leyenberg, "Im Sonderzug zurück nach Bern," *Frankfurter Allgemeine Zeitung*, 16 October 2003.
9. For a succinct account of *Holocaust*'s reception in West Germany, see Anton Kaes, *From Hitler to Heimat: The Return of History as Film* (Cambridge, MA: Harvard University Press, 1989), 28–35, or Michael E. Geisler, "The Disposal of Memory: Fascism and the Holocaust," in *Framing the Past: The Historiography of German Cinema and Television*, eds. Bruce A. Murray and Christopher J. Wickham (Carbondale: Southern Illinois University Press, 1992), 220–60.
10. Jaimey Fisher, "German Historical Film as Production Trend: European Heritage Cinema and Melodrama in *The Lives of Others*," in *The Collapse of the Conventional: German Film and Its Politics at the Turn of the Twenty-First Century*, eds. Jaimey Fisher and Brad Prager (Detroit: Wayne State University Press, 2010), 186–215.
11. See the work of Tino Balio: for instance, *The American Film Industry* (Madison: University of Wisconsin Press, 1976) or "Hollywood Production Trends in the Era of Globalisation," in *Genre and Contemporary Hollywood*, ed. Steve Neale (London: British Film Institute, 2002), 165–84.

12. Randall Halle, *German Film after Germany: Toward a Transnational Aesthetic* (Urbana: University of Illinois Press, 2008), 89.
13. Halle, *German Film after Germany*, 89.
14. Paul Cooke and Marc Silberman, "Introduction: German Suffering?," in *Screening the War: Perspectives on German Suffering*, eds. Paul Cooke and Marc Silberman (Rochester, NY: Camden House, 2010), 2.
15. See Helmut Schmitz, "The Birth of the Collective from the Spirit of Empathy: From the 'Historians' Dispute' to German Suffering," in *Germans as Victims: Remembering the Past in Contemporary Germany*, ed. Bill Niven (Houndmills: Palgrave Macmillan, 2006), 95.
16. See Tim Bergfelder, "Shadowlands: The Memory of the *Ostgebiete* in Contemporary German Film and Television," in *Screening the War: Perspectives on German Suffering*, eds. Paul Cooke and Marc Silberman (Rochester, NY: Camden House, 2010), 123–44.
17. Cooke and Silberman, "Introduction: German Suffering?," 7–8.
18. See Lutz Koepnick, "Reframing the Past: Heritage Cinema and Holocaust in the 1990s," *New German Critique* 87 (2002): 47–82; Lutz Koepnick, "Amerika gibts überhaupt nicht: Notes on the German Heritage Film," in *German Pop Culture: How American Is It?*, ed. Agnes Müller (Ann Arbor: University of Michigan Press, 2004), 191–208; and Kristin Kopp, "Exterritorialized Heritage in Caroline Link's *Nigendwo in Afrika*," *New German Critique* 87 (2002): 106–32. See also Jennifer M. Kapczynski, "Newer German Cinema: From Nostalgia to Nowhere," *The Germanic Review* 82(1) (2007): 3–6.
19. Koepnick, "Reframing the Past," 58.
20. Koepnick, "Reframing the Past," 58.
21. Kopp, "Exterritorialized Heritage in Caroline Link's *Nigendwo in Afrika*," 106.
22. Johannes von Moltke, *No Place Like Home: Locations of Heimat in German Cinema* (Berkeley: University of California Press, 2005), 233.
23. See Katja Nicodemus, "Unsere kleine Traumfabrik," *Die Zeit*, 28 August 2003.
24. Cristina Nord, "Die neue Naivität," *taz*, 20 October 2008.
25. Cristina Nord, "Die neue Naivität," *taz*, 20 October 2008.
26. Dorothea Hauser and Andreas Schroth, "'Das Thema ist erledigt': Romuald Karmakar, Christian Petzold, und Andres Veiel zum Politischen im deutschen Film," *Ästhetik und Kommunikation* 117 (2002): 44–60; here 52 and 45.
27. Among the numerous articles on this subject, see Christine Haase, "Ready for his Close-Up? On the Success and Failure of Representing Hitler in *Der Untergang/The Downfall* (2004)," *Studies in European Cinema* 3(3) (2007): 189–99; Jürgen Pelzer, "'The Facts Behind the Guilt'? Background and Implicit Intentions in *Downfall*," *German Politics and Society* 25(1) (2007): 90–101.
28. Alexander Ruoff, "Die Renaissance des Historismus in der Populärkultur: Über den Kinofilm *Der Untergang*," in *Filmriss: Studien über Der Untergang*, ed. Willi Bischof (Münster: Unrast, 2005), 69–78.
29. Jennifer M. Kapczynski, "Imitation of Life: The Aesthetics of Agfacolor in Recent Historical Cinema," in *The Collapse of the Conventional: German Film and Its Politics at the Turn of the Twenty-First Century*, eds. Jaimey Fisher and Brad Prager (Detroit: Wayne State University Press, 2010), 39–62.
30. Kapczynski, "Imitation of Life," 40–41.
31. Kapczynski, "Imitation of Life," 43.
32. Among the most frequently discussed titles were *The Remains of the Day* (1993), *A Passage to India* (1984), *A Room with a View* (1985), *Artemisia* (1997), *1492: Conquest of Paradise* (1992), *Rob Roy* (1995), and *The Madness of King George* (1994).
33. Ginette Vincendeau, "Introduction," in *Film/Literature/Heritage: A Sight and Sound Reader*, ed. Ginette Vincendeau (London: British Film Institute, 2001), xviii.
34. Attempts to use the English heritage label to describe contemporary German historical productions have overlooked some important differences between trends in the two national cinemas. For example: whereas many English heritage films that British scholars critiqued were largely literary adaptations and period costume

dramas removed from political events, Koepnick's German heritage films transpire around historical events (always World War II) and often include characterization of real political agents—e.g. Goebbels and others in *Comedian Harmonists*. In addition, during the Cold War and on both sides of the Wall there were in fact significant waves of German period costume dramas that aimed to appropriate the common national cultural heritage. In fact, German literary adaptations and period costume dramas comparable in subject matter and aesthetic to the Merchant-Ivory productions are still being made. The domestic cinema continues to produce its share of films that look back to the machinations of wealthy boarding-school pupils from the 1920s (*Was nützt die Liebe in Gedanken* [*Love In Thoughts*, 2004]), imagine the private lives of its most famous writers (e.g. Brentano in *Das Gelübde* [*The Vow*, 2008]), or adapt classic authors (*Buddenbrooks* [2008] is now the fourth German film based on Thomas Mann's novel). If the term "heritage film" is to make sense, it should be only used to describe those films, which promote Germany's self-described heritage as "the land of poets and thinkers." The trouble is that these films are not representative of the surge in postwall German historical productions, which above all turn to the postwar past; thus, scholars would be best advised to discard the label altogether.

35. An important exception is Jaimey Fisher's smart essay on *Das Leben der Anderen*. See Fisher, "German Historical Film as Production Trend"; Adam Muller also attempts to expand the term to *Good Bye, Lenin!* in his "Notes toward a Theory of Nostalgia: Childhood and the Evocation of the Past in Two European 'Heritage' Films," *New Literary History* 37(4) (2006): 739–60.
36. Robert Burgoyne, *The Hollywood Historical Film* (Malden, MA: Blackwell, 2008), 1.
37. Marijke de Valck and Malte Hagener, "Down with Cinephilia? Long Live Cinephilia? And Other Videosyncratic Pleasures," in *Cinephilia: Movies, Love and Memory*, eds. Marijke de Valck and Malte Hagener (Amsterdam: Amsterdam University Press, 2005), 14; see also Paul Willeman, "Through a Glass Darkly: Cinephilia Reconsidered," in *Looks and Frictions: Essays in Cultural Studies and Film Theory* (London: British Film Institute, 1994), 227.
38. De Valck and Hagener, "Down with Cinephilia," 15.
39. De Valck and Hagener, "Down with Cinephilia," 15.
40. Robert Stam, Robert Burgoyne, and Sandy Flitterman-Lewis, *New Vocabularies in Film Semiotics* (London: Routledge, 1992), 203.
41. Stam et al., *New Vocabularies in Film Semiotics*, 204.
42. Stam et al., *New Vocabularies in Film Semiotics*, 204.
43. Julia Kristeva, *Desire in Language: A Semiotic Approach to Literature and Art*, ed. Leon S. Roudiez, trans. Thomas Gora, Alice Jardine, and Leon S. Roudiez (New York: Columbia University Press, 1980), 66.
44. Katherine J. Goodnow, *Kristeva in Focus: From Theory to Film Analysis* (New York: Berghahn, 2010), 13.
45. Stam et al., *New Vocabularies in Film Semiotics*, 207. See Gérard Genette, *Palimpsestes: La Littérature au Second Degré* (Paris: Seuil, 1982).
46. See, for example, James Goodwin, *Akira Kurasowa and Intertextual Cinema* (Baltimore: Johns Hopkins University Press, 1994); or Jefferson T. Kline, *Screening the Text: Intertextuality in New Wave French Cinema* (Baltimore: Johns Hopkins University Press, 1992).
47. Stam et al., *New Vocabularies in Film Semiotics*, 204.
48. Robert Stam, *Film Theory: An Introduction* (Malden, MA: Blackwell, 2000), 202
49. Fredric Jameson, "Postmodernism, or the Cultural Logic of Late Capitalism," *New Left Review* 1(146) (1984): 53–92.
50. Jameson, "Postmodernism," 67.
51. Jameson, "Postmodernism," 66.
52. Jameson, "Postmodernism," 67.
53. Jameson, "Postmodernism," 68.

54. Noël Carroll, "The Future of Allusion: Hollywood in the Seventies (and Beyond)," *October* 20 (1982): 51–81; here 52.
55. Carroll, "The Future of Allusion," 52.
56. Carroll, "The Future of Allusion," 52.
57. Carroll, "The Future of Allusion," 54.
58. Carroll, "The Future of Allusion," 79.
59. Carroll, "The Future of Allusion," 54.
60. Carroll, "The Future of Allusion," 56.
61. Carroll, "The Future of Allusion," 79.
62. Stam, *Film Theory*, 209.
63. See Christian Keathley, *Cinephilia and History, or The Wind in the Trees* (Bloomington: Indiana University Press, 2006).
64. Elena Gorfinkel, "The Future of Anachronism: Todd Haynes and the Magnificient Andersons," in *Cinephilia: Movies, Love and Memory*, eds. Marijke de Valck and Malte Hagener (Amsterdam: Amsterdam University Press, 2005), 153–67.
65. Gorfinkel, "The Future of Anachronism," 155.
66. Gorfinkel, "The Future of Anachronism," 156.
67. Gorfinkel, "The Future of Anachronism," 153.
68. Gorfinkel, "The Future of Anachronism," 160.
69. De Valck and Hagener, "Down with Cinephilia?," 21.
70. Jenna Ng, "Love in the Time of Transcultural Fusion: Cinephila, Homage and *Kill Bill*," in *Cinephilia: Movies, Love and Memory*, eds. Marijke de Valck and Malte Hagener (Amsterdam: Amsterdam University Press, 2005), 69.
71. Carroll, "The Future of Allusion," 72.
72. Thomas Elsaesser, *Fassbinder's Germany: History, Identity, Subject* (Amsterdam: Amsterdam University Press, 1996), 105.
73. See Robert Stam, *Reflexivity in Film and Literature: From Don Quixote to Jean-Luc Godard* (New York: Columbia University Press, 1992), 106.
74. See Gerd Gemünden, *Framed Visions: Popular Culture, Americanization, and the Contemporary German and Austrian Imagination* (Ann Arbor: University of Michigan Press, 1998).
75. "Aperture"—a term that encompasses "open-endedness, overspill, intertextuality—allusion, quotation and parody"—was one of the "cardinal virtues" of the counter-cinema according to Peter Wollen's famous list in his "Godard and Counter Cinema: Vent d'Est," in *Film Theory and Criticism: Introductory Readings*, 6th rev. ed., eds. Leo Braudy and Marshall Cohen (New York: Oxford University Press, 2004), 529.
76. See Dagmar Herzog, "'Pleasure, Sex, and Politics Belong Together': Post-Holocaust Memory and the Sexual Revolution in West Germany," *Critical Inquiry* 24(2) (1998): 393–444; here 398–99. See also Dagmar Herzog, *Sex After Fascism: Memory and Morality in Twentieth-Century Germany* (Princeton, NJ: Princeton University Press, 2005), especially 3–9.
77. Herzog, "'Pleasure, Sex, and Politics Belong Together,'" 440.
78. See Christiane Peitz, "Karl und wie er die Welt sah," *Die Zeit*, 14 January 1999; and Michael Sennhauser, "Hacken in der Eiszeit," *Neue Zürcher Zeitung*, 29 January 1999. See also Katja Nicodemus, "Film der neunziger Jahre. Neues Sein und altes Bewußtsein," in *Geschichte des deutschen Films*, eds. Wolfgang Jacobsen, Anton Kaes, and Hans Helmut Prinzler, 2nd rev. ed. (Weimar: Metzler, 2004), 328; and Merten Worthmann, "Ich bin schuld an Tschernobyl," *Berliner Zeitung*, 14 January 1999.
79. Edward Dimendberg, *Film Noir and the Spaces of Modernity* (Cambridge, MA: Harvard University Press, 2004).
80. See, for example, Dorothée Kohler and Boris Grésillon, "Berlin aus französischer Sicht," *Architektur in Berlin: Jahrbuch 1999*, ed. Architektenkammer Berlin (Hamburg: Junius, 1999), 10.

Chapter 1

REBIRTH OF A NATION
Das Wunder von Bern, the 1950s, and the Reactions to the New German Cinema

For the leftist student movement associated with the generation of 1968, the 1950s was a decade no better than the Nazi period. Indeed, in its radical interpretation of national history, the continuity of former National Socialists' career trajectories and the prevalence of "everyday fascism" in the parenting and education of young people meant that there was in fact no true caesura, no "Zero Hour" in 1945; a more or less submerged Nazism still existed.[1]

This stance is reflected in many of the later New German Cinema's historical films which treat the 1950s. Feminist projects such as Jutta Brückner's *Hungerjahre* (*Years of Hunger*, 1980) and Margarethe von Trotta's *Die bleierne Zeit* (*Marianne und Juliane*, 1981) presented scenes from the decade in which patriarchal structures from the Nazi period remained intact. Von Trotta's film, for instance, implied that the 1970s leftist terrorists were in fact deformed into violence by their upbringing in the 1950s. The narrative of Helma Sanders-Brahms's *Deutschland, bleiche Mutter* (*Germany, Pale Mother*, 1980) suggests that the conditions for German families actually worsened with the return of the fathers from the war. Rainer Werner Fassbinder's *Die Ehe der Maria Braun* (*The Marriage of Maria Braun*, 1979) and *Lola* (1981) associate the Adenauer reign with consumerism, renewed militarism, bourgeois moral hypocrisy, and the lost chance of coming to terms with the past. For leftist filmmakers, the 1950s and its shallow cinema were bad objects to be rejected and fought against.

In the 1990s and through the turn of the twenty-first century, this conception of the 1950s came up for revision. The postwar period resounded strikingly with the postwall years' concerns about national identity and the state's place in new international ensembles. Indeed, as the united Germany slipped into recession and the unemployment rate surpassed 10 percent, a certain nostalgia for the economic miracle and the old Federal Republic's prosperity arose. One event captivated the public memory in particular: the 1954 West German soccer World Cup victory against Hungary in Bern.

In Germany, this "miracle of Bern" has a similar quality to other "epochal" events such as the moon landing, Princess Diana's death, or the collapse of the World Trade Center. In many ways, of course, such "vivid memories" are media experiences. As Thomas Elsaesser has remarked, asking if you remember the day John F. Kennedy was assassinated actually wants to know if you recall the day you watched Kennedy being shot on television.[2]

Leading up to 1994, the fortieth anniversary of the event, the 1954 soccer victory was remembered publicly. Television featured specials and documentaries, such as *WM 1954: Deutschland und die Fußballweltmeisterschaft* (*World Cup 1954: Germany and the Soccer World Cup*, 1990), re-released in 1994 as *Das Wunder von Bern: Deutschland und die Fußball-WM 1954* (*The Miracle of Bern: Germany and the 1954 Soccer World Cup*). In that year, writer Friedrich Christian Delius published his autobiographical novella *Der Sonntag an dem ich Weltmeister wurde* (*The Sunday I Became World Champion*). The story sketches 4 July 1954 from the perspective of an eleven-year-old boy living in a Hessian village. Rebelling against his authoritarian father, who is the village pastor, he experiences the radio commentary of the match and the German victory as a relief from the strict piety at home.

Preceding the fiftieth anniversary in 2004, a much larger spate of articles and television specials appeared. Public channel ZDF produced *Das Wunder von Bern – Die wahre Geschichte* (*The Miracle of Bern – The True Story*, 2003). The documentary features interviews with political luminaries such as ex-Federal Chancellor Helmut Kohl and the President of the Bundestag, Wolfgang Thierse, who reveal their memories in talking-head style. Former players from the national team, such as Helmut Rahn and Horst Eckel, provide the retrospective commentary from the perspective of those who actually were there. A variety of books along these lines, composed primarily of photographs, appeared in 2004.[3] Popular media historian Guido Knopp, who had overseen the 1994 documentary, invited surviving members of the West German and Hungarian teams for a tear-filled walk down memory lane. Weekly magazines described how Hungarian radio reporters cried every time they thought of the game and its Cold War repercussions.[4] In Speyer, a museum exhibition displayed Rahn's game-winning shoe, immortalized in bronze. To commemorate the "eleven from Bern," Adidas introduced a retro-clothing line modelled on the original West German game jerseys from 1954.

The fiftieth anniversary would have been an obligatory occasion to look back to the event, but retrospectively it is clear that Sönke Wortmann's feature *Das Wunder von Bern* (*The Miracle of Bern*, 2003) served as the centerpiece. Before discussing Wortmann's film and the rehabilitation of the 1950s in postwall Germany, however, it is vital to recognize how the memory of the 1954 World Cup final differs from other culture-defining events. National public German television transmission began in December 1952; by 1954 only 11,658 television sets were registered in the Federal Republic of nearly 52 million residents.[5] Today, only eighteen minutes of poor-quality images from this game remain, in part thanks to amateur collectors.[6] Because of the scarcity of televisual coverage both live and afterwards, the memory of the 1954 West German World Cup victory differs from 9/11 or the fall of the Berlin Wall in three crucial ways. First, the primary mode of the game's initial transmission was via radio, and thus non-visual. Second, the lack of quality television footage has denied any one image or set of images iconic status. Unlike the Zapruder film of JFK's assassination, for instance, no single motion-picture record of the World Cup victory has come to stand in for the event. Third, and following on from this, Herbert Zimmermann's radio commentary is the remembered source. In sum, the match is a media memory, but an aural rather than a visual one.

Das Wunder von Bern sets out to fill this visual vacuum with a prosthetic memory. Alison Landsberg uses the term "prosthetic memory" to describe memories that are not products of lived experiences, but derived from engagement with the mediated representation of a film, TV series, museum, and so on. These are interchangeable but ultimately sensuous memories that are experienced by the body. Landsberg has a utopian belief in the possibilities of these memories, speculating that they might help produce "empathy and social responsibility as well as political alliances that transcend race, class, and gender."[7] *Das Wunder von Bern*, however, defies Landberg's utopianism. Here, a prosthetic, mediated memory mythologizes the restoration of a nuclear family as the rebirth of a nation. Mobilizing genres with heavy historical baggage, the film both delivers the missing visual memory of 1954 and tries to erase the subsequent traumatized recollection of the event. It serves as an example of a major strand of postwall German cinema which seeks to recuperate maligned periods of Germany's recent past—especially the 1940s and 1950s—and thus revise the New German Cinema's historical consensus.

A Family Affair

Feature films about culture-defining moments face a significant dramaturgical problem: if everyone knows the story, no one is surprised by its conclusion. Marcia Landy has observed that monumental historical films are robbed of suspense by the spectator's knowledge of the outcome and, for that reason, employ melodramatic strategies.[8] Embedding a family melodrama within a historical epic furthers a feeling of shared experience. Indeed, if prosthetic memories indulge the desire for a sensuous, bodily experience of history, then the melodrama—which Linda Williams terms an excessive "body genre"—is its perfect generic form. The melodrama "seems to endlessly repeat our melancholic sense of the loss of origins—impossibly hoping to return to an earlier state."[9] *Das Wunder von Bern* partakes of the masculine melodrama in its tale of reconciliation and rebirth.

In *Das Wunder von Bern* three narrative strands relate the legend of 1954. The first follows Matthias Lubanski, an 11-year-old boy growing up on the outskirts of Essen. Matthias, his mother Christa, and his older siblings Ingrid and Bruno run a neighborhood pub. When not working, Ingrid fraternizes with American GIs, and young communist Bruno plays in a rock-and-roll band. Matthias's passion is soccer. He follows his home team Rot-Weiß Essen religiously and idolizes striker Helmut Rahn, for whom he serves as a mascot and good-luck charm and in whom he finds a replacement for his own father Richard, who remains a POW in the Soviet Union.

The second line of action involves the West German national team as it prepares for and then participates in the World Cup competition. Focusing on Rahn, goalkeeper Toni Turek, captain Fritz Walter, and coach Sepp Herberger, this storyline shows how the latter whips the amateurs into shape through a mixture of motivation, discipline, and ingenuity. Although the press initially doubts Herberger, the characters of the third strand—*Süddeutsche Zeitung* cub sports reporter Paul Ackermann and his saucy new wife Annette—understand the coach's unorthodox methods as the only way to beat the athletically superior Hungarians.

Meanwhile, Richard Lubanski returns home from war and tries in vain to reestablish his authority. He antagonizes his family so much that Bruno defects to East Berlin and Matthias nearly leaves as well. Attempting to make amends, Richard borrows a priest's car and drives Matthias to Bern. The three narrative strands come together for the final game. The Hungarians score two goals, but by halftime the West Germans even the score. As Annette Ackermannn leads the crowd in cheer, Matthias sneaks into the stadium for the game's final minutes. Rahn, inspired by his presence, scores the winning goal. Using Paul Ackermann's press pass, Matthias and his father board the victory train, where Richard meets Rahn and reconciles with his son.

Striking gender arcs structure this narrative of sport victory and family rapprochement. Chief among these is the trajectory of how the broken Richard Lubanski takes up his responsibilities as provider for Christa and father to Matthias. When Richard makes his first appearance, he is out of step with the times and unable to cope with the postwar order. He returns to the Federal Republic to find patriarchal values called into question by increased female agency. Going back to his former job in the coal mines produces a panic attack: the years as a soldier have left him traumatized, gaunt, and unable to provide for the

Figure 1.1: The Lubanski family's living room in *Das Wunder von Bern*. Image courtesy of Bavaria Film GmbH/Global Screen GmbH.

family. His own war efforts are invalidated by a bureaucracy unwilling to offer a pension for the years he has spent in Soviet captivity. An early composition anticipates this historical tension.

A slow track in long shot shows a black-and-white photograph of a stern Richard Lubanski in his World War II *Wehrmacht* uniform. As the camera continues to track right through the family's living space, the photograph disappears from the frame and we see the Lubanski family sitting at the dinner table. In the scene that precedes this shot, Christa Lubanski reads the letter that her husband is to return, and concludes that "soon [they'll] be a real family again." The triple tension of the shot—between black-and-white and color, still photograph and live family, historical uniform and civilian dress—graphically anticipates the conflict between Richard and his family. The tension finds its most startling prefiguration as an Oedipal constellation. When Richard arrives at the train station in Essen-Katernberg, he thinks he spots Christa. He calls out her name and hugs the woman who resembles the face on the photograph he has in hand. In fact it is his daughter Ingrid; Richard turns and faces his aged wife, and a son who he has never seen.

Richard initially rejects Matthias and treats him harshly. In one memorable scene the father announces that he will cook dinner. As the family assembles at the table it becomes clear that Richard has prepared the meal of rabbit by slaughtering Matthias's pet. The boy begins to cry but Richard remains merciless, telling his son that "German boys don't cry." Matthias responds by doting on Rahn all the more.

The entire community unsuccessfully attempts to integrate Richard. Christa tries to help her husband negotiate the new order, curiously enough, by appealing to his old values. Although Richard scolds his children for being overly sensitive and undisciplined, Christa tells him that he has the least self-discipline of all, indeed that he only considers his own feelings. Richard laments to the local priest that "nothing is like it once was." The priest advises Richard that to be strong he must discuss his memories with his wife and children.

After his initial problems, Richard makes a concerted effort to rejoin his family. He speaks openly about his experiences in Soviet captivity. His rehabilitation is completed in the national team's train after the West German victory. Matthias had once maintained that he would rather have Rahn as his "dad," but in this scene Matthias embraces his real father, an act that moves Richard to tears. Correcting his father's earlier claim that "German boys don't cry," Matthias says, "I think German boys can go ahead and cry sometimes." The strong patriarch regains his son's affection—and, ironically, this becomes possible by the father's feminization, his open expression of emotion. The film presents a post-feminist masculinity that nonetheless is seen as compatible with a 1950s—and even 1930s—conception of manhood.

Richard's is not the only restoration of traditional gender roles. Annette Ackermann is an assertive woman who finds her true femininity—becoming a proper wife and mother—by celebrating a masculine sport. As Paul Ackermann's editor warns him early in the film, "women are the enemies of soccer," a phrase that accurately describes Annette initially. The newlywed demands Paul take her on their promised honeymoon to Africa. Her husband demurs: he has just been assigned to cover the World Cup in Bern. Annette joins him and, despite her disdain for the game, she becomes a quick and enthusiastic study. She bets her husband that the West Germans will win the World Cup and at stake are the names of their possible future children: Annette gambles the fate of her family on the fate of the nation.

This wager sets a narrative in motion in which the reconstituted family fuels the German win. The final match juxtaposes shots of the players on the pitch with crowd shots, depicting several sets of spectators, but especially privileging two: the Ackermanns. The Germans fall behind 0:2 early. Paul tells Annette that if the Germans lose he will name any future daughter Roswitha. Dismayed by Paul's choice, Annette desperately works up the crowd with the rousing cheer, "*Deutschland vor!*" (Go Germany!)

The editing reveals the effect of Annette's efforts: there is a cut to Fritz Walter and the camera tracks in a half-circle around him with the monumentality of the first computer-generated panorama of the crowd and the meticulously recreated Wankdorf Stadium. Walter, inspired by the fans, leads his teammates to charge forward, and the Germans

Figure 1.2: Annette Ackermann cheering on the West German national team in *Das Wunder von Bern*. Image courtesy of Bavaria Film GmbH/Global Screen GmbH.

Figure 1.3: Fritz Walter and the recreated Wankdorf Stadium in *Das Wunder von Bern*. Image courtesy of Bavaria Film GmbH/Global Screen GmbH.

equalize the score by halftime. Paired with Matthias's second-half appearance, which spurs Rahn to score the game winner, the narrative's historiography of Bern 1954 has "family" as the reason for the win.[10]

The German victory, in the case of both the Ackermanns and the Lubanskis, brings a nuclear family into being and produces a masculine (re)birth. The World Cup is the occasion of the Ackermann baby's conception and—because of the German victory—Annette ends up being able to name their first child. The expectant mother is certain that it will be a boy: she "can just feel it." Annette will christen him Dante, a name that recalls the origin of another national culture. Responding to the good news, Paul drops his press pass and leaves the train station, even though he was supposed to interview the West German team. His reason for neglecting his duties echoes his wife's earlier cheer; he says "*Die Familie geht vor!*" (Family comes first!). This turn of events enables the meeting between Matthias and his two fathers—Richard Lubanski picks up the press pass and boards the train with Matthias—and furthers the Lubanski reconciliation. Annette Ackermann has become a mother and Richard Lubanski is once again a proper father: it is only when these traditional gender roles are recovered that the family can be redeemed and, the film implies, that the nation can be reborn.

As a coda to this restoration saga, the ending reanimates the choreography of the *Heimatfilm*. As the sun sets and farmers toil in the fields, the players' train speeds from Switzerland into Germany. Superimposed onto these bucolic images, the closing titles read: "One year later the last prisoners of war returned home. One year later the economic miracle began. The eleven from Bern never played together again." The ragtag team's victory gives rise to the powerful German economy, itself rejuvenated by the return of its lost sons. Heavily criticized by German journalists,[11] the first two sentences from the film's coda were removed in the DVD release. Nonetheless, *Das Wunder von Bern*'s tagline, splayed across the country on posters and replayed on TV airwaves and cinema trailers, could hardly have been more programmatic: "Every child needs a father. Every person needs a dream. Every country needs a legend." The slogan equates child and nation, father and the imaginary. It summarizes the film's Oedipal trajectory and foregrounds the vital, recuperative role of the masculine in nation building. In the German context, "Every country needs a legend" strongly suggests "Every country, *even Germany*, needs a legend." This final line very directly states the film's intended role in 2003 as a national myth.

Male Fantasies

Das Wunder von Bern's blend of historical realism and masculine melodramatic fantasy invokes culturally and historically specific cinematic traditions. Actor Peter Lohmeyer, who plays Richard Lubanski, reported in the DVD's "Making Of" interview that he watched "many returning soldier [*Heimkehrer*] videos" in preparation for his role. One can presume that Lohmeyer's "videos" were "rubble films"—a cycle of domestic productions treating the social problems of the present and recent past that had its heyday between 1946 and 1948—such as *Die Mörder sind unter uns* (*The Murderers are Among Us*, 1946) or *Irgendwo in Berlin* (*Somewhere in Berlin*, 1946).[12]

Like *Das Wunder von Bern*, the rubble/returning soldier films foreground gender issues, and often, the recuperation of "traditional" gender roles. As scholar Robert R. Shandley argues, these films narrate stories of "restabilizing social relations" rather than seriously reflecting on the past, restoring "material security," or reinstalling "men and women into the dominant fiction of conventional gender roles."[13] Many of the rubble films feature a war-weary returning soldier, usually a figure from the working class, and chronicle his passage from cynicism and fatalism to the rehabilitation of his faith in the status quo.[14]

In some of these films this transformation is facilitated by the efforts of a woman. Among the productions in which a woman helps the returning soldier, Hildegard Knef's roles in *Die Mörder sind unter uns*, *Zwischen gestern und morgen* (*Between Yesterday and Tomorrow*, 1947), and *Film ohne Titel* (*Film Without a Name*, 1948) are especially iconic.[15] Erica Carter has written insightfully about the complex constellations of gender, narrative form, and history in rubble films, by which "women are seen as central, then, to the physical labour that erases the traces of war and paves the way to reconstruction in the socio-economic and political domain."[16] Using the iconography of the Madonna figure, these films divest German women from the memory of the war and war guilt, and allow them to be portrayed as the innocent and legitimate bearers of the future national culture.[17] Recently, Hester Baer has made the deepest forays yet into this subject, emphasizing that the importance of women to postwar German cinema was by no means limited to female characters' assistance to men in crisis; she shifts focus toward "the women who emerge as the new focal point both in the stories and formal codes of the films themselves and, extradiegetically, in the cinema audiences."[18]

Besides negotiating a complex functioning of women vis-à-vis the returning males, one important strand of these films, as Jaimey Fisher has argued, deploys boys as the agents of male restoration.[19] *Das Wunder von Bern*'s gender and generational dynamic resounds strikingly with these productions, and a comparison helps us better understand its vision of the postwar past.

In *Irgendwo in Berlin*, just as in Wortmann's film, the roles of women and children are clearly divided. Women detect and attend to symptoms of male weakness; the male child appeals to the returning soldier's sense of pride, honor, and community. For example, Iller's wife in *Irgendwo in Berlin* has her listless and emaciated husband fitted for new clothes, whereas it is his son Gustav who successfully encourages his father to rebuild the family garage. The narrative of *... und über uns der Himmel* (*... And the Sky Above Us*, 1947) follows a similar formula: Hans's neighbor Edith cooks for him, but it is little Werner who convinces him to return to his job as a crane operator, an honorable vocation, rather than continue as a profiteer on the black market. Crucially, these films exclude women from their restoration scenarios.[20] Mrs. Iller is missing from the scenes that lead to her husband's miraculous rehabilitation. *Rotation*'s (1949) Behnke and his son Helmuth reconcile only after the death of the wife and mother Lotte. In *... und über uns der Himmel*, father Hans and son Werner make peace without mother or wife. *Das Wunder von Bern* similarly stages its restoration scene exclusively among men—with Matthias, his father, and Rahn on the homecoming train of the (men's) German national soccer team. During the film's final half hour, Christa and Ingrid only appear briefly as cheering barkeepers.

It would be reductive to claim that all rubble films are simplistically or conservatively reconciliatory;[21] the aforementioned recent commentators on the postwar melodramas have demonstrated how they serve "as a vehicle not for blind manipulation but for the airing of ambiguities, tensions, and contradictions."[22] Rather, I want to point out how *Das Wunder von Bern*'s restorative project appropriates a number of their tropes. The former distills and simplifies the postwar cycle's focus on domestic spheres and family affairs rather than political realms or the realities of reconstruction; its fantasy of returning soldiers who will be rehabilitated and wives who have remained faithful; and its call for reconstruction. By excluding women from this restorative conclusion, *Das Wunder von Bern* follows and retrospectively exaggerates a number of rubble films by seeking to divert attention from permanently altered gender relations. With young boys as agents of restoration, men can look ahead to a rosy future and move beyond the past. However, *Das Wunder von Bern* goes much further in its pursuit of reconciliation than its postwar antecedents. Although the rubble films may have charted the restoration of traditional gender identities and family constellations, Hester Baer notes that "these films virtually always stop short of portraying the harmonious domestic sphere, revoking the fulfillment of private desires by failing to provide the 'happy end' promised by marriage and family."[23] *Das Wunder von Bern*, in contrast, offers a happy ending on all levels of the public and private, from the reconciliation of the recuperated returning patriarch with his son and family, to the coupling of the Ackermanns and the conception of their son, the triumph of Rahn and Herberger, and the unity of a nation. Compared with some rubble films such as Wolfgang Liebeneiner's *Liebe 47* (*Love '47*, 1949), which incorporates a female perspective,[24] Wortmann's appropriation of the returning soldier narrative is particularly nostalgic, conservative, and masculine.

Beyond the rubble film, *Das Wunder von Bern* has another generic genealogy: the soccer film. The subgenre has suffered from a largely dubious history in the Federal Republic. Film producers had long maintained that the sport was unfilmable, box-office poison.[25] Unlike baseball or boxing, which feature a duel structure vital to traditional narrative codes, soccer possesses a team spirit that seems at odds with commercial success. Moreover, a soccer film from Germany has a double hurdle. As Lars-Olav Beier opined in *Der Spiegel*, "in no other land is the resistance against accepting national heroes as great as in Germany, especially when they wear uniforms—be they soldiers, police, or even football players."[26] Indeed, the few post-World War II German soccer movies were modest productions and screened to empty cinemas. Wigbert Wicker's semi-fictional *Libero* (1973), *Die Franz Beckenbauer Story* (*The Franz Beckenbauer Story*, 1983), and *Nordkurve* (*Saturday Action*, 1993) flopped in theatrical release and epitomized the sport's low profile (about twelve films in the postwar period) and poor record in German cinemas. Unsurprisingly, independent projects such as Hellmuth Costard's George Best documentary *Fußball wie noch nie* (*Soccer as Never Before*, 1971) and Helke Sander's *Männerbünde* (*Male Bonds*, 1973) fared no better.

It is only very recently that soccer has made a comeback to the big screen, usually in stories of fandom, family crisis, or social adversity.[27] German features and documentaries abounded.[28] Most prominently, *Die wilden Kerle–Alles ist gut, solange du wild bist!* (*The Wild Soccer Bunch*, 2003), which would spawn four further sequels,[29] proved that the German soccer film could reap sustainable box office in its hybrid generic form.

Indeed, in the wake of Germany's second-place finish in the 2002 World Cup and in anticipation of the 2006 incarnation within its borders, the trend only continued.[30] The 2006 Berlin International Film Festival boasted an Iranian soccer entry in competition (*Offside: The Price of Dreams*, 2006) as well as the German documentary *Warum halb vier?* (*Why Three Thirty – You'll Never Walk Alone*, 2006). Lars Pepe's documentary is exemplary for the way it casts the soccer experience as a narrative in which father–son discord is resolved. Actor Joachim Król recollects his childhood and his father, describing how soccer provided the basis of their emotional communication. Król, best known for his role in Wortmann's *Der bewegte Mann* (*Maybe, Maybe Not*, 1994), reports seeing his father cry for the first time when their team finished at the bottom of the league. Like *Das Wunder von Bern* and the millennial soccer film wave at large, Pepe's project emphasizes soccer spectatorship and the sport's possible agency in masculine reconciliation and redemption. Wortmann himself followed *Das Wunder von Bern* with the nostalgic

World Cup documentary, *Deutschland. Ein Sommermärchen* (*Germany: A Summer's Fairytale*, 2006), which became the highest-grossing German documentary ever. It casts the 2006 German national soccer team—led by the Swabian Jürgen Klinsmann—as a lovable ragtag bunch which, against impossible odds, places third. The "fairy-tale summer" of the title refers to the resurgent patriotism among German citizens during the World Cup.[31]

Soccer films in Germany were indeed scarce and unpopular in the postwar period. A prehistory, however, exists. *Das Wunder von Bern* strongly recalls *Das große Spiel* (*The Big Game*, 1942). The Robert A. Stemmle film premiered on 10 July 1942, the year in which the fictional Richard Lubanski became a Soviet POW. It takes place in the Ruhr area, in the fictional town of Wupperbrück. There, many of the players for the local soccer squad, Gloria 03, have day jobs in the coalmines. Pit foreman Werner Fehling arrives in town from Gleiwitz and joins the team as a striker. With a reputation for undermining team spirit at his former club, he quickly falls in love with Grete Gabler, the daughter of one of the club's founding members, the sister of one of its players, and the team goalkeeper Jupp Jäger's girlfriend. Jupp resents Werner because of Grete's attraction to the man from the East, but he realizes that team spirit is more important than romance and accepts Werner as a teammate. Gloria 03 eventually advances to the championship match in Berlin, where the young men from Wupperbrück triumph over the opposing side, FC Nord, with the score 3:2.

Stemmle's film resembles *Das Wunder von Bern* not only in terms of setting, milieu, and final score. A crucial similarity abides in the film's thematic emphases and narrative designs, which chart a trajectory toward the cohesion of family, team, and nation. Like *Das Wunder von Bern*, Stemmle's project champions amateurs—men who toil in mines but then become stars. It too begins with a father–son relationship and depicts the team's relationship to the club's parallel under-16 squad. Father Gabler encourages his young son Heini to join the team, who makes a decisive intervention in the championship match, much like Matthias in *Das Wunder von Bern*. Furthermore, both narratives are integration stories. The Ruhr folk initially distrust Werner from Gleiwitz: "A foreign body [*Fremdkörper*] remains a foreign body, it harms the game community [*Spielgemeinschaft*]." In the end, they are won over and agree that "he's a German too." Much in this vein, Wortmann's film also foregrounds cultural difference as a temporary obstacle to be overcome via team spirit, fandom and spectatorship, and nation-building. The story of Herberger's eleven emphasizes their initial differences of temperaments but above all regional origin: the Essener Rahn, the Walter brothers from Kaiserslautern, and the other footballers' distinct accents. Herberger's feat is to unite the group as a truly national squad.

Nevertheless, it is curious that each film elides the actual heritage of its characters. Even journalist Ulrich von Berg, who sets out to rescue Stemmle's film from the readings of leftist "part-time night-school film studies teachers," admits the portrayal of an "Aryan" Ruhr-area soccer team strays far from reality.[32] A turn-of-the-century census revealed that 80 percent of area residents were of Masurian or Polish descent.[33] Furthermore, nearly all the footballers who played for Schalke 04—the real team upon which Gloria 03 is based—were the sons of immigrants from those areas.[34] In *Das Wunder von Bern*, although some spectators may well surmise that the Lubanskis, by virtue of their surname, belong to this Polish-Catholic minority which immigrated to the Ruhr area in the late nineteenth and early twentieth century, their ethnic background never becomes an issue.

As in the story of Bern, in *Das große Spiel* spectatorship plays a central role in the narrative of integration. Anticipating *Das Wunder von Bern*, Stemmle provides a montage of listeners, depicting the family and friends back in the Ruhr region huddled around their radios. Like Matthias and his friends, Heini's father acts out the game. During the final match in Berlin, Stemmle obsessively cuts back to the spectators, showing a man wiping the sweat from his face with a woman's veil, or a fan who has taken off his shoes trying to extinguish a cigarette. The era's stars are in the stands: boxing champion Max Schmeling and *Reichstrainer* Herberger make cameo appearances in the crowd. Half of the national team took part in the film as extras: Fritz Walter, Hermann Eppenhoff, Ernst Lehner, Erich Goede, and Otto Tibulski. Furthermore, the story stages a similar transformation of women who take to soccer just as Annette does in *Das Wunder von Bern*. Annette first chides her husband for wasting his time on "24 [sic] men chasing a ball" only to realize soccer's importance; likewise, Grete initially claims "Soccer is just a game!," only to become emotionally involved in the final match. Similar to Annette's role in pressing the national squad on to victory, women's cheering inspires Gloria 03 to victory. As Werner outruns the FC Nord defenders and approaches to score in the last moments, Grete and Annemarie (Werner's former lover) chant together, "Werner, Werner!" Suddenly, Grete turns her gaze to the goalkeeper who loves her and yells "Jupp!" Werner scores, Jupp is appeased, and the romantic quadrangle is somehow resolved.

Examining *Das große Spiel* may explain the postwar distaste for soccer films as too nationalistic. Contrary to most Nazi genre films, *Das große Spiel* features many overt references to contemporary politics.[35] We see a portrait of Hitler in the team's pub and in the hotel ballroom, as well as party pins on fans at the final match; we hear two shouts of "Heil Hitler." Stemmle, who began his career writing the screenplay for Luis Trenker and Kurt Bernhardt's ideologically suspect historical film, *Der Rebell* (*The Rebel*, 1932),[36] devotes much more screen time to a celebration after the semi-final than to the football match itself.

This scene features much pomp and fascist ideology as well as several sayings that would in the postwar period be called Herbergerisms— for example, "You can only play as well as your opponent lets you" and "You have to be eleven friends." Herberger was a major creative force behind the film. The coach staged the soccer scenes; Fritz Walter's autobiography reveals that Herberger functioned as co-director.[37] The lines, attributed to the coach, appear a decade before they became household expressions. Their origin, among salutes to the Führer, belies *Das Wunder von Bern*'s sanitized history. In the 2003 version, as I will examine further in the next section, the witticisms are supposed to have arisen in a nocturnal exchange between the coach and a Swiss cleaning woman during the 1954 World Cup.

Clearly, neither Sönke Wortmann nor co-screenwriter Rochus Hahn (a comic-book publisher and former announcer for a professional wrestling program on RTL) harbors National Socialist sentiments. Indeed, it is unlikely that either has even seen Stemmle's film.[38] But what shall we make of a German soccer film from 2003 that re-animates the restorative animus of the rubble film and the choreography of a Nazi feature from 1942? Vivian Sobchack's comments on the American baseball film are helpful to understand the nationalist component in the German soccer film. Sobchack analyzes how the American baseball film plots nostalgia for a "pure" American identity.[39] Examining the inventory of post-World War II American baseball films, she uncovers curious cycles and patterns. Although twenty baseball features were released between 1942 and 1958, the next fifteen years saw only one addition. A new cycle arose in 1988; here the utopian national space of previous baseball films is nostalgically redeemed. By analogy one can see how *Das Wunder von Bern* participates in a postwall cycle of soccer films not out of step with this nostalgic redemption.

The appropriation of the rubble film—a historical cycle rather than a genre as such—constitutes an act of displacement in 2003. The rubble films responded to their social present and immediate past; invoking them almost six decades later is to transpose their social agenda. If the 1950s *Heimatfilm* translated the rubble film's programmatic slogan, "we will be normal again," into the present tense ("we are somebody again"), Wortmann's retrospection operates in the historical future tense: "It was to turn out that we became proud to be Germans again." This logic, however, subscribes to a normalizing revision. "Every child needs a father, every person needs a dream, every country needs a legend": this third part of *Das Wunder von Bern*'s program imposes this necessity onto Germany. The film asks, "What would it be like if today, in 2003, we could recover our pride to be Germans again?" The recourse to the rhetoric of the rubble film and the echoes from *Das große Spiel* participate in transforming this "legend" into a parable, an example to be enacted by the German nation of the twenty-first century.

Animating Memory: Authenticity and the Desire to See

The production of a compelling prosthetic memory is not merely a function of characters and genre formulae. It entails satisfying a desire to experience history in a sensuous way. In practice this means attending to the period's shapes, colors, and sounds (i.e., "authenticity"), providing access to hitherto inaccessible events or details, and employing special effects to enhance the visual realism.

Indeed, Wortmann uses a catalogue of forms and styles to affect a nostalgic look. He re-creates newsreel footage of the World Cup team training with a grainy black-and-white digital effect accompanied by a campy voice-over, ending the sequence with an iris shot. During the final match, each goal is re-created precisely. In addition, the film intimates how the match might have been filmed; many shots recall the conventions of 1950s television soccer broadcasts, for example, in their use of an aerial perspective. In spite of these nods to authenticity, the title match is not presented in a televisual format. Filmed in saturated colors, this crucial moment in the narrative and German cultural memory is transmitted in a mythical form. Although the camera remains static for nearly the entire film, avoiding close-ups and conspicuous angles,[40] the big game possesses an exceptional aesthetic aura: circular camera movements, quick cuts, slow motion, and dramatic uses of CGI technology. Rahn's game-winning goal is divided into no less than three shots, each from a different perspective. This of course transcends what live television reportage could have delivered, both in 1954 and even in 2003.

Das Wunder von Bern would be unimaginable without the numerous television documentaries from the 1990s on the 1954 World Cup victory; it reiterates their themes and even borrows their compositions.[41] In the DVD interview, the director claims to have screened all of the newsreels from the World Cup summer in order to understand the era's "complexion." He carefully selected Sascha Göpsel, whom he calls the "reincarnation" of Helmut Rahn, because Göpsel, like Rahn, comes from Essen and speaks the local dialect. According to the DVD, the production crew spent October through December 2000 casting semi-professional football players from Germany's minor leagues as the West German and Hungarian squads. Costume and make-up crews went through "waves of family albums" to design the style for their clothes and determine precisely how long women wore their nails. Wortmann even invited the aging Horst Eckel to the film set so that he might countenance the production. The "Making Of" unit captures Eckel gleefully exclaiming that his actor counterpart looks and moves just like he did.

Das Wunder von Bern does not merely recreate period costumes or offer actors who look and sound like their real-life characters. The narrative allows privileged access to these historical figures, speculating on their motivations and private lives. This quenches a sensuous desire to learn more about these stars and to see what they "were really like." For example, the film imagines the origins of Sepp Herberger's famous witticisms such as "the ball is round and the game lasts 90 minutes" or "the post-game is the pre-game," which have long entered into everyday German discourse. In Wortmann's apocryphal history, these sayings stem from a late-night conversation with a Swiss cleaning woman. The sleepless coach wanders the hotel halls wondering whether to punish the recalcitrant Rahn for his drunken insubordination. Herberger asks the maid for advice on his "22 children" and the two engage in a friendly exchange of phrases. The next day the coach charms the testy press corps with his new-found witticisms.

The representation of Herbert Zimmermann's reportage further indicates the film's drive to provide visual historical pleasures. The radio commentator's play-by-play coverage of the World Cup final reached 50 million listeners. His ebullient delivery became synonymous with the event, and *Das Wunder von Bern* draws on this cultural memory. Zimmermann's signature broadcast accompanies the end of the film's credits as well as the teaser-trailer shown in German cinemas. These disembodied but "real" appropriations of Zimmermann have a clear function: first, to "authenticate" the Wortmann film via the pre-existing cultural memory of the event and, second, to lure spectators into theaters to *see* what Zimmermann was doing.

Figure 1.4: Andreas Obering embodying announcer Herbert Zimmermann in *Das Wunder von Bern*. Image courtesy of Bavaria Film GmbH/Global Screen GmbH.

Michel Chion's theory of a voice that becomes embodied in the course of a film provides a way to approach one of the most remarkable aspects of *Das Wunder von Bern*: when the film debuted, Germans finally got to see the face behind the voice, because actor-comedian Andreas Obering intoned excerpts from Zimmermann's original commentary. According to Chion, an acousmêtre is a being whom we hear but do not see.[42] People speaking on the radio are acousmêtres, for instance, because there is no way of seeing them. Films deploy this tactic to dramatic effect: characters can enter or leave the frame while talking, or the director might delay the character's entrance into the visuals as a tool of suspense: "An entire image, an entire story, an entire film can thus hang on the epiphany of the acousmêtre" (23). Chion speaks of de-acousmatization, the eventual embodiment of the disembodied voice. Fantasy, thriller, or gangster pictures regularly use de-acousmatization—for example in *Kiss Me Deadly* (1955), when the hitherto invisible Big Boss becomes embodied, and because he is now visible, he is also vulnerable.

But what happens when the genre is the historical film and the narrative re-tells a story that had existed as an acousmatic media memory? For Chion, de-acousmatization is "a sort of symbolic act, dooming the acousmêtre to the fate of ordinary mortals" (28). Although this thought is borne out in films like *The Wizard of Oz* (1939) (when the "Great Oz" is revealed to be an ordinary man) or in the aforementioned genres, there seems to be another effect at work here. The visual representation of Herbert Zimmermann in *Das Wunder von Bern* allows Germans who had experienced the final match over the radio to partake of Obering's gestures and contorted facial expressions. Even younger viewers not alive in 1954 can see the man whose voice they have heard in documentaries and reportages. The representation of Zimmermann is the visceral dimension that fills out the sonic memory.

It is important to note that Zimmermann is not—unlike in Chion's examples—merely withheld by the director over the course of a film. The announcer had been previously denied to the public imagination by a medium and a moment in history. Accordingly, I call this unveiling "historical de-acousmatization." Unlike in *The Wizard of Oz* or *Kiss Me Deadly*, this effect makes the historical figure all the more monumental. By using the Zimmermann character's voice and face to narrate *Das Wunder von Bern* in voice-over, the film "promotes" Zimmermann. Once Zimmermann is historically de-acousmatized, he is no longer a radio announcer, but rather a television commentator. The final scenes at the Lubanski's pub and in Bruno's East Berlin hangout confirm this insofar as the Zimmermann character's voice emanates from the television. The historical Zimmermann's insufficient ability to narrate a "picture of the game"—a fault for which professional colleagues have retrospectively taken him to task[43] and one to which Zimmermann himself admits in his post-game commentary—is covered up in this retro-vision by the re-created images of the game. The imagined Zimmermann comes into being prosthetically enlarged.

To appreciate *Das Wunder von Bern*'s creation of a sensuous public memory, it is useful to turn briefly to its color design. In a recent article, Jennifer M. Kapczynski insightfully examines *Das Wunder von Bern*'s nostalgic "Agfacolor effect": "a palette of graying greens, darkly saturated reds, and wan blues," which attempts to "animate the past through the act of aesthetic restoration."[44] Exploring the industrial history of Agfacolor and especially parent company IG Farben's complicity with the Hitler regime, Kapczynski shows how the stock was deployed in major exemplars of "national self-imaginings," such as test footage for coverage of the 1936 Berlin Olympics, Josef von Baky's *Münchhausen* (1943), and Veit Harlan's *Kolberg* (1945). Thus, deploying the Agfacolor look in 2003 represents "a form of nostalgic remembrance, closely bound up with questions of trauma as well as normalization."[45] In an analysis of Wortmann's film, she comments on how *Das Wunder von Bern* changes its color scheme from the gray tones of the Ruhr area to the vibrant "Agfacolor effect" of Switzerland and the big game.[46]

One film that Kapczynski does not mention, but also served as a "national self-imagining" once again anticipates the prosthetic memory from 2003: *Das große Spiel*. Stemmle's film showcases its own technological invention in a similar manner. The titular big game is withheld until the last twenty minutes; after an entire film in black and white, it appears in striking Agfacolor. Everything that happens during the final match and after—for the players, the announcer, the crowd, as well as the listeners in Wupperbrück—is polychrome. The new epoch has arrived; color signals a utopian historicism. The film confirms Paul Virilio's remarks about how color, increasingly used during final years of the Third Reich, provided Germans with a distraction from their black-and-white existence.[47] The similarity to *Das Wunder von Bern* abides in the latter's enhanced access to historical figures, painstaking period "authenticity," and prominent use of CGI in the final match: both projects deploy technology as a telos and a spectacle. These larger-than-life representations monumentalize football, bind the society together, and make the event much more than "just a game."

1954 – 1979 – 2003

Das Wunder von Bern re-visualized—and thus revised—the past. Its prosthetic memory was compelling for Germans, as demonstrated in its reception history. The film recorded over 3.5 million viewers in its domestic theatrical run and, even if movie critics were often skeptical, it found resonance with the general press on account of its cultural importance. *Der Spiegel* ran three special articles on the feature in three separate issues; *Die Zeit* devoted an entire "Dossier" section to the movie and the memory of the historical match.[48]

The film was a national and political event. Wortmann screened a rough cut to Gerhard Schröder and proudly reported that the "macho" chancellor had cried three times. Schröder, in turn, encouraged his fellow Germans to weep. Indeed, the Essen premiere of *Das Wunder von Bern* became a site of nostalgic recollection. Wortmann chose the industrial city because it had been hometown of Rahn, who had died not long before the premiere. The principal actors rolled into the Essen central station in the same train wagons that transported the championship 1954 team back from Switzerland. Schröder, Interior Minister Otto Schily, Northrhine-Westphalia Minister President Peer Steinbrück, the Consul-General of Switzerland, and the Hungarian Ambassador attended the red-carpet premiere at the Lichtburg cinema.[49]

In the meantime, *Das Wunder von Bern* has left its mark as the central reference point for the event. When the *Süddeutsche Zeitung* released a book-length World Cup 1954 history, its dust jacket thanked "Sönke Wortmann's film, which turned the black-and-white memories into color. The soccer World Cup even helps in history class and connects generations."[50] Indeed, the Federal Agency for Civic Education published a teachers' booklet so that the film might be used in school history lessons. One leftover from 1994's smaller memorial of 1954, F.C. Delius's novella *Der Sonntag an dem ich Weltmeister wurde*, got a *Wunder von Bern* make-over in the twenty-first century: Peter Lohmeyer—Richard Lubanski in Wortmann's film—recorded the audiotape version. In sum, the film appears to have assumed the cultural function that Elsaesser ascribes to the Zapruder home movie: although *Das Wunder von Bern* was released years after the event it represents, the German public recalls it as the historical antecedent's ground zero.

And yet, as this chapter has detailed, *Das Wunder von Bern* imagines the World Cup through a variety of genres and cycles and with the aid of television documentaries, period photographs, and newsreels. It is crucial to note that the film not only interprets 4 July 1954, but also comments on that event's previous interpreters. In order to understand what it is saying about the course of German film history we must first examine the biography of Sönke Wortmann and his attitude toward the New German Cinema.

Wortmann established his commercial reputation with relationship comedies which—according to commentators writing in the ideological-symptomatic vein—although initially piquant, resolve with the restoration of social conformism and traditional gender values; like sitcoms, the "protagonists are often placed in an initially hostile environment, which leads to inevitable misunderstandings and conflicts until a compromise brings harmony."[51] His debut theatrical feature,

Allein unter Frauen (*Alone Among Women*, 1991), which tells the story of a macho who must share a flat with a group of feminists, attracted over a million Germans. The follow-up hit, *Kleine Haie* (*Little Sharks*, 1992), also features the tribulations of a young man dumped by his girlfriend; the protagonist is forced to eke out an existence as an actor with male friends in a (putative) politically correct "women's world." The best-attended domestic picture for both 1994 and 1995, with nearly seven million admissions, *Der bewegte Mann* adapted Ralf König's graphic novels but without the source's subversive wit. Featuring the then ascending star Til Schweiger, Wortmann's adaptation chronicles a handsome rake, Axel, who, after being thrown out of his flat by his girlfriend, moves in with a smitten gay friend, Norbert. Although several scenes hint at Axel's potential bisexuality, this initial sexual turbulence gives way to a final confirmation of heterosexuality. *Der bewegte Mann*, in particular, anticipates the gender "tasting" of *Das Wunder von Bern*. In the former film, Axel encourages his Norbert to be confident and assertive; in return, the gay man teaches the heterosexual hunk about shopping and cooking. After these flirtations with non-normative regimes of gender and sexuality, however, the status quo is reinstated. This, what Randall Halle calls the "temporary-gay narrative,"[52] corresponds to the criss-crossed gender trajectories in *Das Wunder von Bern*: Richard Lubanski and Annette Ackermann are temporarily "feminized" and "masculinized," respectively, only then to reassume their normative gender positions.

Wortmann's early features, alongside the work of his contemporaries Detlev Buck and Doris Dörrie, epitomized the carefree spirit of early 1990s German cinema and became synonymous with the death of the New German Cinema.[53] Wortmann's box-office magic disappeared after *Der bewegte Mann*, however, and his subsequent films suffered scathing reviews and diminishing returns. These included *Das Superweib* (*The Superwife*, 1996), a reactionary tale about an empowered woman who finally "accepts" domestication; *Der Campus* (*Campus*, 1998), about a university professor falsely accused of rape and a send-up of political correctness in academia and the public sphere; and *St. Pauli Nacht* (*St. Pauli Night*, 1999). *The Hollywood Sign* (2001), starring Burt Reynolds and Tom Beringer, went straight to video in North America and did not have a German release until 2004.

Wortmann became bitter that the relationship comedy he had pioneered was displaced by the more "sophisticated" productions of X-Films and other "art films." The director was explicit about this in interviews, and vented his frustrations by taking on screenplays with snide remarks about the course of German film history.[54] Will Groß, the arrogant rake who wrongs Veronica Ferres's character in *Das Superweib*, is referred to as a former director of New German Cinema. Now taken to delivering formulaic genre films, during a shoot he wonders, nearly apoplectic, "What are we making here? *Deutschland, bleiche Mutter* or something?"

Given the aesthetics and politics of Wortmann's work and his comments on the New German Cinema, it is perhaps unsurprising that *Das Wunder von Bern* responds most explicitly to a production released during the twenty-fifth anniversary of Bern, Rainer Werner Fassbinder's *Die Ehe der Maria Braun*. In the latter, the 1954 World Cup final also provides a dramatic finale and the backdrop for a domestic melodrama. The final minutes of Herbert Zimmermann's radio broadcast play over the title character's unhappy reunion with her long-absent husband, and climax as the house explodes because Maria has left a gas burner on. Fassbinder interprets the Bern victory as a site of a lost opportunity, the Federal Republic's missed chance at a new beginning, and the continuation of totalitarianism from Hitler to Helmut Schmidt. A closer inspection of the two films' final scenes is instructive.

The last minutes of the game in *Das Wunder von Bern* represent a harmonious dénouement. Andreas Obering's Herbert Zimmermann play-by-play dominates the soundtrack. His voice-over commentary is authoritative and dynamic. As the film cuts between shots of Matthias outside the Wankdorf Stadium, inside the arena, and on the edge of the field itself, and finally to Zimmermann in his press box, the "source" and function of Zimmermann changes from a voice emanating from the radio, to a *Dr. Mabuse*-esque semi-diegetic voice-over, to a de-acousmatized narration. The re-created Zimmermann is constant and the central point of sonic attention in a soundtrack that otherwise consists of crowd noise and Marcel Barsotti's expressive score. In the historic match, the referee's decision to begin the game eight minutes early meant that Zimmermann had to scramble in the first minutes to narrate the action and announce the line-ups. Wortmann's version begins with Zimmermann calmly listing the cast of characters on the field. Only one moment defies media saturation: the look between Rahn and Matthias, just before the winning goal. In these ten shots, the Barsotti score swells and Zimmermann's voice vanishes.

Otherwise, Zimmermann's re-enacted voice permeates the diegetic space and, by extension, the entire nation. Immediately following Rahn's goal, a montage of spectatorship begins. It consists of cheers scenes from all over Germany, frontal perspectives relayed with an immobile camera. Each location typically receives a single shot, and the effect offers a photographic flipbook reminiscent of the coffee-table records of the event: Annette in the stands, the Lubanski pub in Essen, Herberger and the player's bench in Bern, Matthias, and the players. Using suspenseful music as Zimmermann appeals to the game clock to tick more quickly, Wortmann stages the redemption of Germany. Several more stock images follow, some directly copied from 1954 World Cup documentaries—for example, crowds watching the game in the shop window of Radio Spiess. The editing is relentless and literal, depicting the empty desk of the bureaucrat who denied Richard

Lubanski his war pension, the soccer field where the boys re-enacted the Austria game, the vacant Essen-Katernberg train station, Bruno watching the game on television with his FDJ comrades in East Berlin (even Lenin, in a mural behind the boys seems to be looking on), the vacated *Süddeutsche Zeitung* building, monks in a monastery intensely facing the radio (a crucified Jesus observes the scene from behind), and back to the game itself for Zimmermann's "It's Over! It's Over! Germany are World Champions!" *Das Wunder von Bern* retrospectively unifies all areas of East and West Germany so that it becomes the imagined community of "one nation."

In contrast, Fassbinder deploys the Zimmermann radio commentary in the last ten-and-a-half minutes of *Die Ehe der Maria Braun* as an element of disjunction. The coverage of the final match begins upon Hermann Braun's return. Unlike in *Das Wunder von Bern*, where the authentic Zimmermann recording is relegated to the film's trailer and the very end of the film's credits, Fassbinder uses the original throughout. However, Fassbinder takes sonic liberties, cutting up and rearranging the play-by-play to startling effect.[55] Zimmermann's voice comes as part of a multi-layered soundtrack that includes character dialogue (often itself multi-layered as when, for example, the will is read while Maria and Senkenberg converse) and sound effects (e.g., the door bell and the hiss of the gas stove). The commentary competes with the characters' conversations and the other effects; because individual tracks increase and decrease in volume, the sound focus is in constant flux. Rather than a vehicle of Zimmermann's commentary, Fassbinder provides a sonic cacophony. Whereas Barsotti's score creates anticipation for the final whistle, Peer Raaben's sound design engenders a feeling of doom and dread when Zimmermann expresses the concern that there are "only five minutes left!"

Contrary to *Das Wunder von Bern*, in Fassbinder's film it is unclear whether the track is diegetic or non-diegetic. The potential source radio is never identified, only glossed over by a quick tracking shot; the fact of concentrated listening, likewise, is never depicted. At times, the characters seem to respond to the narrated events of the game. Indeed, the end of the preceding scene both highlights this diegetic/non-diegetic ambiguity and makes an explicit parallel between the Bern game and nascent German nationalism. As Maria eats in a restaurant, Chancellor Konrad Adenauer announces West German rearmament on the radio, a move that he had explicitly rejected earlier in history (and in the film). Maria becomes ill—perhaps at hearing this hypocrisy—and Adenauer's address concludes with a radio voice announcing the next day's World Cup final against Hungary. Although radio transmits the political sphere incessantly over the course of the film, the family almost always ignores it.

This contrasts to the general role that the media play in *Das Wunder von Bern*. In Wortmann's 1954, the media are the seminal sites of mass culture—sports and pop music—and his Germans are avid, enthusiastic spectators and listeners. The media, in a variety of forms, bind the family and the body politic. The first scene shows a carrier pigeon delivering Matthias and his pals the score of the Rot-Weiß Essen game. When Matthias's brother Bruno smuggles a radio into his room so that he can listen to one of the opening round matches, the act brings Matthias closer to his brother and provides him with an—aural—window to the world, especially because his father has grounded him. The pub, which supports the family during Richard's absence and unemployment, is only profitable because local men come to watch soccer games on their television. Via editing and camera movements, television maintains an intimate relationship with the Lubanskis. In one broadcast, German national goalkeeper Anton Turek advertises for the *Spätheimkehrer* (late returning soldiers) charity, which directly addresses Richard Lubanski's problem. The film cuts between Turek on the pub's black-and-white television to Turek in the studio. A tracking shot reveals that this perspective is not that of the television camera, but rather of a filmic camera-eye in the studio. The film then cuts back to a concerned Ingrid Lubanski. *Das Wunder von Bern* thereby establishes a narrative link between the Lubanskis and history writ large, pitting television as an interlocutor with the family.

Unlike *Das Wunder von Bern*, in which the re-created Zimmermann becomes the uncontradicted, single voice of an entire nation, the final scene of *Die Ehe der Maria Braun* takes place within the confines of Maria's mansion. Michael Ballhaus's cinematography favors claustrophobic and disorientating tracking shots and zooms. In long takes the camera meanders through rooms, and the editing between shots is in total disregard of the classical 180°-axis convention; each time Ballhaus photographs Maria in her bedroom, his camera shoots from a different distance and perspective. The two takes outside of the house—depicting Senkenberg and the French notary turning toward the exploded building—evade Zimmermann's sonic reach. Rather than bringing a country together, the disjunctive sound design serves to intensify the scene's drama of disunity. Hermann and Maria talk twice about the fact they have not yet kissed. They try to initiate sex but are always interrupted. The film ends with Zimmermann's "It's over!" coupled with the dial tone of a phone that is off the hook: quite literally, a missed connection.

The two sound schemes characterize two films of different times, productions that are directed to different audiences and which offer different interpretations of 1954. Surely, both projects tie the fate of a family and a team to the fate of the German nation. But whereas the final victory in *Das Wunder von Bern* means reconciliation for father and son Lubanski, in *Die Ehe der Maria Braun* it parallels Maria and Hermann's death. For Fassbinder, Bern means a woman's self-destructive act that negates a futile lifetime goal of familial reunion (based as it was on a marriage that lasted half a day and a whole night). Allegorically, it constitutes a continuity with Nazism. The historical audience that Fassbinder addresses is of a particular political persuasion (progressive to radical); the where-were-you-when sentiment—so vital to Wortmann's project—is beside the point. The concluding montage, negative photographs of the postwar chancellors (with the exception of Willy Brandt), is exemplary in its unabashedly leftist take on the 1950s. Including Helmut Schmidt, the leader in power in 1978, it moves beyond the story's setting, 1954, to suggest an unbroken fascist continuum from the leader portrayed in the opening shot, Adolf Hitler, to the present. Zimmermann's post-game apology for his sparse play-by-play, the last words in Fassbinder's film, echoes ironically as a historical diagnosis of the Federal Republic: "You can't imagine what went on here." For Wortmann, the same event precipitates German economic might and the triumphant reunion of a German family and nation.

Das Wunder von Bern's final titles—"One year later the last prisoners of war returned home. One year later the economic miracle began. The eleven from Bern never played together again."—stand outside diegetic time as well, authoritatively passing judgment on history by "outliving" their subject. But rather than presenting a death scene, *Das Wunder von Bern* seeks to revive the innocence of the notion of *Heimat* so that the concluding image of a team's train speeding into the sunset can be presented without irony. In so doing, it excises the traumas of 1968 and the leaden years of left-wing terrorism, and revises the 68ers' interpretations of Bern, 1954, the economic miracle, and the Adenauer–Erhard–Kiesinger years.

The chemistry of emotional masculinity at work in *Das Wunder von Bern* characterizes a host of postwall revisionist films about the 1940s and 1950s, including *Stalingrad* (1993), *Comedian Harmonists* (*The Harmonists*, 1997), *Der Untergang* (*Downfall*, 2004), and *Die Fälscher* (*The Counterfeiters*, 2007). This applies also to television documentaries on the postwar period, such as ARD's *Die Vertriebenen* (*The Displaced Persons*, 2001) and *Unsere 50er Jahre* (*Our 1950s*, 2005). *Der Untergang*'s representation of a "human" Hitler garnered particular media and academic attention, but in general all of these projects impose a New Age sentimentality onto its historical subject. Indicative of this tendency is the advice that the priest gives to Richard Lubanski: "Many of the former prisoners I talk to have these problems. Most of them are ashamed of their time in misery. They shut out their families, try to pretend that they're strong, but in reality they are afraid to show what captivity did to them." Long a staple of the 1980s relationship comedies such as Dörrie's *Männer...* (*Men...*, 1985) or Wortmann's own

Der bewegte Mann, this pop psychology is nonetheless a jarring revision of 1950s masculinity. The portrayals of tearful men hugging their sons contrast strikingly with the New German Cinema's cold, often violent fathers. One need only think of Ernst Jacobi's brutal Hans in *Deutschland, bleiche Mutter* or Franz Rudnik's turn as pastor and father to Marianne and Juliane in *Die bleierne Zeit* to realize the singularity of a Richard Lubanski. Sanders-Brahms and von Trotta presented these men as part of a malignant generation without investigating the motives for their harsh or even evil behavior. Psychoanalysis was reserved only for the children, the filmmakers' own generation and their ultimate focus. Postwall revisions such as *Stalingrad, Das Wunder von Bern*, or *Der Untergang*, in contrast, apologize for the war generation by providing their fathers with psychological detail and emotional depth. The memories of the war and the immediate postwar period are sufficiently distant to allow this retrospection; the political stakes have vanished and the soldiers' generation has nearly died off. The following chapter examines a set of films which imagine the old Federal Republic's other major historical trauma, the children's inheritance of their parents' fascism: left-wing terrorism.

Notes

1. For an English-language account of this "continuity thesis," see Hans Kundnani, *Utopia or Auschwitz: Germany's 1968 Generation and the Holocaust* (London: Hurst, 2009).
2. Thomas Elsaesser, "Subject Positions, Speaking Positions: From *Holocaust, Our Hitler,* and *Heimat* to *Shoah* and *Schindler's List*," in *The Persistence of History: Cinema, Television, and the Modern Event*, ed. Vivian Sobchack (New York: Routledge, 1996), 146.
3. See, for instance, Lothar Schirmer, *Das Wunder in Bildern. Bern 1954. Deutschland – Ungarn 3:2. 73 Reportagephotographien vom Endspiel* (Munich: Schirmer/Mosel, 2004), as well as the book that accompanied the Knopp documentary, Sebastian Dehnhardt, *Das Wunder von Bern: Die wahre Geschichte* (Munich: Heyne, 2004).
4. See Oliver Link, "Das Spiel ist niemals aus," *Der Stern*, 2 October 2003, 188–94.
5. Knut Hickethier, *Die Geschichte des deutschen Fernsehens* (Stuttgart: Metzler, 1998), 112.
6. See the 2004 ZDF documentary *Das Wunder von Bern: Die wahre Geschichte (The Miracle of Bern: The True Story)*, which fetishizes the color footage of goals it unearthed.
7. Alison Landsberg, *Prosthetic Memory: The Transformation of American Remembrance in the Age of Mass Culture* (New York: Columbia University Press, 2004), 20–21. See also Celia Lury, *Prosthetic Culture: Photography, Memory and Identity* (London: Routledge, 1998).
8. Marcia Landy, *Cinematic Uses of the Past* (Minneapolis: University of Minnesota Press, 1996), 24.
9. Linda Williams: "Film Bodies: Gender, Genre, and Excess" *Film Quarterly* 44(4) (1991): 10–11.
10. Christof Siemes's novelization of the film makes an even more explicit connection. Once West Germany has won, he speculates on the reactions and futures of the fictional family members: Bruno Lubanski, for example, packs his bags and moves to West Berlin. In the same manner, however, the novel incorporates real anecdotes from historical personages. For instance, "When Germany becomes world champion, the 23-year-old Johannes Rau sits in a small French train station…On 23 May 1999

Johannes Rau will become the eighth Federal President of the Federal Republic of Germany." Christof Siemes, *Das Wunder von Bern* (Cologne: Kiepenhauer & Witsch, 2003), 242–52; here 244.

11. See, for example, Fritz Göttler, "Hallo, Helmut!," *Süddeutsche Zeitung*, 16 October 2003, or the *Die Zeit* "Dossier" section, 28 August 2003.

12. He might have also seen Wolfgang Liebeneiner's *Taiga* (1958), which dramatizes the Siberian POW situation that Richard Lubanski escapes.

13. Robert R. Shandley, *Rubble Films: German Cinema in the Shadow of the Third Reich* (Philadelphia: Temple University Press, 2001), 185.

14. Peter Pleyer estimates that 60% of rubble films feature a *Heimkehrer* figure. See Peter Pleyer, *Deutscher Nachkriegsfilm 1946–1948* (Münster: Fahle, 1965), 143.

15. See Ulrike Sieglohr, "Hildegard Knef: From Rubble Woman to Fallen Woman," in *Heroines without Heroes: Reconstructing Female and National Identities in European Cinema, 1945–1951*, ed. Ulrike Sieglohr (London: Cassell, 2000), 113–27.

16. Erica Carter, "Sweeping Up the Past: Gender and History in the Post-War German 'Rubble Film,'" in *Heroines Without Heroes: Reconstructing Female and National Identities in European Cinema, 1945–1951*, ed. Ulrike Sieglohr (London: Cassell, 2000), 91–110: here 101.

17. See Carter, "Sweeping Up the Past," 104ff. as well as Tim Bergfelder, "German Cinema and Film Noir," in *European Film Noir*, ed. Andrew Spicer (Manchester: Manchester University Press, 2007), 147.

18. Hester Baer, *Dismantling the Dream Factory: Gender, German Cinema, and the Postwar Quest for a New Film Language* (New York: Berghahn, 2009), 7. Baer builds on and complicates the argument about the importance of postwar German female film spectatorship in Heide Fehrenbach, *Cinema in Democratizing Germany: Reconstructing National Identity after Hitler* (Chapel Hill: University of North Carolina Press, 1995).

19. One writer reports that more than 25% of German films made between 1946 and 1949 have children as protagonists. See Bettina Greffath, *Gesellschaftsbilder der Nachkriegszeit: Deutsche Spielfilme 1945-1949* (Pfaffenweiler: Centaurus, 1995), 215. But surely a much greater proportion of rubble films from this period feature children as agents of restoration: e.g.... *und über uns der Himmel* (... *And the Sky Above Us*, 1947), *Rotation* (1949), *Der Ruf* (*The Last Illusion*, 1949), *1-2-3 Corona* (1948), *Die Kuckucks* (*The Cuckoos*, 1949), *Wege ins Zwielicht* (*Paths in Twilight*, 1948), and *Irgendwo in Berlin*, among others. See Jaimey Fisher, "Deleuze in a Ruinous Context: German Rubble-Film and Italian Neorealism," *Iris* 23 (1997): 53–74 as well as Jaimey Fisher, *Disciplining Germany: Youth, Reeducation, and Reconstruction after the Second World War* (Detroit: Wayne State University Press, 2007).

20. See Carter, "Sweeping Up the Past," 104ff. as well as Erica Carter, *How German Is She? Postwar German Reconstruction and the Consuming Woman* (Ann Arbor: University of Michigan Press, 1997), 178.

21. This was often implied in the research on the rubble film (Pleyer, Greffath). For the first significant attempt to redeem the genre from purely ideological critique (while simultaneously participating in such a critique), see Thomas Brandlmeier, "Von Hitler zu Adenauer," in *Zwischen gestern und morgen: Westdeutscher Nachkriegsfilm 1945–1961*, ed. Hilmar Hoffmann and Walter Schobert (Frankfurt: Deutsches Filmmuseum, 1989), 32–59.

22. Carter, *How German Is She?*, 179.

23. Baer, *Dismantling the Dream Factory*, 8.

24. Baer, *Dismantling the Dream Factory*, 73–100.

25. Lars-Olav Beier, "Der Traum vom großen Kick," *Der Spiegel*, 14 July 2003: 136–38. In the subsequent discussion, the page number is provided in the text. See also Nora Sayre, "Winning the Weepstakes: The Problems of American Sports Movies," in *Film Genre: Theory and Criticism*, ed. Barry K. Grant (Metuchen, NJ: Scarecrow, 1977), 182–94.

26. Beier, "Der Traum vom großen Kick," 138.

27. The German productions were prefigured by prominent and successful international contributions. An early instance is the UK film *Fever Pitch* (1997), based on the Nick Hornby novel, which thematizes father–son soccer spectatorship and the effect of fandom on a romantic relationship. *Bend It Like Beckham* (2002), a UK–German co-production, is similar. Portraying a young British-Indian girl's struggles with her orthodox Sikh parents over her insistence on traveling to Hamburg with her team, the film is as much about generational and cultural tension in England as it is a movie about soccer. Indeed, this also would be a strategy for *Das Wunder von Bern*, which arrived in a surge of sport films to hit German theaters. Besides *Bend It Like Beckham*, these included the Australian film *The Cup* (1999), the Hong Kong feature *Shaolin Soccer* (2001), and *The Game of Their Lives* (2002).

28. For example: *Fußball ist unser Leben* (*Football Rules Ok*, 2000), Romuald Karmakar's short *Die Nacht von Yokohama* (*The Night of Yokohama*, 2002), *Befreite Zone* (*Liberated Zone*, 2002), *Die Champions* (*The Champions*, 2003), *Männer wie wir* (*Guys and Balls*, 2004), *Aus der Tiefe des Raumes - ...mitten ins Netz!* (*A Pass from the Back*, 2004), and a co-production with Honduras, *Adelante Muchachas!* (*Let's Go, Girls!*, 2004). German television boasted, furthermore, the eight-part WDR documentary *Der Ball ist rund – 40 Jahre Fußball-Bundesliga* (*The Ball Is Round – 40 Years Soccer-Bundesliga*, 2003).

29. *Die wilden Kerle II* (2005), *Die wilden Kerle 3* (2006), *Die wilden Kerle 4* (2007), and *Die wilden Kerle 5* (2008).

30. See, for example, the German re-make of the Finnish *FC Venus* (*FC Venus – Made in Germany*, 2006), *Das Wunder von Mühlenbeck* (*The Miracle of Mühlenbeck*, 2006), *Fußballgöttinnen* (*Soccer Goddesses*, 2006), *Futbol Fanatico* (2007), *Gate 8 – Fußball im Ungleichgewicht* (*Gate 8 – Soccer Out of Balance*, 2007), *Fan-Demanium* (2007), *Die Fans sind wir* (*We Are the Fans*, 2007), and *Jesus liebt Dich* (*Jesus Loves You*, 2008). In addition, 2006 featured the Swedish Jonas Karlsson star vehicle and soccer film *Offside*.

31. For an ideological reading of the film, see Lutz Koepnick, "Public Viewing: Soccer Patriotism and Post-Cinema," in *The Collapse of the Conventional: German Film and Its Politics at the Turn of the Twenty-First Century*, eds. Jaimey Fisher and Brad Prager (Detroit: Wayne State University Press, 2010), 63–80.

32. See Ulrich von Berg, "Raritäten: *Das große Spiel*, der beste aller Fußballfilme," *Steadycam* 23 (1992): 14.

33. von Berg, "Raritäten," 19.

34. von Berg, "Raritäten," 18–19.

35. See Eric Rentschler, *The Ministry of Illusion: Nazi Cinema and Its Afterlife* (Cambridge, MA: Harvard University Press, 1996), 7.

36. Eric Rentschler reports that the "energy and élan" of *Der Rebell* "excited Hitler and [Goebbels], prompting the latter to praise it as a film so powerful that it 'could even bowl over non-National Socialists.'" See Rentschler, *The Ministry of Illusion*, 81.

37. Fritz Walter, *Der Chef – Sepp Herberger* (Munich: Copress, 1964), 36–38, 53. Other recent sources (e.g., von Berg, "Raritäten," 19) credit Herberger with inventing the "behind-the-goal camera."

38. Michael Althen nonetheless also notes this parallel in "Die Wahrheit liegt auf dem Platz," *Frankfurter Allgemeine Zeitung*, 15 October 2003.

39. Vivian Sobchack, "... Baseball in the Post-American Cinema, or Life in the Minor Leagues," in *Out of Bounds: Sports, Media, and the Politics of Identity*, eds. Aaron Baker and Todd Boyd (Bloomington: Indiana University Press, 1997), 175–97.

40. The one exception is the stylized scene in the mine shaft, where Richard Lubanski suffers a nervous breakdown, a spectacle Wortmann stages with back projection, slow motion, and shaky visuals.

41. Nonetheless, the information it elides from those productions is even more telling. The film pointedly lacks, for instance, the 1994 documentary's lengthy discussion of the negative nationalism catalyzed by the event. Nor does Wortmann's version

show how the German spectators in Bern sang the forbidden first stanza of the German national anthem immediately after the victory. This is especially curious since *Das Wunder von Bern* plays the entire *Deutschlandlied* before the game and omits the Hungarian anthem. There is also no mention of the German team's controversial doping, a scandal treated thoroughly in, among others, Guido Knopp's documentary.

42. Michel Chion, *The Voice in Cinema*, trans. and ed. Claudia Gorbman (New York: Columbia University Press, 1999), 21. In the following discussion, page numbers are provided in the text.
43. Manni Breuckmann faults "zu wenig Spiel-Bild" ["too little play-by-play"] in Zimmermann's broadcast. See his foreword to Erik Eggers, *Die Stimme von Bern: Das Leben von Herbert Zimmermann, Reporterlegende bei der WM 1954* (Augsburg: Wißner, 2004), 5.
44. Jennifer M. Kapczynski, "Imitation of Life: The Aesthetics of Agfacolor in Recent Historical Cinema," in *The Collapse of the Conventional: German Film and Its Politics at the Turn of the Twenty-First Century*, eds. Jaimey Fisher and Brad Prager (Detroit: Wayne State University Press, 2010), 39–62; here 41.
45. Kapczynski, "Imitation of Life," 41.
46. Kapczynski, "Imitation of Life," 52–53.
47. Paul Virilio, *War and Cinema: The Logistics of Perception*, trans. Patrick Camiller (London: Verso, 1989), 7–8. See also Rentschler's discussion of Nazi color productions in *The Ministry of Illusion*, 203.
48. Lars-Olav Beier, "Der Traum vom großen Kick,"*Der Spiegel*, 14 July 2003, 136–38; Nikolaus von Festenberg, "Der beseelte Mann," *Der Spiegel*, 28 September 2003, 150–54; Klaus Brinkbäume, "Der Chef und sein Boss," *Der Spiegel*, 6 October 2003, 146–51; and *Die Zeit*, 25 September 2003.
49. See Fritz Göttler, "Hallo Helmut!," *Süddeutsche Zeitung*, 16 October 2003; Richard Bernstein, "Germany's Grief and Glory, Wrapped Up in a Soccer Ball," *New York Times*, 10 November 2003; and Hans-Joachim Leyenberg, "Im Sonderzug zurück nach Bern," *Frankfurter Allgemeine Zeitung*, 16 October 2003. The Social Democratic Chancellor, who often appeared juggling a soccer ball during political campaigns, became associated with the film. Newspapers parodied his Agenda 2010 as Agenda 1954 and cartooned him among his cabinet members in a retro-jersey, spoofing the passage of his Hartz III and Hartz IV measures as "The Miracle of Berlin." (See Göttler and the front page of the 18–19 October 2003 edition of *Neues Deutschland*.) This was, after all, the man who had had a piece of the pitch from the demolished Bern Wankdorf Stadium planted in the lawn of the Federal Chancellery.
50. *1954. Süddeutsche ZeitungWM-Bibliothek* (Munich: Süddeutsche Zeitung, 2005).
51. "Sönke Wortmann," in *The Concise CineGraph: Encyclopaedia of German Cinema*, eds. Hans-Michael Bock and Tim Bergfelder (Oxford: Berghahn, 2009), 539–40.
52. Randall Halle, "Happy Ends to Crises of Heterosexual Desire: Toward a Social Psychology of Recent German Comedies," *Camera Obscura* 15(2) (2000): 12.
53. See, for example, Halle, "Happy Ends to Crises of Heterosexual Desire," 1–39.
54. See Milan Pavlovic, "Ein Wunder, das noch immer Wunden heilt," *Süddeutsche Zeitung*, 6 October 2003.
55. The film appeared just as the possibilities for sound multi-tracking had taken off. Besides Hollywood blockbusters like *Star Wars* (1977) and *Close Encounters of the Third Kind* (1977), New Hollywood directors like Francis Ford Coppola were spending as much time mixing sound on *The Conversation* (1974) or *Apocalypse Now* (1979) as in shooting the film. See Michel Chion, *Audio-Vision: Sound on Screen*, trans. and ed. Claudia Gorbman (New York: Columbia University Press, 1994), 153.

Chapter 2

POP RETRO-VISION
Baader, Der Baader Meinhof Komplex,
and the RAF Film

In the first years of the new millennium, the Red Army Fraction (RAF), West Germany's homegrown terrorists of the 1970s and 1980s, enjoyed a renewed prominence. The iconography of the Baader-Meinhof Group was transformed into what the popular press termed "radical chic." The "RAF goes pop," diagnosed journalist Reinhard Mohr while describing the commercial appropriation of the German criminal organization which had coordinated scores of bombings, kidnappings, and murders before formally disbanding in 1998.[1] A new take on the group was clearly underway. In the year of the World Trade Center attacks, the designers Maegde und Knechte marketed underwear adorned with slogans such as "Prada Meinhof," "German Angst," and "Mein Kampf." *Tussi Deluxe* and *Max*, lifestyle magazines, featured fashion photographs which re-created the poses of the dead Stammheim inmates; "the time is ripe for RAF pop stars," declared the latter. In many ways, however, this pop iconography was already part and parcel of the group's own memory. Former RAF-member Astrid Proll published a coffee-table volume of photos, alternately called *Hans und Grete* or *Photos on the Run*, depicting Andreas Baader and Gudrun Ensslin in French cafés like tourists on holiday. In interviews, Proll recalled the heady days of illegality just as graying hippies might recall sit-ins and Rolling Stones concerts.[2] Leander Scholz occupied the bestseller list for weeks with his novel *Rosenfest*, a fictionalization of Baader and Ensslin's romance. German theaters, which had already anticipated the wave in the 1990s, presented a profusion of RAF plays and performance pieces.[3] The RAF even became the subject of a pop song when recording artist Jan Delay released a reggae track ("The Sons of Stammheim") with lyrics such as: "The terrorists are finally gone / and there's peace and quiet / And you can drive your Mercedes safely / without it exploding."

In the first three years of this century, the RAF returned on German screens in documentaries and features such as *Große Freiheit – Kleine Freiheit* (*Big Freedom – Little Freedom*, 2000), *Die innere Sicherheit* (*The*

State I Am In, 2000), *Die Stille nach dem Schuß* (*The Legend of Rita*, 2000), *Black Box BRD* (*Black Box Germany*, 2001), *Was tun, wenn's brennt?* (*What to Do in Case of Fire*, 2001), and *Starbuck – Holger Meins* (2002). The most controversial release was Christopher Roth's *Baader* (2002). A quarter of a century after Andreas Baader's 1977 death in the Stammheim prison, the feature imagines the RAF terrorist perishing in gunfire with police in 1972. Even though it won the Alfred Bauer Prize for New Perspectives of Film Art at the 2002 Berlin International Film Festival, Roth's film failed as a commercial venture. A meager 27,570 viewers saw it in German cinemas; it ranked 54th among the year's domestic productions and was nowhere near the top 100 overall.[4] The lack of success is at least partly attributable to the very poor reviews it received. With very few exceptions, German critics panned the film, almost exclusively for one of two reasons.

Many reviewers rejected the story's deviation from the historical record or its rosy memory—a tactic, they protested, that glorified the RAF and made it cool. Bernd Haasis claimed the film "invented history rather than dealing with it."[5] For sociologist Detlev Claussen, *Baader* "exploit[s] history˙for the sake of spectacular, show business."[6] The journal *Schnitt* attacked the film's conflation of "fact and fancy" and its mythification of the RAF, while a commentator in the left-liberal *Frankfurter Rundschau* bemoaned the feature's historical "mistakes" and its trivialization of German terrorism, and castigated the "late-born" filmmakers for their "ignorance and impertinence."[7] Abroad, the Austrian daily *Der Standard* saw merely "the set of a fashion photo layout, for which a resourceful editor gave out the assignment 'Terrorist Chic.'"[8]

Other reviewers, writing mostly for middle-brow newspapers, specialty film magazines, or academic journals, accepted *Baader*'s deviations from the historical record, but concluded that the film lacked both a larger conception and a regard for the political gravity of the subject. Jan Schulz-Ojala regretted the inattentiveness to the RAF's founding purpose, and concluded that Roth's effort was a "vague psychogram of a petty criminal car lover."[9] Harald Martenstein said that the film had "no opinion about its source material, just vague fascination." For the director and screenwriter, according to Martenstein, the RAF was merely a "cool brand name from the supermarket of German history."[10] The cinephile journal *Kolik.film* deemed *Baader* an unironic pastiche "leeching" on the European auteurist counter-cinema and New Hollywood. The film forgets history in order to let a "perfect mélange of retro-chic and hipster-spirit arise."[11] The *taz*'s Stefan Reinecke complained that the "directionless" film delivered clichéd montage à la Guido Knopp, the German journalist and television documentarist, infamous for his "historytainment" treatment of Hitler and World War II.[12]

Even if most commentators concluded this was not the appropriate way to represent the history of the RAF, everyone—including Roth himself—agreed that *Baader* was no conventional biopic.[13] In fact, *Baader* distills, exaggerates, and drives the essence of the biopic to extremes. Its pop historiography represents a highly complex engagement with the RAF and above all with previous representations. Neither hagiography nor condemnation, the film is part of a new group of terrorist pictures which reject the weighty ruminations on the RAF delivered by the later and "mature" New German Cinema. Instead, *Baader* returns to that cinema's less illustrious beginnings. It dramatizes a life composed of and motivated by film-derived dreams, casting the Baader-Meinhof Group as a *bande à part*.

Young Mr. Baader

Despite many allegations as to its historical heresy, *Baader* is indeed a biography of Andreas Baader and must be contextualized within the biopic genre and the recent proliferation of biographical films. By the early 1990s, leading commentators on the biopic had pronounced the genre dead. A veritable boom, both in Hollywood and internationally, soon proved such judgments premature.[14] German productions included *Marlene* (2000), *Abschied – Brechts letzter Sommer* (*The Farewell*, 2000), *Luther* (2003), and many others.[15]

One of the biopic's essential charcateristics, according to Henry Taylor, is weak narration with episodic form, number dramaturgy, and seriality. Weak narration entails a terse narrative that strings together a series of short episodes less by causality than by chronology. This narrative economy enables the film to transmit a sense of the life of the "historical star," or—as is often the case—a portion of his or her life, over the course of a feature-length film.[16] *Baader* both follows and exaggerates these conventions. Although the type and order of the plot points resemble many biopics, it represents these with a particularly elliptical narrative, slight characterization, and recourse to quotation. Rather than political warriors, it depicts the Red Army Fraction as performers playing a part.

Baader's narrative form is a tried and tested biopic structure. After a prologue and title sequence, the story picks up in 1972 with the title character in a BMW, reading a *Bild-Zeitung* headline that announces he will turn himself in. A policeman approaches him and requests identification. Baader fires at the officer and flees. A flashback to a series of tableaux between 1967 and 1972 follows. Baader's initial meeting with Gudrun Ensslin, the trial for the 1968 Frankfurt department store bombing, escape to France, renewed escape from prison with the help of Ulrike Meinhof, guerilla training in Jordan, and various bank robberies

Figure 2.1: Frank Giering as Baader in *Baader*.
Image courtesy of Christopher Roth.

and bombings in West Germany after the group goes underground: this section constitutes the bulk of the running time. By the time the film returns to the initial 1972 scene, BKA chief Kurt Krone (clearly based on real-life boss Horst Herold) has assumed a prominent role. Finally, in the film's two large deviations from the historical record, Baader and Krone meet furtively before the character Baader dies in a hail of bullets in front of the Frankfurt garage where the historical Baader was in fact wounded by the police and apprehended.

The basic structure (an introductory scene followed by a flashback that returns to the initial event in a dramatic conclusion) has a long tradition. The Billie Holiday biopic *Lady Sings the Blues* (1972), for example, begins with a scene from 1936 of the drug-delirious singer being straightjacketed. Oliver Stone's *Nixon* (1995) begins with and then catches up to the Watergate break-in. In particular, *Wyatt Earp* (1994) resembles *Baader*'s structure. It begins with a scene in which the title character sits at his sheriff's desk with a glass of whiskey and a gun. When the plot later returns to this point in the story we realize that the moment comes just before the showdown in the O.K. Corral. *Baader*'s irritation, however, is that biopics as a rule use this structure in order to chart the subject's trajectory toward the achievement for which he or she is most famous.[17] *Baader* adheres to this pattern, but then fictionalizes the final event. A plot summary from the soundtrack CD booklet depicts graphically the *Wyatt Earp*-esque "showdown" teleology:

Andreas Baader from 1967 to 1972... His great love Gudrun Ensslin, the Frankfurt department store bombings... Paris, drugs, Ulrike Meinhof, jail, the Fatah, bank robberies, BMWs, explosives... Trying out illegality... His enemy Kurt Krone, boss of the BKA... and then, in May 1972... in Frankfurt... they face each other... the RAF and the State

The literal ellipses of this summary intimate how *Baader*'s narration is spare and hard to follow. Scenes often begin in the middle of an action, in mid-sentence, and without establishing shots. Within the larger flashback sequence comprising most of the diegetic time, there are very short flashbacks and cut-aways of ambiguous historicity and narrative perspective. During the courtroom scene, for instance, the film flashes back momentarily and repeatedly to Baader and Ensslin's meeting with Kurt Wagner, as well as other scenes from the events surrounding the Frankfurt department store bombing. Later, the editing interrupts the visuals of Krone's discussion with his BKA subordinates about crime prevention in order to show displays of Baader's new weapons cachet. Compared with contemporary biopics such as *Nixon*, in which dates guide the viewer through the labyrinthine narrative, *Baader*'s references to historical time are decidedly subtle. The film contains only six titles: "1972" (directly after the title sequence); "5 Years Earlier – 1967" (signaling the flashback after the introductory scene); "GDR Transit Autobahn"; "1969 Paris"; "East Berlin Airport"; and "1970 Jordan." Surely, newspaper title pages, posters, news reports, or the viewer's own familiarity with the events also provide indices of historical time. Nevertheless, *Baader* supplies the bare minimum of the narrative cues, historical information, and period effects necessary to make sense of the film's plot and characters.

Rather than historical realism, *Baader* provides quotation as a means to convey its portrait of the terrorists. Instead of naturalistic dialogue, the characters often intone excerpts from interviews, articles, speeches, prison notes, or other sources from the historical record. One example is a scene late in the film. While shooting rounds, Meinhof turns and calmly says, "When the time is ripe for the revolution, it will be too late to prepare it." Similarly, one-shot "scenes" featuring Kurt Krone punctuate the RAF sequences. Krone appears only long enough to deliver a sound bite from Horst Herold's speeches and writings. In one shot, couched as a TV interview and cut discontinuously into the Frankfurt trial proceedings, Krone says, "If the revolution does not come from above, it will certainly come from below." These are Horst Herold's words which appeared in *Der Stern* in 1968.

The prologue strongly foregrounds the penchant for quotation. Ensslin's dialogue comes from Brecht's poem "Wenn das so bleibt," while *Baader*'s first shot restages the iconic photograph, "Youth with Mao bible and red flag in the Wetterau, Hesse, July 1969," a key image in Astrid Proll's book of Germany's leaden years. The composition in which Meins films in the background resembles a photo in Proll's volume which depicts the historical Holger Meins and Michael Ballhaus.[18] Indeed, this 47-second film itself recalls the early politically didactic dffb (Berlin's Film Academy) films in which Meins took part, such as the omnibus project, *Die rote Fahne* (*The Red Flag*, 1968) or Harun Farocki's *Die Worte des Vorsitzenden* (*The Words of the Chairman*, 1967). The biopic's beginning is traditionally the point where it makes its non-fiction claim to historical authenticity and uses iconographic means to introduce the protagonist's career.[19] Instead, *Baader* undermines such a claim by offering an exaggerated form of quotation rather than historical realism.

The weak narration and estranging use of quotation foreclose dynamic characterization and thus exaggerate a typical attribute of the classical biopic. Given this narrative economy, figures remain static; according to Taylor, they "emerge rather than develop" (130). The film leaves motivations—including Baader's—largely in the dark. History unfolds rather than develops logically. *Baader*, to the chagrin of critics, does not explain what drives these historical personages. Moreover, moral dilemmas are largely absent. To this day professional historians wonder how Ulrike Meinhof, a prominent and successful journalist, could have abandoned her children to become a terrorist. In the film, Baader and Ensslin appear at her house for dinner, and Meinhof asks how Ensslin could give up her son and go underground; she could never part from her two daughters. In a later scene, just before taking part in Baader's jailbreak, there is a brief shot of Meinhof lingering over a photograph of her children, but no further information. Commenting on *Baader*'s lack of drama, one journalist reported that Roth instructed actress Birge Schade to make Ulrike Meinhof's escape after the Baader's breakout (which the written record recounts as the dramatic "birth of the Baader-Meinhof group") "look as if she were considering whether she had already bought milk today."[20] The abbreviated Baader–Ensslin courtship is similarly curious. One sequence portrays briefly their initial encounter at a political meeting. After Baader interrupts pacifist participants ("We got to kick their ass"), the camera cuts to an admiring Gudrun Ensslin. But the film ignores what has traditionally been the key question surrounding the pair: how could an intelligent and deeply moral daughter of a Swabian pastor become a central figure in a terrorist organization and the lover of a loutish petty criminal?

As we have seen, *Baader* has a thin exposition and provides little to no character psychology. The "why?"—always the most fascinating question in accounts of the RAF—is missing. Instead of a psychology of a terrorist, *Baader* opts for a phenomenology of a pop star. It examines how a young man grows into the role of a revolutionary, how he learns the part he aspires to perform. In Paris, Baader inspects Ché Guevara books and wears Régis Debray's monographed silk shirt in the latter's apartment. Both are figures Baader clearly aims to emulate. The set design abounds with posters of idols, including Mao and Walter Benjamin. Nevertheless, they are primarily important as iconographic emblems, rather than intellectual examples. Although Baader justifies his actions with Marxist jargon, the film implies this is more pose than conviction. Class warfare takes a back seat to Baader's enthusiasm for fast cars. In one scene near the end, Baader trains the new recruit Karin Rubner: "Being 'against' isn't enough. Look at the SPD. The strategic function of the Social Democrats is securing the initiative of capital in crisis. Got it?" Directly thereafter, however, the more important lesson becomes clear—the benefits of stealing BMWs: "The BMW 2500…or the old square 1800, or the convertible here, that's a top car: wood, leather, fast," Baader coos as he caresses the steering wheel. This scene suggests Baader's politicization has not changed the former petty criminal, but instead has provided him with a rationale for his machinations.

The terrorists' actual "work" is represented as theater: they commit bank robberies and prison breaks with masks and costumes. Over the course of the film, it becomes clear that this is more a performative dressing-up than simply a practical disguise. The level of detail involved exceeds the level sufficient to conceal their identity. One of the women quite convincingly pretends to be a flight attendant in order to steal a rental car. Baader and Ensslin play tennis at a country club at the height of the nationwide manhunt; in another scene they sit in a train compartment and pose as a bourgeois couple: they have even faked a wedding photo. Baader takes this role-playing very seriously. He barks at Ensslin to put on some lipstick; otherwise she will "look like a terrorist."

Accompanied by demands emanating from a portable cassette player, the terrorists' coordinated audiovisual acts resemble performance art. Indeed, Baader first notices Ensslin in a newsreel as she participates in the famous Albertz art-action protest.[21] When the group travels to Jordan in order to train as "urban guerillas" with Fatah, the scene is represented as grand spectacle. Much to the chagrin of their Muslim drill commanders, the female German "guerillas" sunbathe topless rather than fire rounds. Baader prances through basic training in bright red velvet pants and traipses around in leather jackets, fur coats, and sunglasses (even in the dark). The later Frankfurt trial scene is also typically theatrical. The four defendants carry on for their audience, playfully quoting from *Spartacus* (1960): "I'm Baader. No, I'm Baader…." The group is shown making 8mm films of itself; the prologue introduces the terrorists as moviemakers.

Baader's recourse to performance is not limited to theme and character; the style and form are performative in their own right. The cinematography privileges a cinema verité hand-held camera, close-ups dominate the shot scale, and the editing is overwhelmingly high-speed. Furthermore, there are sudden switches to super-8, flashbacks and flashforwards, as well as collages with documentary excerpts. Non-diegetic music conspicuously accompanies nearly every scene. The song selection—which includes numbers by Suicide, CAN, The Stone Roses, Trans Am, Turner, as well as Beethoven and Shostakovich—is decidedly anachronistic. Excluding MC5's 1969 song "Kick Out the Jams" and seminal Krautrockers CAN's release "Sing Swan Song" from 1972, the pop music emanates from a point in time much later than the story. In the mise en scène, Baader and Ensslin are often grouped together in shots, framed like popular images found in contemporary media culture. Compositions are arranged in tableaux that resemble album covers or publicity photos for bands such as Cream, Mike Bloomfeld and Al Cooper, MC5, or The Doors.

There is, additionally, an unusually high frequency of montage sequences. Some of these passages are not out of step with traditional biopics in that they telegraph Baader's public "career." The RAF's 1972 "May Offensive," for example, is rehearsed in spurts of images: bombings at the officer's casino of the US Army in Frankfurt and the detonation of a car in front of the Munich police headquarters. More curious is the second variety of montage sequences, which works toward an opposite effect and is much more prominent in *Baader*. In contrast to the excessive information and historical commentary provided by "progress" sequences, these scenes communicate a feeling

Figure 2.2: Baader flanked by Meinhof and Wagner in *Baader*.
Image courtesy of Christopher Roth.

Figure 2.3: Pop stars? The Baader-Meinhof gang, drugs, and cars in *Baader*. Image courtesy of Christopher Roth.

or lifestyle. In so doing, they offer pure spectacle. Furthermore, whereas the first kind of montage portrays Baader's public interventions (e.g., the RAF's bombings), these sequences depict private moments between Baader and his associates. One example is the scene directly after the group's release on parole. The camera captures the band at sunset sitting around a car on the edge of a river or lake, smoking dope and shooting opium, accompanied on the soundtrack by CAN's "Sing Swan Song." Another example is the sequence of Baader, Ensslin, Diedrich, and Inga on a Paris rooftop at sunset. They film each other to the non-diegetic backdrop of Trans Am's "Motr." Much of the footage is in slow motion and some is actually in 8mm format, replicating a music video or advertisement aesthetic.

In many ways *Baader*'s montage sequences hark back to the psychedelic films of the period such as Donald Cammell and Nic Roeg's *Performance* (1970) and Klaus Lemke's *Brandstifter* (*Firestarters*, 1969). The latter film, based on the Baader–Ensslin–Söhnlein–Proll Frankfurt department store fire as well as the director's own experiences sharing a flat with Baader and Söhnlein in Munich, anticipates *Baader*'s music video aesthetic. Lemke's production concludes with The Rolling Stones' "Paint it Black" on the soundtrack, and three of the students strut down the Cologne pedestrian zone in their psychedelic finest, filming each other with a hand-held 8mm camera. Furthermore, *Brandstifter*'s film-within-the-film strongly resembles that of *Baader*. Accompanied by the Stones' song "Street Fighting Man," it presents a montage of newsreel footage of American bombers over Vietnam, protests, the Axel Springer building, and so on. Christopher Roth deploys many of the exact same images in *Baader*'s title sequence montage.[22]

The "music video" montage sequences exaggerate biopic conventions and cast the life of Andreas Baader, best known in the public eye as a terrorist, in the generic form of the "performer" narrative. According to Taylor, actor, singer, dancer, and musician biopics contain a large amount of "performance-inserts with a high show-value or spectacle character." These scenes do not develop the story as much as they "serve primarily the visual and acoustic pleasure of the audience" (275). The Baader in *Baader* is a pop idol; the Baader-Meinhof Group appears here as a band on the run.

Helping Genres

As biopics are weakly coded, they rely on other "helping" genres. Hollywood scriptwriting manuals insist that successful biographical films must interpret the lives of their subjects through formulas such as the court drama, modern epic, disillusionment plot, or punitive plot; in no event may the biopic become a mere chronology.[23] For instance, 23 (1999), besides chronicling the life of Karl Koch, employs aspects of the paranoid thriller and the spy film, and elements from productions about the computer and internet.

We have seen how *Baader* incorporates sequences that resemble music videos and television commercials. It also borrows idioms from the gangster film in its depictions of bank robberies, terrorist actions, and jail breakouts. More astonishing, however, is the way in which it mobilizes generic traditions in the final showdown between Baader and Krone.

By the time the plot has caught up to the January 1972 incident in which Andreas Baader fires upon an approaching policeman, the mise en scène and tone have become dark and sinister. There are few long shots, and claustrophobic close-ups follow in quick succession. The voice-over of a radio newsreader and the editing present Baader and Krone as "enemies": in parallel montage, Krone and Baader watch television or monitor computers. The film stands still, accompanied by tense incidental music, in the dark German countryside. Baader joins Krone in the latter's car and the two smoke cigarettes. In polite conversation they reveal their familiarity with one another. "You need us to step up your armament," says Baader. "You need me," says Krone, "in order to intensify the existing contradiction. To deepen the gap between the State and the masses." Baader pretends to be Krone: "I, Kurt Krone, am the man who has to conduct war. Give me an organization, power, and money." Krone seems to acknowledge this;

he neither arrests nor kills the state's public enemy. "If you hadn't killed anyone, you might have achieved your goal. Rudi Dutschke could have succeeded. The time just wasn't ripe yet. He could have toppled the State. But nobody should have been killed."

The film's final scene deserves close attention. Baader, Meins, and Raspe drive up to an apartment block in Frankfurt in a white Porsche 911. Baader and Meins enter the garage, while Raspe stands lookout. Baader discovers that the getaway Lancia has been disabled. Meins simultaneously feels that the explosive powder waiting for them has been switched. The two draw their guns and partially open the garage. Baader spots a civilian-clad policeman among the cars parked outside. "This is a 1-A trap!" says Baader to Meins, who promptly fires his gun. There is a cut to the sleeping Krone at the BKA headquarters. The bullet sound seems to wake him. Indeed, Krone is depicted as having a mental connection to Baader; he "senses" that his adversary is in danger. In front of a large political map of Germany, Krone answers the telephone and orders the caller to insure that "no one lies dead on the concrete."

In Frankfurt the standoff continues and the police demand that the duo come out. The terrorists laugh and begin firing while Baader smokes. The editing quickens as the shootout continues. Up to this point the Frankfurt scene is shot in a cinema verité style, in hand-held, shaky shots of approximately two seconds, mostly close-ups of Baader and Meins, and sometimes their POVs of the police. Krone arrives on a balcony and, speaking via 2-way radio, orders the police to cease fire. A cameraman and sound technician recording this spectacle also stop shooting. Baader requests to see his daughter Jule. He turns to Meins: "I'll write a book for Jule. Gun Talk. And now let's get out of here, okay?" Meins doubts that they will survive, but Baader is confident: "Bullshit. Of course we will. See you in Hanoi." Meins says he would prefer Havana, and the pair begin firing again. Baader emerges from the garage in slow motion. The film cuts to a close-up of Krone, who instructs his force to exercise restraint, and then to the hard-hat clad police officers with rifles drawn, before cutting back to Baader in a low-angle long shot. The music swells in a tense chord. Baader discards his cigarette before he is shot in the leg by a police sniper. In slow motion the terrorist staggers, stills himself, and discards his gun. The police rise, visibly relieved, before the film cuts to Meins, still in the garage, looking directly into the camera and shooting two imaginary pistols in slow motion. As Krone leaves the balcony (where a star-struck woman in curlers gazes at Baader), Baader recites a Brecht poem in voice-over. Meins enters the Lancia and turns on the car stereo to CAN's "Sing Swan Song." Baader draws two guns and begins firing, at which point the music stops. The police shoot down Baader in an excessive hail of bullets, in slow motion. Krone cradles the dead and still sunglass-clad

Baader, and looks to the heavens. The credits begin with a quote from the historical Andreas Baader: "If someone says I got shot while on the run, or one of us got shot while on the run, don't believe him."

The curious Baader/Krone constellation, it would seem, pushes the conventions of the biopic to the extreme. In biographical films, according to Taylor, "the antagonist is complex, it embodies less an individual figure than a negative mirror of the protagonist,"— an emblem of the subject's dividedness (131). The Krone figure, perversely, seems to take on the figure of the older mentor typical of biopics (102). *Baader* is classical insofar as it "end[s] the narration as quickly as possible in order to produce a mythical ending which allows no earthly compromises" (133). A drastic death functions as the last "performance in public" (264). Indeed, similar to musician biopics, which often conclude with a "best-of" number (e.g., *The Buddy Holly Story* [1978]), in *Baader*, performance is "the kinetic climax of the film: a movement and music euphoria, which lets us enjoy their body. The specifically historical disappears...until [only] cinematic pleasure and pure spectacle [remains]" (183). This "final performance," the transcendence of death, is doubled. Dying like a hero in the film, Baader assumes a mythic presence that is spared the humiliation and suffering in Stammheim. *Baader* parodies the truism that biopics progress toward the point for which protagonists are best known. It is precisely when the initial frame structure of the January 1972 scene is completed that the film engages in its most obvious and stylized deviations from fact. The film begins (Baader's letter) and ends (the death scene and the final quote) with Baader's declaration that he will never turn himself in. In this counter-history, Andreas Baader keeps his promise.

Beyond this reading, however, a rigorous analysis of these scenes must also focus on their recourse to helping genres. The exchange regarding Baader's daughter is what outlaws are "supposed" to ask for. Indeed, the next snatches of dialogue quite explicitly come from the cinema. The Meins/Baader buddy sequence is a parody of *Butch Cassidy and the Sundance Kid* (1969), when the bandit duo, about to face an impossible mass of authorities, discuss going to Australia. In that film, too, knowing they are surrounded, they burst out of their hideouts. The image freezes into a photograph and transmutes into a sepia black-and-white, immortalized despite the sound of massive gunfire which suggests their death. In *Baader*, however, the demise is not only aurally implied. The film depicts Baader losing in a very graphic way. It draws on the violent ending of Sam Peckinpah's *The Wild Bunch* (1969) and the pyrotechnic conclusion of the spaghetti western, *Il grande silencio* (*The Great Silence*, 1968). Meins cues us to the quotation with his direct look into the camera and the two imaginary guns.

The ending also recalls playful moments from *Pierrot le fou* (1965) and *Bonnie and Clyde* (1967).[24] Arthur Penn's film also ends with rapid-fire montage, slow motion, the unreal sound of bullets, and a shootout replete with stylized fake blood. Baader and Ensslin, like Clyde and his female accomplice, are provincial terrorists. *Baader* employs car scenes with Baader and Ensslin that allude to the ironic, back-projected shots of Bonnie and Clyde. Like Clyde, Baader is a small-time car thief fresh out of prison, a media-savvy self-promoter, and a snappy dresser. Like his counterpart in *Bonnie and Clyde* ("I'm somebody they're going to remember!"), Baader reads and responds to his own reportage and place in history. Just as Arthur Penn's bandits hide out in a cinema to the non-diegetic tune of "We're in the Money" (which Bonnie subsequently sings), in *Baader*, cinema dreams and reality converge and blur.

In *Baader*'s final scene, reporters filming the event direct our attention to the documentary footage that we know—the historical "reality"—and create a distance between *Baader* and that material with its correspondent claim to authenticity. The point at which they stop filming is precisely when *Baader* takes leave of the historical record. In addition, the CAN tune "Sing Swan Song" certainly has a programmatic function in this last scene, much like "Dream Baby Dream" had in the 1967 sequence and in its later reprises, or even Shostokovitsch's "Dedicated to the Victims of Fascism and War." Commenting quite literally on the unfolding events, it is the only song that might have been on the radio in 1972. This is also nearly the only diegetic music in a film that so rigorously takes recourse to a video-clip aesthetic. In this mythic cinematic moment, the music video comes to life and

Figure 2.4: Baader and Ensslin like Bonnie and Clyde in *Baader*.
Image courtesy of Christopher Roth.

links the textual inside and the historical outside: the song is first heard diegetically, stopping momentarily before continuing non-diegetically.

Rather than simply employing helping genres like the gangster film or urban thriller, *Baader* mobilizes a historically specific tradition: the gangster and exploitation films from the period in which the film takes place. This ensemble includes *Bonnie and Clyde, Butch Cassidy and the Sundance Kid*, Peckinpah and the spaghetti westerns, as well as Godard, but above all the Munich School, especially the early Rainer Werner Fassbinder and Klaus Lemke, as well as the gangster films of Jean-Pierre Melville. *Baader* imagines Andreas Baader through the films that he had seen at the time.

Like *Baader*, a central feature of the Melville and Munich School films is the self-absorbed male figure who plays the part of the gangster. As Stella Bruzzi writes about gangster pictures in general, masculinity in these films is a performative act measured by narcissism. The law of the genre is "the smarter the clothes, the more dangerous the man."[25] The Melville and Munich School examples, however, exaggerate this generic rule. One thinks of Alain Delon's roles as Jeff Costello in *Le Samouraï* (*The Samurai*, 1967) and Corey in *Le Cercle rouge* (*The Red Circle*, 1970). Melville's criminals are often depicted checking their reflection and fixing their clothes—even, as in the memorable dénouement to *Le doulos* (1962), when they are about to die. Fassbinder's crooks are just as vain: for example, Bruno and Franz in *Liebe ist kälter als der Tod* (*Love Is Colder Than Death*, 1969) or Harry Baer's turn as Franz (in *Götter der Pest* [*Gods of the Plague*, 1970]) with his leather jacket, finely coiffed hair, and sideburns. One of the most compelling preoccupations of these dapper figures is their deference to the past. As Bruzzi writes about the characters in Melville and other Franco-American gangster flicks, their "traditions hinge on a constant, ultimately futile striving for a stereotyped, idealized and unattainable image of masculinity… [the gangster] create[s] his identity by comparing himself to past icons" (xviii). These "heroes" are unabashed in their reverence for their idols. Gerd Gemünden describes Bruno in *Liebe ist kälter als der Tod* as Ulli Lommel "imitating Alain Delon imitating Humphrey Bogart."[26] *Rocker*'s (1972) Gerd Kruskopf channels the knockoffs of Marlon Brando in *The Wild One* (1953) that we find in *Scorpio Rising* (1964) and *The Wild Angels* (1966). Just as when Baader wears Régis Debray's silk shirt embroidered with the revolutionary's initials, in this tradition the hero knows that the clothes make the man.

In the Munich School's gangster films, vain "wannabe" criminals inhabit a sorry "underworld." In Fassbinder's *Liebe ist kälter als der Tod* and *Götter der Pest*, the gangster existence is mundane and unsexy. These productions feature quotidian scenes in supermarkets and shots of trenchcoat-clad figures taking walks down well-lit suburban streets. They focus on the time in between the backroom deals and violent confrontations, and lay bare a profound boredom. The gangsters play pinball machines in *Liebe ist kälter als der Tod* and slot machines in *Götter der Pest*. In the former, Franz toys with his gun; he cannot be bothered to acknowledge Johanna's money or her naked body. Ennui also permeates Lemke's *Brandstifter*, which presents a series of quotidian tableaux from a "radical" commune in Cologne. Lemke exaggerates the lethargy with pans over the collective's bored faces. This strategy recurs in *Baader*, where the group finds Paris tedious and sits around watching television. In other scenes, Baader and Ensslin bide their time taking LSD at Meinhof's house; Baader shorts the toaster, just to make a small fire. Baader spends his downtime, much like Karl in *Brandstifter*, reading Mickey Mouse comics. Indeed, *Baader* seems to take its representation of the terrorists' ideological beliefs from the Munich School of *Rote Sonne* (*Red Sun*, 1970) or *Zur Sache, Schätzchen* (*Let's Get Down to Business, Darling*, 1968). A scene on the train in *Liebe ist kälter als der Tod* exemplifies the movement's carefree mixture of pop and politics. Bruno asks a stripping coed, "What are you thinking about? Sex?" Her reply: "About the revolution!" In a similar scene from *Baader*, Karin Rubner happily reports performing oral sex to distract someone as Baader steals his BMW. She jokes that next time she might try reading Lenin.

In Melville's crime pictures, the milieu is less bored than in Fassbinder's Bavaria. It includes an assortment of criminals and the state, two sides which lack a clear distinction. Indeed, the relationship between Baader and Krone strongly recalls the friendly symbiosis between cop and crook in the films of Melville. In his cinema, the opposing camps often meet without any sign of conflict and they often wear nearly identical clothes. Indeed, when Krone holds Baader, the tableau replays the "father–son" *pietà* of Bob and Paolo from *Bob le flambeur* (1956). One might say that *Baader* emulates the Melville films with a similar, but opposite, moral ambiguity. In *Le Cercle rouge*, Mattei's boss, the chief of police, famously utters the last words of the film: "All men are guilty." In *Baader*, by contrast, both hunter and hunted are left-wing, utopian, and struggling for a better world. In the pair's automobile conversation, Krone reveals himself to be someone who not only wants to understand the terrorists, but himself subscribes to dialectical logic and utopian designs articulated by Rudi Dutschke; he knows the work of Marx better than Baader. As Mattei, a cop battling a corrupt chain of command, Krone believes that his computer system of criminal geography will democratize the police force and eliminate hierarchy in German law enforcement. Like Mattei, whose only emotional contact is with his cats, Krone overlooks that it is Christmas Eve in the midst of his workaholism. Vadim Glowna's Krone follows in the tradition of the dying actor André Bouvil's asthmatic interpretation of Mattei.

Figure 2.5: Vadim Glowna as *Baader*'s Kurt Krone à la André Bouvil in *Le Cercle rouge*. Image courtesy of Christopher Roth.

Casting Vadim Glowna as Kurt Krone accentuated this ideological and moral ambiguity. Glowna, himself a former radical, is known for playing leftists in several roles, such as in the classic omnibus project about the RAF and the Federal Republic, *Deutschland im Herbst* (*Germany in Autumn*, 1978). In that film he is Freiermuth, a young man who police stop at a border checkpoint to France. The policeman delivers a monologue in broad Baden dialect: Freiermuth's girlfriend could be one of the terrorists, the policeman muses, before concluding, "no, [she] doesn't have the fanatic eye." The check is quite necessary, the officer says to Freiermuth, because "this is the type of car that they [i.e., the terrorists] prefer: fast and with two doors." (The echoes of this sequence in *Baader* are not to be missed; in fact, the film replays it.) In *Die Unberührbare* (*No Place to Go*, 2000), Glowna plays Hanna's ex-husband Bruno, an old 68er who, in the midst of a drinking binge several decades later reveals that he had placed his utopian hopes in the RAF.[27]

The camaraderie between criminal and state is part of the primarily male constellations and the often misogynistic and homosocial behavior that is common to all of these films. Fassbinder's works bring the underlying homoerotic current of the classical gangster film to the fore. In *Liebe ist kälter als der Tod*, for example, Franz caresses Bruno, and *Götter der Pest* features a lengthy, sexually suggestive wrestling scene between men. *Der amerikanische Soldat* (*The American Soldier*, 1970) concludes on a similarly homoerotic note. Commentators have written much on the "homophilia" in Melville's films, noting how women play almost no part and all strong emotional ties are between men.[28] In this tradition, the spectator learns almost nothing about character backgrounds or motivations, and the camera attends above all to sorrowful male countenances, anticipating the many close-ups of the melancholy Baader's face in Roth's film.[29] This form of masculinity ends in futility in Melville (particularly in *Le Cercle rouge*) and in *Götter der Pest*'s unglamorous final death scenes on the supermarket floor and in the porno shop. In *Baader*, melancholy masculinity leads to loneliness (Krone) and death (Baader).

Many reviewers took Roth to task for casting Baader as a womanizing macho, criticizing the character's repeated use of the word "cunt." In contrast, Ulrike Meinhof receives minimal attention, Gudrun Ensslin is little more than a "galpal," and otherwise, summarized critics, women appear as fawning groupie-terrorists.[30] Doubtless, as the film approaches its conclusion, the women disappear and a male bond is the love story. After the cursory courtship between Baader and Ensslin, the relationship becomes steadily one-sided and Ensslin increasingly desperate, as Baader loses interest in women. The topless female German terrorists in Jordan fail to attract his attention; at best he suggests that the liberated women sleep in the same tent as the men. Late in the film, Ensslin's "I love you" goes unanswered. When Karin Rubner confesses her affection for the RAF-honcho ("I like you so much!"), Baader harshly brushes her off ("What is that for a sob story? Do you want a Christmas present from me or something?") and fires a round.[31] He snaps and snarls at the female members of the group, referring to each woman on the "Anarchistic Criminals" poster individually as a "cunt." Conversely, he shows more attraction to men. In one scene near the end he sits in a car with a male member of the group and caresses the man's head. The film's final scene with Meins studiously partakes of the buddy movie's homosociality.[32] Baader and Krone have by far the film's longest and most intense conversation. The scene between the pair is the most important expression of love and the final *pietà* configuration is its most tender embrace.

Life Made of Cinema Dreams

Revisiting the work of Melville, Fassbinder, and Lemke, *Baader* returns to the cinema of 1967–1972 in its depiction of that period. It replicates the performativity of these texts: playing gangsters, pretending to be film heroes, enacting big-screen dreams. But although both Melville (before) and Fassbinder (after) made a number of historical pictures, the works from which *Baader* draws are all set in the late 1960s and early 1970s. Indeed, this is a major point in these films. Characters like Franz Walsh and Corey are living anachronisms. They owe themselves to Humphrey Bogart or Marlon Brando. What does it mean, then, to paraphrase a biography through this specific film history?

The recourse to "helping" genres and the deployment of pop culture as an alternative to historical authenticity are, despite critics' complaints, hardly arbitrary in the case of the Baader-Meinhof Group. There was a concrete relationship between radical activism (as well as terrorism) and cinema. Christoph Wackernagel had acted for Johannes Schaaf in *Tätowierung* (*Tattoo*, 1967) and with Fassbinder in Franz Peter Wirth's *Al Capone im deutschen Wald* (*Al Capone in the German Forest*, 1969) before going underground with the Red Army Fraction. The French-German student leader Daniel Cohn-Bendit made *Le Vent d'Est* (*East Wind*, 1970) with Godard. RAF member Petra Schelm was an aspiring make-up artist who had been recruited by her boyfriend Manfred Grashof, a film student. Ulrike Meinhof, who had established herself as a journalist before she submerged into illegality, produced a number of television reports and wrote the film *Bambule* (*Trouble*, 1970). Dorothea Hauser reports that Gudrun Ensslin acted in a sex film. One wonders whether Hauser has in mind "the experimental film," *Das Abonnement* (*The Subscription*, 1967). A production still of the topless Swabian "actress" graces Astrid Proll's volume.[33]

Various sources discuss Horst Söhnlein and Andreas Baader's involvement in Fassbinder's theater group and social circle. Baader's active nightlife in Munich in the 1960s saw him frequenting the same cafés and bars as Fassbinder, Schlöndorff, and Herzog. Klaus Lemke, who lived with Baader and Söhnlein in Munich, reports that he and his group looked down on these "jokers": they were desperate to get into film.[34] Later, after Baader had moved to West Berlin, he became acquainted with Rosa von Praunheim. Indeed, many commentators describe Baader as a movie star. For some, Baader's "enormous physical presence and magical sex appeal" recalled Marlon Brando, for others, James Dean.[35] Stefan Aust has the future public enemy "cruising Kurfürstendamm with the wide-brimmed hat of his admired Humphrey Bogart deep over his face"; acquaintance Peter Homann wrote that Baader saw himself in terms of his "role models from cinema" (above all Bogart) and regularly quoted lines from films.[36] Historians and other commentators who examined the group around the turn of the millennium, with the knowledge that the RAF had disbanded and the Cold War had ended, tended to describe the terrorists in the manner normally reserved for starlets. Baader and Ensslin became "celebrities" through their "performance" at the Frankfurt department store bombing trial, a farce that one commentator described as a "justice happening."[37] Sober journalistic reports referred to the Baader-Meinhof Group in Jordan as "anti-authoritarian Pop-Teutons" and to the RAF as a having a "Bonnie and Clyde existence with a political substructure."[38] Of course, this implied genealogy is correct insofar as the initial actions of the Kommune I, Bewegung 2. Juni, and RAF—before 1972, in other words up to the point where *Baader* ends—grew out of a performance art tradition of Go-Ins, Sit-Ins, and other innovative demonstration traditions.[39]

If one believes historical witnesses, Baader and Ensslin regarded their exploits in terms of films they had seen. Stefan Aust describes the group taking in a screening of *Easy Rider* (1969) in Amsterdam, the original English version with Dutch subtitles.[40] Another account claims that Baader and Ensslin saw *Pierrot le fou* and afterwards exclaimed, "That's just a film. We do that in real life!"[41] The pair clown around and quote poses from *Bande á part* (*Band of Outsiders*, 1964) in Proll's snapshots from Paris cafés.[42] Indeed, when one reads that Baader had had the chance to sneak out of prison in 1970, but refused, wanting the drama of the breakout,[43] one cannot help but think of lines from Godard's film about a robbery that "must wait until nightfall, thus respecting the tradition of bad B-pictures." Like Franz in that picture, the historical Baader seemed "uncertain whether reality is becoming a dream or dream becoming reality." Baader and Ensslin's initial flight to France in 1969 was in fact a parody very much like *À bout de souffle* (*Breathless*, 1960). Before they had gone "underground," they lived a farce of illegality, switching cars, dying hair and changing identity. Hauser describes the group's time in France and Italy as a honeymoon or Grand Tour, the "role of Baader's life."[44]

Figure 2.6: *Baader*'s final showdown à la Leone.
Image courtesy of Christopher Roth.

According to fellow travelers, Baader's favorite movie was *Il grande silencio*. One cannot help but speculate what attracted Baader to Corbucci's spaghetti western, which critic Hans-Christoph Blumenberg once called "the acme of this genre...in that it demonstrates that in a world of total terror only chaos can prevail" and a film in which "dramaturgy outflanks authenticity."[45] Perhaps Baader identified with Klaus Kinski's brutal dandy bounty hunter Tigrero, a.k.a. "Loco," a man who wears, as the sheriff in the film describes, "a priest's hat and a woman's fur coat." The conversations between the two about the blurring between law and lawlessness and their tentative truce certainly recall the meeting between Krone and Baader in Roth's film. The historical Baader (who as previously mentioned once said, "If someone says that I was shot while on the run, don't believe him") would have scoffed at the cowardly bandits at the beginning of the film who would "rather be taken alive" because at least "it's warm in jail." Baader's macho swagger and tough-guy rhetoric always outpaced his actions, however. He may have admired the absolute destruction of *Il grande silencio*'s blood-and-guts dénouement, an ending that certainly anticipates that of *Baader*; yet in reality he died by his own hand in a warm jail.

Although Baader and Ensslin were more or less aspiring performers, other members of the group had more potential to become film artists. Holger Meins offered the most serious and sustained connection between filmmaking and postwar terrorism. Gerd Conradt's *Starbuck – Holger Meins* presents Meins' biography and its links between political activism and West German filmmaking. Meins was a student in the dffb's inaugural 1966 class, alongside Conradt, Wolfgang Petersen, Harun Farocki, Bernd Fiedler, Helke Sander, and Hartmut Bitomsky. A promising cinematographer, he worked under the wing of Michael Ballhaus and made a legendary short that showed how to build a Molotov Cocktail. After forswearing mainstream culture for life with the group, his experiences at the film academy played a role in his new "career." On various occasions, the RAF would purchase explosives and other materials with the excuse that these were props for a film they were making. When an unwitting metalworker asked Meins what the project was about, he called it "a sort of revolution fiction." Snapping at the metalworker who anticipated needing more time and money to finish the device, Meins reportedly said, "The couple hundred extra marks are insignificant. The whole film succeeds or fails with the props."[46]

The experiences of the filmmakers Meinhof and Meins, and the "failed actors" Baader and Ensslin, are those of young people who turned to terrorism precisely after facing the disappointment of their utopian belief in film as a catalyst for social change or a vehicle for performative self-expression, respectively. In this context, one thinks of

Fassbinder's comment about *Die dritte Generation* (*The Third Generation*, 1979): "I don't throw bombs. I make films." In this formulation, filmmaking functions as an expressive alternative to physical violence. Harun Farocki and many of the early dffb students successfully made this transition—Meins, Meinhof, Baader, and Ensslin did not.

The German Genre and *Der Baader Meinhof Komplex*

Baader and Ensslin fulfilled their film-star dreams posthumously. Various filmmakers turned their attention to the group in features made during or in the five years after Baader's time in Stammheim, the most important of which include *Die verlorene Ehre der Katharina Blum* (*The Lost Honor of Katharina Blum*, 1975), *Mutter Küsters' Fahrt zum Himmel* (*Mother Küsters' Trip to Heaven*, 1975), *Das zweite Erwachen der Christa Klages* (*The Second Awakening of Christa Klages*, 1977), *Messer im Kopf* (*Knife in the Head*, 1978), and *Die bleierne Zeit* (*Marianne and Juliane*, 1981).[47]

Harald Martenstein suggests that "the terrorism film is a German genre like the *Heimatfilm*."[48] Although this comment is meant to be ironic, the West German terrorist films of the late 1970s and early 1980s do indeed have a unique narratological code. They concentrate on the victims of terrorism—not necessarily the actual victims of terrorist acts, but rather those who, due to affinities or family ties, are caught in the war between the outlaws and the state.[49] For example, the title figure in *Die verlorene Ehre der Katharina Blum*, after a one-night-stand with a suspected terrorist, is hounded and tormented by police and the boulevard press. Bruno Ganz's character in *Messer im Kopf* is seriously wounded by an overzealous cop while pursuing his estranged wife, who is involved with a young radical. These stories about moral choices appeal to spectators' emotions and, above all, to their sympathies. Even if the films usually cast the terrorists in a relatively unfavorable light, the perpetrators are nonetheless positioned as "victims" of Germany's Nazi past and a repressive postwar upbringing.

In this context, it is useful to compare the quite different depictions of Gudrun Ensslin's father in *Die bleierne Zeit* and *Baader*. In the former film he is overbearing and wastes little time trying to understand his daughters; he represents continuity with a repressive Nazi patriarchy. In Roth's film, Helmut Ensslin seems supremely reasonable in comparison to the impulsive Gudrun. He gently advises his topless daughter to turn herself in, and accedes to her demand that he speak with both her and Baader together. Quoting from an interview that the historical Helmut Ensslin gave after the department store bombing, the figure even praises her critique of the West German state: "You've moved us all with your deed [the Frankfurt bombing]. You've shown us that this state is weak and corruptible."

The older films always contextualize the politics of terrorists within a broader and more viable leftist spectrum. The former lover of Marianne and father of her child (based on Bernward Vesper) says to Juliane, a feminist journalist (a stand-in for Christiane Ensslin), in *Die bleierne Zeit*: "Her damn ideas are in us too, it's just we're too cowardly or reasonable [to act on them]." In an atmosphere of a political (i.e., leftist) national minor cinema, this stance-taking was necessary. The fundamental difference in the treatment of the Nazi generation (in the 1970s wave always the underlying antagonist) suggests that for the later generation such a critique is no longer necessary, whether because it has been rejected or because it has become internalized as self-understood; in any event, it has undergone revision.

A few films, such as *Die dritte Generation* and some scenes in *Der subjektive Faktor* (*The Subjective Factor*, 1981), used comedy, fantasy, or distanciation to depict the (future) terrorists with much less respect.[50] Subsequently, Hauff's *Stammheim* (1985) worked within the documentary theater tradition and located its drama almost exclusively in the windowless courtroom at the Stammheim prison. The dialogue is based on courtroom transcripts reproduced in Stefan Aust's account, *The Baader Meinhof Complex*. Similarly, the docudrama *Todesspiel* (*Death Game*, 1997) held millions of German television viewers captive with its historical recreationsand its interviews with politicians as well as crew members and passengers of the hijacked Lufthansa passenger airplane Landshut. *Todesspiel* became a media event accompanied by the obligatory title story in *Der Spiegel*. Both films were epic efforts that attempted to exhaust the subject RAF, and display their loyalty to the historical record (*Stammheim*) or documentary representations (*Todesspiel*) as measures of their quality.

Among the 1970s German terrorist films, *Deutschland im Herbst* constitutes a special case. Its heterogeneous form and content intended to respond to the German autumn of 1977 (the kidnapping of Hanns-Martin Schleyer, directorof Daimler-Benz and the "boss of Germany's bosses" in early September; the hijacking of the Landshut; the deaths of Baader, Ensslin, and Raspe in their Stammheim cells during the night of 17–18 October; and the subsequent discovery of Schleyer's corpse near Mulhouse) while it was still happening. Its episodes include theories and observations, fiction and document, the public and (especially in Fassbinder's portion) the deadly personal, all of which Alexander Kluge and his editor Beate Mainka-Jellinghaus assembled into dialectical montage. Commentators have drawn attention to Soviet influences as well as the film's challenge to contemporary West German television culture. *Deutschland im Herbst*, submits Miriam Hansen, "stakes out claims for a communicative praxis, which is the basis for an alternative organization of the public sphere."[51]

Writing about the difference between the New German visions of left-wing terrorism and the culture of memory emerging at the very end of the twentieth century, Thomas Elsaesser has suggested that the transition can be seen as the shift of focus from the victimhood of the leftist terrorists to the heroics of the West German state, and from the space of art cinema to the televisual electronic medium.[52] In the films of the late 1970s, according to Elsaesser, "the initiative for representing the RAF was with the liberal left, who saw the group as misguided idealists who were themselves victims of German history – Hitler's children, as they have been called – and victims of a repressive state."[53] The release of the TV-movie *Todesspiel*, however, represented a radically new commemoration: "it restaged the events of the Hot Autumn [of 1977] as a contemporary media event, and by doing so, it re-wrote one of the films from the 1970s, namely *Germany in Autumn*: not literally, of course, but on the level of myth and ideological fantasy."[54] Elsaesser suggests that "terror" and "trauma" are "Siamese twins in political discourse," by which "real, symbolic, somatic, and semantic violence can not be separated."[55] In this way, too, discourses of victim and perpetrator are reversible and symbiotic; Elsaesser notes how capitalist democracies depend on terrorist opposition in order to define themselves.[56] Both the RAF terrorists and the Federal Republic competed as media phenomena and as managers of mass media.[57] The shift in identification from the terrorists' generation to the generation of Helmut Schmidt and the German soldiers of World War II as seen in *Todesspiel* served, in Elsaesser's reading, as "a very useful piece of election propaganda for Helmut Schmidt's pragmatic heir Gerhard Schröder."[58]

I agree with Elsaesser's diagnosis that the RAF must be understood as a pop phenomenon and that "a significant element in the RAF's popular appeal to members of their own generation lay in the kinds of vicarious violence and protest they permitted young people to engage in, which were not so much political as they were cinematic."[59] Nevertheless, because his analysis concludes with the release of *Todesspiel*, it does not take into account the new cycle of films depicting left-wing terrorism, which peaked in Germany between 2000 and 2004.[60]

Many of these new features are not historical films as such; several engage with the pop and media issues that Elsaesser emphasizes were constituent of the historical phenomenon; and many, *pace* Elsaesser's predictions in his analysis of *Todesspiel*, do not create regimes of identification with the generation Schmidt. Indeed, the perspective on the RAF has shifted toward the sons and daughters of the first and second generation of the group. *Die innere Sicherheit*, for example, follows two terrorists and their daughter on the lam in present-day Europe. The focus and sympathy are clearly with the girl, who must come to terms with a youth spent in hiding from the authorities because of her parents' past actions. Not once does anyone mention the RAF; indeed, in Russia, the film was thought to be a depiction of former Stasi members.[61] *Die fetten Jahre sind vorbei* (*The Edukators*, 2004) also takes place in the present, and features two young men and a woman who mimic the political actionism of the late 1960s and 1970s. They kidnap a former activist who has long since become bourgeois. One of the young men, Peter, suggests, "What about a political kidnapping in the style of the 70s? We can hang a sign around his neck…film it, and send it to a TV station." These are *Nachahmungstäter*, copycat culprits engaged in an imitation of life. For commentator Roger F. Cook, *Die fetten Jahre sind vorbei* represents the subjectivity of a generation caught between a romanticism for the generation of 1968 in theory, and a disillusionment with the outcome of that older generation's long march to power in practice: neoliberalism and globalization.[62]

In this vein, scholar Rachel Palfreyman notes that the new films "allude to the cinematic traditions of the New German Cinema both by taking up the genre of the terrorist film and by consciously alluding to the aesthetics and politics of the earlier films."[63] By gesturing to the 1970s and 1980s terrorist films, the new productions seek to use both the history and film history of the old Federal Republic as an archive "to investigate questions of contemporary Germany and a relationship of cinema both to its own past and to its current political context."[64] In sum, Palfreyman sees the terrorist films as part of a "quest for identity": the new terrorist films reckon with the West German past and East–West relations in order to imagine a "pan-German identity" by reworking both the DEFA canon and the New German classics.[65] Chris Homewood's scholarly work has been similarly preoccupied with the resonances of the New German Cinema in the new terrorist films.[66] He shows, for example, the parallels between *Die bleierne Zeit* and *Die innere Sicherheit*, postulating that Petzold's project functions as an unofficial sequel. The latter "relocates the terrorist aberration to the Berlin Republic and in light of a new social context" and imagines the 1970s through the perspective of a child, "for whom the personal history of her family's terrorist legacy has become a suffocating anachronism."[67] Like Palfreyman, Homewood analyzes the new productions as meditations on generational identity in united Germany: they assess "to what extent it is possible for [today's young generation] to find a usable and sustainable identity of its own in light of the legacy of the 68ers."[68]

The new films take perspectives close to the terrorists. Nevertheless, the features assume knowledge in keeping with the profusion of information on the RAF that is now in circulation. In almost all of the German terrorist productions since 1972, one speaks of the RAF only indirectly. These narratives can afford to be elliptical because of the widely known historical record as well as the many previous films on the subject. This is simply how the "German genre" works.

Of course, a few films have attempted to treat the RAF directly and in detail, most notably the docudramas *Stammheim* and *Todesspiel*. The most recent high-profile RAF project, *Der Baader Meinhof Komplex* (*The Baader Meinhof Complex*, 2008), also pursues this strategy. Using journalist Stefan Aust's 667-page book as a source text, director Uli Edel and producer Bernd Eichinger distilled a screenplay that telegraphs ten years of terrorist activity in 150 minutes. The narrative is less opaque than *Baader*, and the dramaturgy indulges conventional re-creations, such as the demonstrations against the Shah's visit to West Berlin, the anti-war rally in the Audimax at the Freie Universität Berlin, and the protest outside the Axel Springer building after Dutschke was shot. Nevertheless, because of the epic scale needed to be faithful to Aust's dense history, the story races in seconds from chapter to chapter. Pressed for time, Edel delivers the story in soundbites and by dutifully re-creating iconic photographs or newsreel footage: Benno Ohnesorg's lifeless body, Baader and Meins's arrest in Frankfurt, and Baader's corpse after his suicide in Stammheim.

Largely a chronicle, *Der Baader Meinhof Komplex* makes little use of "helping" genres beyond the action film. Stylistically, it takes cues from recent Hollywood pictures, rather than previous German accounts of the RAF. The editing is relentless; the camera rarely pauses. The filmmakers mobilize a prodigious arsenal of automatic weapons and bullets, bombs, and stage blood. Likening the project to *The Bourne Identity* (2002), commentator Robert Sklar objected to the mixture of authenticity and getaway caper: "Its idea of interpreting the past is to try to match on screen the same number of bullets that were expended in the actual event."[69]

Character development is subordinated to gunfire, car chases, and recycled documentary footage. Because of the sheer number of figures who made up the group's first, second, and incipient third generations, individual introductions are sparse. Time and again, sequences end with a pan across a circle of committed terrorists, until the camera rests on the face of a nameless new recruit who—one realizes on a second viewing—will lead the next cell's illegal activity. Moritz Bleibtreu's Baader is shriller than Frank Giering's melancholy turn in *Baader* and just as unsympathetic, but the Eichinger–Edel script gives him much less screen time. Rather than the macho duel with Herold, it is more concerned with the bitchy squabbles between Ensslin and Meinhof. Characterized schematically, the two women represent the hot heart and the cool brains of the organization. The very first scene depicts Meinhof reading a book in the shade, while her daughters and husband swim. She is a frigid intellectual: on the nude beach in Sylt, she is the only clothed woman. We first see Ensslin as the feisty daughter of religious parents; she gesticulates wildly as she accuses her father's generation of tacit complicity with the National Socialists. Later, she bathes and flirts with the very young Peter-Jürgen Boock; Baader enters the bathroom and begins to fondle his topless lover, while, in one critic's words, "the pop-eyed lad gazes on like a choirboy who has just woken up on tour with Led Zeppelin circa 1973."[70] By the time the group leaders are imprisoned in Stammheim, Ensslin's vicious attacks on Meinhof have begun to have an existential effect. Listless and depressed, Meinhof loses her will to live after Ensslin accuses her of "theoretical masturbation" and rewrites her texts; Meinhof is "the knife in the RAF's back." The political and generational stakes of the era evaporate into a jealous catfight over Andreas.

The sexiness of the production was increased by the distractingly star-studded stable of actors Eichinger recruited. The major actors include Bleibtreu as Baader, Martina Gedeck as Meinhof, Stipe Erceg as Meins, Alexandra Maria Lara as Petra Schelm, Jan Josef Liefers as Peter Homann, Nadja Uhl as Brigitte Mohnhaupt, and Bruno Ganz as Herold. Even bit parts are mimed by major domestic players, such as Tom Schilling's second-long role as the deranged nationalist who shot Dutschke, Michael Gwisdek's brief appearance as Ensslin's father, Hannah Herzsprung as Susanne Albrecht, and Katharina Wackernagel as Astrid Proll. The re-created wanted poster with the actors, which served as the design for promotional posters and the DVD menu, resembles a Who's Who of German actors, head shots with retro haircuts, and certainly has none of the desperation of the "Anarchist Criminals" original. The film's music does not dispel the rock-star feel. The soundtrack includes Janis Joplin's "Mercedes-Benz" and two songs that The Beatles and The Who made famous: "Dizzy Miss Lizzy" and "My Generation." Given the picture's action-film aesthetic, Bob Dylan's peace mantra "Blowin' in the Wind" jars when it plays over the final credits. The choice, however, is a common one in Hollywood movies that remember the hippie era—for example, *Forrest Gump* (1994). Using it here confirms that Edel (born in 1947) and Eichinger (born in 1949) remember the Baader-Meinhof Gang less as a site of trauma than as a nostalgic part of "[their] generation," like a VW Beetle or hot pants. Critics by and large objected to this "glorification." Ryan Gilbey criticized the "black-leather glam" and gratuitous focus on sex, likening the project to *This is Spinal Tap* (1984). In his mind, it made the story of Germany's most-feared terrorists feel like an "account of the wildest rock band ever to wield Kalashnikovs instead of Rickenbackers."[71]

As we have seen, the nostalgic, pop retrospection of the RAF was not new and neither was the critical discourse of historicism or "gilded memory." Certainly, *Der Baader Meinhof Komplex* takes on the RAF with perhaps the most ambitious scope and surely the largest budget ever. It digests the subject matter of at least five previous German films on the subject that, for instance, deliberate on the political and gender dynamics of why individual members might have joined the struggle (*Die bleierne Zeit*) or document their trial in painstaking detail (*Stammheim*). Nevertheless, its severely elliptical narrative is in keeping with previous accounts. By tearing through the most complex chapter of West German history between the war and the wall, the film demands either the perspective of an older German (who will recognize the historical agents without prompts) or a young, international audience, which neither needs nor cares to know why these children of the middle class turned to armed combat against the state; *Der Baader-Meinhof Komplex* chronicles (who, what, when) rather than analyses (how, why). Such a large-scale production is perhaps most revealing less for what it shows than for what it excludes. The story withholds curious facts from its surfeit of memory. For example, key lawyers for the group, who are depicted smuggling in messages and weapons to the prisoners, are never named. Neither does the film indicate that some of these lawyers, such as Otto Schily and Hans-Christian Ströbele, went on to hold key positions in government and that some (e.g., Horst Mahler) represented ideological viewpoints far from their original leftist utopianism. Even after Edel's movie, the RAF will continue to serve as a contested site of memory for the generation of 1968 and its legacy.

Late-Born Memory

To comprehend the singularity of *Baader*'s historical project, we must return to the negative responses that the film received in the German press. The first criticism, of misrepresentation of history or "gilded memory," seems at first to be a somewhat puzzling response. Fictionalization is part and parcel of the biopic: names are changed, characters are made into composites, and events reordered or invented.[72] Why, then, is it wrong for Roth to alter history but permissible for John Ford to do so in *Young Mr. Lincoln* (1939)? After all, Ford invents entire episodes about Lincoln as a young man. Likewise, critics failed to protest when Oskar Roehler imagined his mother dying in 1989 in *Die Unberührbare*, when in fact Gisela Elsner lived on for two years in the united Germany. At best only a few of Karl Koch's old pals pointed out that Hans-Christian Schmid's 23 does not entirely adhere to the hacker's life.[73] The meeting between Krone and Baader was a sore point for critics and yet such a contrivance is not unprecedented in a German historical film: for example, Ulli Lommel's *Adolf und Marlene* (*Adolf and Marlene*, 1977). This satire imagines a fictive encounter between Dietrich and Hitler, who has become so enamored of the screen actress that he sends Goebbels to retrieve her from America. The dictator—played by Kurt Raab as a hysterical, obsessive Wagner freak and animal lover— even travels to the United States with the hope of consummating his imagined relationship.

It may well be that the problem critics had with *Baader* was not that it distorted the facts but that—unlike the Lommel film, which places Hitler and Dietrich in a stylized art cinema universe—it took recourse to more popular genre traditions. For, contrary to the critics who objected to a misrepresentation of history, *Baader* represents nearly word for word and image for image the written historical record. One could correctly call the film an adaptation of Stefan Aust's standard work on West Germany's leaden years, *The Baader Meinhof Complex*, so slavishly does it rely on the anecdotes and quotations from the volume's first and second chapters. Indeed, one way to explain the critical reaction is that the film wavers between fiction and an excessive form of fidelity. *Baader* enlists quotation rather than "authenticity" as a means to remember. It alludes to pop culture (films, genres, album cover compositions) and cites the historical RAF's "dialogue" (Ulrike Meinhof's *konkret* articles, prison correspondence, tableaux from iconic photos, passages from Brecht underlined in their books, and so on). The two fictionalized events take this historiographical principle of quotation to a logical extreme. This movie-mad, movie-made individual's metaphorical death as generic quotation, one might argue, is truer to the history than the painstaking attention to period detail would have been.

The German press's rejection of the pop representation of Baader (and German audiences' refusal to see *Baader*) point to a larger, underlying battle for the memory of 1968. This struggle involves both what the generation of 1968 was and is, but also who is entitled to narrate this history. Although the RAF's violence came to pervert the peaceful aims of Dutschke and the student protestors, the group stems from these movements: according to one commentator, the RAF from 1970 to 1972 was the only true "German" cultural and political remnant of 1968.[74] One must not forget that previous RAF films had also dictated the "reception" of the terrorist organization—for example, von Trotta's attempts to "understand" Ensslin and terrorism in *Die bleierne Zeit*. Rather than reduce the RAF to a family saga, Roth uproots the group's sociology and its political program, and dwells on the signs and the symbols, on the media coverage as such, rather than, as in *Katharina Blum* for instance, concentrating solely on renegade reporters. Roth dwells on the RAF's sunny halcyon days rather than the members' sordid childhood or their tragic legacy. *Baader* addresses the time that came before the period in which *Stammheim* and *Die bleierne Zeit* invested their emotional capital: the prison conditions, the suicide/murder scenarios, and so on. As Arthur J. Sabatini notes, the conflation of terrorists as individuals with their symbolic value—that they "stand" for something—is what makes them dangerous to the societal order.[75] The New German films about the RAF, even those that were very critical of the group, had tended to conflate real and symbolic bodies. This explains in part the harsh critical response to *Baader*. The film did not respect the "German" tradition, but rather showed Baader taking a day off.

Rather than creating an exact chronicle of Baader and the RAF, *Baader* re-channels the story through another generation. The film's style is dark, ephemeral, and imprecise, like the "late-born" director's own memory of the RAF. Baader is a historical untouchable, just out of reach behind his flash clothes and dark shades. The focus on a struggle between him and Herold does surely, as one critic charged, "privatize and ego-fy what was experienced as a collective German drama."[76] However, it is precisely the generation of 1968 which, even in academic histories, as Dorothea Hauser points out, tends to "privatize their experience as personal inheritance."[77]

Baader synthesizes polarized historiographies into a palimpsest, reflecting the fact that the historical record has been guided by a series of divergent memories, including the "official record," journalistic versions, and counterculture myths.[78] Its historical project hinges on the superimposition of unlike entities. The contradictory portrait of the RAF reveals its self-important coolness but also its private emptiness. This logic also extends to the film's form. *Baader* lacks the clear lines of *Deutschland im Herbst*, such as the two framing funerals that echo each other in their opposition. *Deutschland im Herbst* shows competing historiographies with a clear sympathy for the left. Indeed, this antimony between the burial of the RAF members and the state Schleyer funeral is vital to the film's dialectical project. It keeps the fronts separate and clear-cut; in Roth's feature, Baader and Herold actually meet. And when they do, it is clear that neither is fully guilty or innocent: everyone is, somehow, on the left.

The dénouement offers two interpretations. The death in front of the Frankfurt garage is both a homicide and a suicide, Baader is both a "murderous desperad[o] without higher political motives,"[79] as well as a pop hero. It is precisely the death scene that must be faked, because Baader's actual death in 1977 was the subject of so much historical speculation and contestation.[80] Baader's final performance provides a grand spectacle of suicide made to look like murder. And indeed, his disappearance from the underground to the confines of Stammheim represented a symbolic death and afterlife as a martyr of the West German justice system.

Baader speaks to a national audience that had the privilege of a quarter-century's distance and an altered perspective on the height of leftist terrorism. The film stands for the position of those old enough not to have first read about Baader in a textbook, but not old enough to have understood him as part of a social phenomenon (such as von Trotta, Fassbinder, and Schlöndorff did). This generation partook of the evening news about Baader and *Derrick* episodes with the same level of seriousness; the "Anarchistic Criminal" wanted posters might as well have been a "promo" for an upcoming concert. This generation later saw films like *Die bleierne Zeit* and *Stammheim*, and felt a discrepancy with its own blurred memories. This is Roth's generation: in interviews, the director speaks badly of *Stammheim* and refers to von Trotta's film as "Die breierne Zeit" (the mushy time).[81]

Nevertheless, *Baader* is hardly a reactionary opposite of *Deutschland im Herbst*. It neither ridicules terrorists like *The Raspberry Reich* (2004), nor does it glorify Krone or the police: *Todesspiel* had already served this function in its redemption of Helmut Schmidt and his fellow politicians from the World War II generation, who rescue the nation from radicals. Roth's film is aware both of its cinematic predecessors as well as the ironies of history that have in the meantime complicated the New German Cinema's response. (For example, renaming Horst Mahler—prominently interviewed as a radical leftist and former RAF co-founder in *Deutschland im Herbst*—as the character "Wagner" in *Baader* refers to the NPD leader's postwall conversion to anti-Semitism.) In the course of time and with the revelations of history, the status of the omnibus film has transformed alongside the retrospective meaning of German left-wing terrorism. Witness the comments of Wolfgang Langraeber after re-viewing *Deutschland im Herbst* in 1997:

> The scene at the Stuttgart cemetery impressed me and many others greatly back then – now, after ex-terrorists like Peter Jürgen Boock [*sic*] have described how coldly the four Stammheim prisoners planned their suicides, in order to hold the movement together and incite the "fighters" of the second RAF generation to murder Schleyer and commit further attacks – now, from the distance, this emotional final scene produces a stale taste.[82]

In spite of the many critics who accused Roth of having produced a slick postmodern pastiche, *Baader* maintains at least one deep sense of loss. Its nostalgia is hardly for the terrorists' violence and certainly not for their radical politics. Rather, it mourns the era's much more personal connection to culture. We must not forget that West Germany in the late 1960s and early 1970s was the birth hour of the New German Cinema and the golden age of cinephilia in Germany; the period saw the flowering of rock and the bloom of album cover art.[83] The materiality of celluloid and vinyl has been largely lost in the age of digital projection and the MP3. Although Christian Petzold's work with Harun Farocki on *Die innere Sicherheit* as well as Bertolucci's *The Dreamers* (2003) also meditate on this historical juncture, *Baader*'s terrorist-cinephile nostalgia is the boldest and most rigorous endeavor in this vein. The film's figures are alienated loners imprisoned by history, locked in poses behind ideological fronts. Baader and Krone could have been father and son, the film implies, if it had not been for the rigid politics of postwar West Germany.

Notes

1. Reinhard Mohr, "Die Prada-Meinhof-Bande," *Der Spiegel*, 25 February 2002, 202–4. See the cover of *Der Spiegel* from 29 January 2001 ("The Spirit of the 70s – The Present of the Past"). For other summaries, see Natalie Lettenewitsch and Nadine-Carina Mang, "Helden und Gespenster: Die RAF untot auf der Leinwand," *Ästhetik & Kommunikation* 117 (2002): 29–34; Holger Liebs, "Die Söhne Stammheims," *Süddeutsche Zeitung*, 17 October 2002; or Niels Werber, "Die Prada-Meinhof-Bande," *Literaturen* 12 (2001): 28–31. For an English-language assessment, see Paul Hockenos, "Hindsight turns German militants into T-shirt icons," *Christian Science Monitor*, 31 October 2002.
2. See quotations in Mohr, "Die Prada-Meinhof-Bande," 202–4 and Holger Liebs, "Die Söhne Stammheims," *Süddeutsche Zeitung*, 17 October 2002.
3. See Henrik Pedersen, "RAF auf der Bühne. Inszenierung und Selbstinszenierung der deutschen Terroristen," *Trans* 9 (March 2001), http://www.inst.at/trans/9Nr/pedersen9.htm.
4. See the market data of the Filmförderungsanstalt at http://www.ffa.de.
5. Bernd Haasis, "Eine vertane Chance: Die Lüge vom deutschen Desperado," *Stuttgarter Nachrichten*, 17 October 2002.
6. Claussen's comments are quoted and translated in Paul Hockenos, "Hindsight turns German militants into T-shirt icons," *Christian Science Monitor*, 31 October 2002.
7. Oliver Baumgarten, "Mythos als Lektion," *Schnitt.de*, http://www.schnitt.de/202,1161,1; "Rein zufällig," *Frankfurter Rundschau*, 29 October 2002.
8. Isabella Reicher, "Es muss auf die Fresse geben," *Der Standard*, 3 December 2002.
9. Jan Schulz-Ojala, "Kleinbürger, überlebensgroß," *Tagesspiegel*, 17 October 2002.
10. Harald Martenstein, "Die Rückkehr der Killer-Tomaten," *Tagesspiegel*, 16 February 2002.
11. Alexandra Seibel and Christian Höller, "Was tun…? Inszenierungsformen des Politischen im aktuellen Spielfilm," *Kolik.film* 3 (2005): 8.
12. Stefan Reinecke, "Einsamkeitshelden unter sich," *taz*, 18 October 2002.
13. See, for example, Ralph Eue, "Alles Feeling!," *Tagesspiegel*, 17 October 2002; or Barbara Schweizerhof, "Überblendung," *Freitag*, 18 October 2002.
14. For a pronouncement on the demise of the biopic, see George F. Custen, *Bio/Pics: How Hollywood Constructed Public History* (New Brunswick, NJ: Rutgers University Press, 1992), 2.
15. E.g., *Comedian Harmonists* (*The Harmonists*, 1997), *Aimée & Jaguar* (1999), *23* (1999), *Le roi danse* (*The King Is Dancing*, 2000), *Bonhoeffer* (2000), *Die Unberührbare* (*No Place to Go*, 2000), *Taking Sides* (2001), *Rembrandt* (2001), *Happiness is a Warm Gun* (2001), *Führer Ex* (2002), *Mein Name ist Bach* (*My Name Is Bach*, 2003), *Rosenstraße* (2003), *The Pianist* (2003), *Der Untergang* (*The Downfall*, 2004), *Der neunte Tag* (*The Ninth Day*, 2004), *Sophie Scholl* (2005), *Klimt* (2006), *Das wilde Leben* (*Eight Miles High!*, 2007), *Die Fälscher* (*The Counterfeiters*, 2007), *Strajk – Die Heldin von Danzig* (*Strike*, 2007), and *Der rote Baron* (*The Red Baron*, 2008).
16. See Henry M. Taylor, *Rolle des Lebens: Die Filmbiographie als narratives System* (Marburg: Schüren, 2002), 18, 91–101, and 114; as well as Custen, *Bio/Pics*, 248–55.
17. See Mary Joannou and Steve McIntyre, "Lust for Lives: Report from a Conference on the Biopic," *Screen* 24(4–5) (1983): 147. For more on the biopic's structure, see Taylor's discussion of *Lady Sings the Blues* and some of these examples (*Rolle des Lebens*, 253–54).
18. Astrid Proll, ed., *Hans und Grete: Bilder der RAF 1967–1977* (Berlin: Aufbau, 2004), 66 and 44 respectively.
19. Taylor, *Rolle des Lebens*, 248–49. (Page numbers hereafter cited in the text.) See also Custen, *Bio/Pics*, 8.

20. See Rainer Gansera, "Bewusst, wie ein Projektil," *Süddeutsche Zeitung*, 17 October 2002. Stefan Aust's standard work on the RAF, *Der Baader Meinhof Komplex*, rev. ed. (Munich: Goldmann, 1998), begins *in medias res* with the Baader breakout to demonstrate its importance.

21. In protest of West Berlin mayor Heinrich Albertz's handling of the Shah visit and Benno Ohnesorg's death on 2 June 1967, Peter Homann organized an art-action protest. White T-shirts were painted with large letters and each person involved (including Gudrun Ensslin) wore a letter on his or her shirt. Standing in a row together on one side was the name of the mayor, A-L-B-E-R-T-Z, on the back A-B-T-R-E-T-E-N ["resign"]. The action was carried on the evening news, and photographs appeared in the morning newspapers. See Aust, *Der Baader Meinhof Komplex*, 60.

22. The connection between Roth and Lemke is no elective affinity. Roth cut class to go to the Café Capri, the elder bon vivant's notorious hangout on Leopoldstraße in Munich's Schwabing district. Roth describes some of these encounters with "the director Klaus L." in his pop novella *200D*. In the book the film producer BERND E (30) parties with KLAUS L (40) and the TV director HELMUT D (33). See Christopher Roth, *200D* (Munich: Belville, 1982), here 46ff. Roth later edited Lemke's *Zockerexpress* (1991) and was a primary force behind the publication of a comprehensive volume on the director. See Brigitte Werneburg, ed., *Inside Lemke: Ein Klaus Lemke Lesebuch* (Cologne: Schnitt, 2006).

23. Robert McKee, *Story: Substance, Structure, Style and the Principles of Screenwriting* (London: Methuen, 1999), 84.

24. Laura Tonke resembles less the historical Ensslin, and more Godard's female leads, such as Anna Karina in her roles in *Pierrot le fou* and *Made in U.S.A.* (1966) and Anne Wiazemsky in *La Chinoise* (1967).

25. Stella Bruzzi, *Undressing Cinema: Clothing and Identity at the Movies* (London: Routledge, 1997), 91, 93 (hereafter cited in the text).

26. Gerd Gemünden, *Framed Visions: Popular Culture, Americanization, and the Contemporary German and Austrian Imagination* (Ann Arbor: University of Michigan Press, 1998), 99.

27. "It is so shitty! It is so shitty, I could cut off my hand out of rage. Gudrun, Ingeborg, Rita, Ulrike! I can understand them so well, those girls! They knew what was going on. You have no idea how much I loved Gudrun! I loved them so much, those girls!" For more on Vadim Glowna's radical past, see his memoir, *Der Geschichtenerzähler: Erinnerungen* (Berlin: Ullstein, 2006).

28. See Ginette Vincendeau, *Jean-Pierre Melville: An American in Paris* (London: British Film Institute, 2003), 21, 196.

29. See Vincendeau, *Jean-Pierre Melville*,165, 181ff. See also Thomas Elsaesser on Fassbinder's early gangster films: "Gaps in the characters' motivation as well as their depravity and casual evil are dignified in these films by the stark schematism which love seems to impose on all the protagonists, male and female" (Thomas Elsaesser, *Fassbinder's Germany: History, Identity, Subject* [Amsterdam: Amsterdam University Press, 1996], 269.) See also Jan Distelmeyer, "Baader: Christopher Roths Terroristen-Biographie scheitert an ihren Vorgaben," *epd Film* 19 (10) (October 2002): 44. For Distelmeyer the many close-ups of Baader's face were a "waste of time."

30. See, for example, Distelmeyer, "Baader: Christopher Roths Terroristen-Biographie scheitert an ihren Vorgaben," 44. Even Birge Schade, the actress who played Meinhof in *Baader*, complained about this in interview. See Cristina Nord, "Beinahe kaberettistisch," *taz*, 18 October 2002.

31. *Baader* very much echoes *Brandstifter* in these scenes of disaffection. In Lemke's film, when Anka declares to Karl—in spite of his overwhelming unlikeability—"I love you," Karl retorts nonchalantly "Oh, forget it!"

32. See Eve Sedgwick, *Between Men: English Literature and Male Homosocial Desire* (New York: Columbia University Press, 1985). See also Molly Haskell, *From Reverence to*

Rape: The Treatment of Women in the Movies, 2nd ed. (Chicago: University of Chicago Press, 1987), 187–88: "It is the rapport between Newman and Redford in *Butch Cassidy* rather than between either one of them and Katharine Ross, that has all the staples—the love, the loyalty, the yearning and spirituality, the eroticism sublimated in action and banter, the futility and fatalism, the willingness to die for someone—of women's fantasies as traditionally celebrated by the woman's film."

33. Aust, *Der Baader Meinhof Komplex*, 106 and 188; Dorothea Hauser, *Baader und Herold: Beschreibung eines Kampfes* (Frankfurt: Fischer, 1998), 128; and Proll, *Hans und Grete*, 42–43.

34. See, for example, Pedersen, "RAF auf der Bühne," n.p.; Hauser, *Baader und Herold*, 111, 81; and Ulrich Kriest, "Der Fernsehfilm *Brandstifter*," in *Inside Lemke: Ein Klaus Lemke Lesebuch*, ed. Brigitte Werneburg (Cologne: Schnitt, 2006), 104–19; here 117.

35. The quotation is from Hauser, *Baader und Herold*, 123. See also Hauser, *Baader und Herold*, 114 and Thomas Elsaesser, "From Censorship to Over-Exposure: The Red Army Fraction, *Germany in Autumn* and *Death Game*," in *I limiti della rappresentazione/ The Bounds of Representation*, eds. Leonardo Quaresima, Alessandra Raengo, and Laura Vichi (Udine: Forum, 2000), 289–308; here 307n22.

36. Aust, *Der Baader Meinhof Komplex*, 46; see Peter Homann, "Volksgericht im Wüstensand," *Der Spiegel*, 19 May 1997, 52–59; here 53. See also Peter Homann, "Aber nicht andere nur, auch uns töten wir," *Der Spiegel*, 21 October 2002, 170–78; here 174.

37. See Hauser, *Baader und Herold*, 147 and 152, as well as Pedersen, "RAF auf der Bühne," n.p.

38. See Hauser, *Baader und Herold*, 168 as well as Wolfgang Roth, "Das stille Einverständnis mit dem Terror," *Süddeutsche Zeitung*, 5–6 April 2007.

39. One famous example is the Kommune I's plan to pelt American Vice-President Hubert Humphrey with pudding. See Pedersen, "RAF auf der Bühne," n.p.

40. Aust, *Der Baader Meinhof Komplex*, 98.

41. See Peter Körte and Nils Minkmar, "Das Wesentliche am Terrorismus ist die Inszenierung," *Frankfurter Allgemeine Zeitung*, 17 October 2002.

42. See Proll, *Hans und Grete*, 80–89.

43. Hauser, *Baader und Herold*, 162.

44. Hauser, *Baader und Herold*, 155ff.

45. The leadership of the SDS and the Baader-Meinhof group were serious cinephiles. The rebels' favorite films had much to say about their courses through history: Rudi Dutschke's favorite was *Viva Maria!* (1965), Cohn-Bendit's was *À bout de souffle* (*Breathless*, 1960). According to Cohn-Bendit, "The filmic ideal in the SDS in 1968 was the Western *Viva Maria*." See the interview with Roth and Cohn-Bendit, Heide Platen, "'Baader war ein rührender Verlierer,'" *taz*, 15 February 2002, as well as Ralph Eue, "Alles Feeling!," *Tagesspiegel*, 17 October 2002. Cf. Rainer Gansera, "Bewusst, wie ein Projektil," who reports that Baader's favorite film was in fact *C'era una volta il West* (*Once Upon a Time in the West*, 1968), which certainly shares an affinity with the Corbucci film. The quotation is from Hans-Christoph Blumenberg, "Der italienische Western – ein Fazit nach sechs Jahren," in *Um sie weht der Hauch des Todes: Der Italowestern – die Geschichte eines Genres*, ed. Studienkreis Film, 2nd rev. ed. (Bochum: Schnitt, 1999), 7–13; here 12.

46. This story is cited in Aust, *Der Baader Meinhof Komplex*, 223–24, 230. Harun Farocki takes up this motif in *Etwas wird sichtbar* (*Before Your Eyes: Vietnam*, 1981).

47. For journalistic accounts of West German films about terrorism, see Stefan Reinecke, "Verrückte Märchen, Gespenster aus der Vergangenheit: 25 Jahre Deutscher Herbst und das Kino," *epd Film* 19 (10) (October 2002): 18–23, and his "Keine Stille nach dem Schuss: Terrorismus im deutschen Film," http://www.filmportal.de/df/7e/Artik el,,,,,,,FC5331E6248E2C3EE03053D50B376058,,,,,,,,,,,,,,,,,,,,,.html; as well as Felix Ensslin's article "Die doppelte Verdrängung," *Die Zeit*, 22 March 2007. A standard work on the terrorist films up to 1997 is Petra Kraus et al., eds., *Deutschland im Herbst:*

Terrorismus im Film (Munich: Münchner Filmzentrum,1997). See also Lettenewitsch and Mang, "Helden und Gespenster," 29–34. English-language articles include Olaf Hoerschelmann, "'*Memoria Dextera Est*': Film and Public Memory in Postwar Germany," *Cinema Journal* 40(2) (2001): 78–97.

48. See Harald Martenstein, "Die Rückkehr der Killer-Tomaten," *Tagesspiegel*, 16 February 2002. See also Barbara Schweizerhof, "Überblendung," *Freitag*, 18 October 2002.

49. This is also a hallmark of this generation's literary accounts of the RAF. See Julian Preece, "Between Identification and Documentation, 'Autofiction' and 'Biopic': The Lives of the *RAF*," *German Life and Letters* 56(4) (2003): 363–76.

50. As did, later, Christoph Schlingensief's *Terror 2000 – Intensivstation Deutschland* (*Terror 2000*, 1992) and Philip Groening's *Die Terroristen!* (*The Terrorists!*, 1992).

51. See Miriam Hansen, "Cooperative Auteur Cinema and Oppositional Public Sphere: Alexander Kluge's Contribution to *Germany in Autumn*," *New German Critique* 24–25 (1981–1982): 36–56; here 53.

52. See Thomas Elsaesser, "From Censorship to Over-Exposure," 289–308; as well as Thomas Elsaesser, *Terror und Trauma: Zur Gewalt des Vergangenen in der BRD* (Berlin: Kadmos, 2006).

53. Elsaesser, "From Censorship to Over-Exposure," 290.

54. Elsaesser, "From Censorship to Over-Exposure," 290.

55. Elsaesser, *Terror und Trauma*, 1.

56. Elsaesser, *Terror und Trauma*, 12–13.

57. Elsaesser, "From Censorship to Over-Exposure," 291–92.

58. Elsaesser, "From Censorship to Over-Exposure," 296.

59. Elsaesser, "From Censorship to Over-Exposure," 296.

60. The features from this period included *Die innere Sicherheit*, *Die Stille nach dem Schuß*, *Was tun, wenn's brennt?*, *Baader*, *The Raspberry Reich* (2004), *Die fetten Jahre sind vorbei* (*The Edukators*, 2004), and *Der Baader Meinhof Komplex* (*The Baader Meinhof Complex*, 2008). There were also a series of documentaries, among them *Große Freiheit – Kleine Freiheit*, *Black Box BRD*, and *Starbuck – Holger Meins*. In addition, there has been a number of films which reflect on Islamic terrorism and the aftermath of 11 September, such as *September* (2003), *Fremder Freund* (*The Friend*, 2003), and *Schläfer* (*Sleeper*, 2005).

61. See Barbara Schweizerhof, "Überblendung," *Freitag*, 18 October 2002.

62. See Roger F. Cook, "*Die fetten Jahre sind vorbei*: Edukating the Post-Left Generation," in *The Collapse of the Conventional: German Film and Its Politics at the Turn of the Twenty-First Century*, eds. Jaimey Fisher and Brad Prager (Detroit: Wayne State University Press, 2010), 309–32.

63. Rachel Palfreyman, "The Fourth Generation: Legacies of Violence as Quest for Identity in Post-Unification Terrorism Films," in *German Cinema: Since Unification*, ed. David Clarke (London: Continuum, 2006), 11–42; here 12.

64. Palfreyman, "The Fourth Generation," 13.

65. Palfreyman, "The Fourth Generation," 15.

66. See Chris Homewood, "Von Trotta's *The German Sisters* and Petzold's *The State I Am In*: Discursive Boundaries in the Films of the New German Cinema to the Present Day," *Studies in European Cinema* 2(2) (2005): 93–102; Chris Homewood, "The Return of 'Undead' History: The West German Terrorist as Vampire and the Problem of 'Normalizing' the Past in Margarethe von Trotta's *Die bleierne Zeit* (1981) and Christian Petzold's *Die innere Sicherheit* (2001)," in *German Culture, Politics and Literature into the Twenty-First Century: Beyond Normalization*, eds. Stuart Taberner and Paul Cooke (Rochester: Camden House, 2006), 121–35; Chris Homewood, "Challenging the Taboo: The Memory of West Germany's Terrorist Past in Andres Veiel's *Black Box BRD* (2001)," *New Cinemas* 5(2) (2007): 115–26; and Chris Homewood, "Making Invisible Memory Visible: Communicative Memory and Taboo in Andres Veiel's *Black Box BRD* (2001)," in *Baader-Meinhof Returns: History and Cultural Memory of*

German Left-Wing Terrorism, eds. Gerrit-Jan Berendse and Ingo Cornils (Amsterdam: Rodopi, 2008), 231–49.

67. Homewood, "Von Trotta's *The German Sisters* and Petzold's *The State I Am In*," 101.
68. Homewood, "Von Trotta's *The German Sisters* and Petzold's *The State I Am In*," 102.
69. Robert Sklar, "*The Baader Meinhof Complex*," *Cineaste* 34(4) (2009): 42–44; here 42.
70. Ryan Gilbey, "Killing to Be Cool," *New Statesman*, 17 November 2008, 43.
71. Gilbey, "Killing to Be Cool," 43.
72. Many commentators have disputed claims of "historical misrepresentation" in historical feature filmmaking as naïve film criticism. See, for example, Marcia Landy, *The Historical Film: History and Memory in Media* (London: Athlone, 2001), 12ff. For a journalistic account of the problems with criticizing feature historical movies based on historical accuracy, see Caryn James, "These Are Works of Art, Not Children's Schoolbooks," *New York Times*, 21 May 1995.
73. See Barbara Jung and Holger Stark, "Als die Hacker ihre Unschuld verloren," *taz*, 6 February 1999.
74. See Matteo Galli, "Paralleoli Bioi: Andres Veiel, *Black Box BRD* (2001)," in *Da Caligari a Good Bye, Lenin! Storia e cinema in Germania*, ed. Matteo Galli (Florence: Le Lettere, 2004), 539–57; here 542.
75. See Arthur J. Sabatini, "Terrorismus und Performance," *Kunstforum International* 117 (1992): 147–51; here 148–49.
76. Jan Schulz-Ojala, "Kleinbürger, überlebensgroß," *Tagesspiegel*, 17 October 2002.
77. Hauser, *Baader und Herold*, 15.
78. Aust, *Der Baader Meinhof Komplex*, 650.
79. See Hauser, *Baader und Herold*, 14.
80. As Roth says, "The whole thing is, like the national soccer team, a subject about which everybody has something to say. Everybody knows best." See Christopher Roth, "Der Stil des Terrorismus," *Süddeutsche Zeitung*, 17 March 2001.
81. See Hanns-Georg Rodek, "Verfilmt den RAF-Terroristen Baader als Popstar: Christopher Roth," *Die Welt*, 18 October 2002.
82. Wolfgang Landgraeber, "Das Thema 'Terrorismus' in deutschen Spielfilmen 1975–1985," in *Deutschland im Herbst: Terrorismus im Film*, eds. Petra Kraus et al. (Munich: Münchner Filmzentrum,1997), 11–21; here 17.
83. See Michael Rutschky, *Erfahrungshunger: Ein Essay über die siebziger Jahre* (Frankfurt: Fischer, 1982), especially 167–92.

Chapter 3

THE AMBIVALENT VIEW
23, Historical Paranoia, and the 1980s

In September 1998, after sixteen years of conservative CDU/FDP rule under the helm of Chancellor Helmut Kohl, the Social Democrats and Greens won elections that allowed them to govern the country in a coalition for the first time. The election precipitated a change of political parties, but also marked a generational shift. With Chancellor Gerhard Schröder, Interior Minister Otto Schily, and Foreign Minister Joschka Fischer, the central figures of the new government were politicians whose past had an intimate connection to the project of 1968 and its consequences.

A few months later, according to the film critics of the era, the spirit of change spread from Germany's political offices to its cinema screens. When 23 premiered in Germany in January 1999, a new respect for domestic filmmaking suddenly arose in the press. Film critics ecstatically hailed the story of a 1980s computer hacker from Hannover as a breakthrough. 23 "makes you believe in German Cinema again," wrote one critic. "No other German film," according to a notice in *Die Zeit*, "has brought us closer to a young person…[23] belongs to the best that German cinema has to offer." A commentator for the *Neue Zürcher Zeitung* even likened Hans-Christian Schmid's thriller to the work of Rainer Werner Fassbinder.[1]

Although the latter comparison may well be overstated, it reflected the frustrations of leftist critics who found the very few signs of critical volition within German cinema at the time. 23 was an aberration in a national cinema in which genre films tended to lack historical or geographical specificity.[2] Relationship dramas, detective movies, and above all comedies abounded in the decade's domestic production. Even the previous year's coup, *Lola rennt* (*Run Lola Run*, 1998), surely a breakthrough moment for post-New German Cinema, was seen by some contemporary critics as a clever exception to the lackluster rule. Tobias Kniebe spoke of Tykwer and Schmid as a sort of Méliès and Lumière, the former eager to invent a compelling fantasy, the latter aiming to capture the existing world: "Tom Tykwer wants to adrenalize his images until the filmmaker's pure fun therein explodes…Hans-Christian Schmid is a master of restraint and precision: he wants to disappear behind his images and characters."[3]

The journalists were above all surprised that a German production had attempted to thematize the *recent* past. A reviewer for the *Berliner Zeitung* saw *23* as an "exceptional German film" because it was a true story from the twentieth century.[4] Historical films in Germany, according to *23*'s many advocates, were by and large limited to relationship studies from the age of Goethe, Schiller, or Brentano or, when the twentieth century came into play, historical films set in the Nazi period. In contrast, maintained a critic in the *Berliner Morgenpost*, *23* "reflects the West German political realities of the 80s…it takes this period on, like almost no other of our directors."[5]

The film *23* figures among productions that, with varying degrees of fondness, recalled 1980s West Germany and West Berlin.[6] Schmid and writing partner Michael Gutmann's script presents a nightmare conspiracy within a labyrinth of trap doors and dead ends, and depicts the corruption of the internet into a front for the Cold War. In this way, the film both mourns the left's higher purpose and at the same time casts it as uncannily distant. Structured around the circle, the coming-of-age story channels 1980s West Germany through the 1970s American paranoid thriller and reflects on a loss of national innocence in the wake of the reunification, as well as a larger dissatisfaction with the late 1990s "end of history" rhetoric. *23* and the postwall prospects of the 1980s reframe the question of *Heimat* for people living in an age of globalized capitalism.

Coming of Age

The film *23* is a loose biopic of Karl Koch, a key player in a German spy scandal. It opens on one of Koch's final days, 23 May 1989, before flashing back to demonstrations at the West German nuclear power plant at Brokdorf in 1985. Together with the contemporary expansion plans for Frankfurt Airport,[7] Brokdorf, the first new nuclear power plant to go online after the Chernobyl meltdown, represented the political litmus test of a generation. This first scene transports the spectator back to the Cold War and into the midst of the social turmoil that characterized mid-1980s West Germany. Rather than advocating the dreams of Marx and Mao, German youth of that era focused its energies on protesting the use of rockets and atomic energy by the West German state.

In his first leading role, August Diehl plays Karl, a gangly, markedly insecure teenager from Hannover. When his father dies, he sets up a "research station for free living" with his DM 50,000 inheritance. Karl throws extravagant parties for friends from the leftist school newspaper and a host of crashers. He laughs off a DM 570 pizza delivery bill, even if his landlord dislikes his tenant's wayward behavior and lack of restraint. The Green generation activist is the only one at the Brokdorf demonstration who climbs the plant's wire fence and confronts a stream of water from police hoses. Later, he purchases a car after he and buddy David are ejected from a train, so that the latter can get to a biology exam on time. Both scenes characterize a young man prone to excess and self-indulgence.

Karl desperately wants to impress his peers and not feel alone. The incipient internet with its capacity for "knocking on doors in the global village," as Karl calls it, offers the perfect means of communication. Teaming up with David and guided by the cult sci-fi book *Illuminatus!*, Karl begins to hack into computer networks. Although his ostensible aim is to create a democracy or anarchy of information, Karl is flattered by attention from journalist Maiwald and thug Lupo. Convinced to make intrusions into military and nuclear computer systems by these and other unsavory characters, Karl descends into drug-fueled paranoia. He thinks he sees the number 23 everywhere, both in his own environment as well as in the larger world. After a final hack for the Soviets, he deems himself responsible for the Chernobyl disaster and suffers a nervous breakdown. David, Maiwald, Lupo, and the police interrupt his "rehab" stay. Karl decides to recount his story in exchange for a new life as a civil servant. The past once again haunts this retreat and the film returns to the opening. In the final images, Karl flees into the countryside and the titles note that the real Karl Koch was found dead in his car a few days later.

Director Schmid made his initial mark with distinctive period pieces that focused on growing-up in the old Federal Republic's small towns and big cities. *Nach fünf im Urwald* (*It's a Jungle Out There*, 1995) and *Crazy* (2000) explore Bavarian city–country tensions within coming-of-age trajectories. *Requiem* (2006) imagines 1970s provincial Swabia as a desolate setting for a troubled young woman who has left her family to study in Tübingen. In sum, Schmid's features concern the difficult separation of children from their parents. In *23*, Karl's relationship with his father is seriously troubled; this dysfunction casts a shadow over much of the story. The generational struggle becomes evident early on in a dinner-table scene with Karl and his parents. Father Koch is editor of the local newspaper, the *Hannoveransche Rundschau*, and confronts Karl with photographs of his activities at Brokdorf. Koch senior used his journalistic connections to prevent publication of the pictures and is furious that his son could have ruined the family's reputation. Karl is unrepentant; he is "against the crap of [his father's] generation." In a voice-over, Karl envisions only two possibilities for people of his age: to "conform or rebel."

The West Germany of 23 is a stifling place in which to grow up. Karl and David sit in the restaurant carriage of a train, smoke a joint, and brashly sing the folk song, "Die Gedanken sind frei" (Thoughts are Free). Their fellow passengers—seniors and other middle-class citizens—have little in common with the young men. The film's implication is: don't trust anyone over thirty. Indeed, a cast of older figures prey on Karl and David. Lupo appeals to their utopianism, even though they ultimately will function as tools in service of his greed. One night Lupo urges them to stop wasting their talent: "It's time to start with redistribution and hack into atomic facilities." Lupo's associate, Pepe, is a jaded drug dealer with a penchant for expensive suits and Argentinean leather bags. In his high-rise apartment, the four discuss a partnership. Pepe has little interest in Karl and David's internet ethics; he rolls a giant joint and changes his daughter's diaper. Lupo is cannier and feigns interest, urging the young idealists to help the Soviet bloc out of fairness to the principle of bipolarity vis-à-vis the Americans. Karl hesitates because he thinks the plan is proceeding too rapidly; David worries that they will be apprehended. Very quickly, however, Lupo comes up with a compelling question: "Are you spectators or do you want to take things in hand yourselves?" Later, Lupo and Pepe will insist that the boys' lucrative hacking is "fighting for world peace."

Karl's relation to Maiwald follows a similar pattern. The ambitious journalist, like Lupo, approaches Karl at a computer conference. From then on he pursues the teenager, bargaining exclusive stories on dangerous hacks for money, attention, and "friendship." Ultimately, however, Maiwald betrays Karl in order to save himself from prosecution. He arranges for Karl to give him and Weber the story and then to turn himself in. In addition, Maiwald offers what proves to be cynical advice about the German witness protection law: "They made that for the RAF terrorists. If you talk you get immunity and a new identity. You begin anew with a new name. And before that we'll make a killer TV-program…Good for me and for you. Among friends. That's how it goes." Weber—played by Burghard Klaussner, who portrays an absent father and a duplicitous manipulator in *Crazy* and *Die fetten Jahre sind vorbei* (*The Edukators*, 2004)—supplies Karl with an attorney, and delivers him to the authorities. An avuncular official lets Karl read a statement. The office reveals the micro-conspiracy at play in this German family. In addition to a print of an Illuminati hand hanging on the wall behind the agent's desk, the camera rests on a photograph of the official, Weber, and Karl's lawyer playing tennis together: state, press, and defender—an entire generation—are all in cahoots.

A story about the circulation of information, money, and ideology, 23 is structured by the circle. Tracking the film's recurrent circles, one quickly runs the risk of replicating Karl's own paranoia. There is the circularity of travel in the film between Hannover and Berlin, or the

Figure 3.1: Circular paranoia: the conspiracy of state, press, and defender in *23*. Image courtesy of Claussen + Wöbke Filmproduktion.

symmetry Karl and David discover in Bach's music: it can be played forward or backward. The film portrays the internet's beginnings where the circulation of information and capital became a global question. The Cold War was a conflict scenario based on the circular idea of mutually guaranteed destruction. Even the narrative form is circular: the film begins with the narrative end point and returns to it as the film closes. Schmid and Gutmann's shooting script has a circular pattern of characterization scenes followed by montage sequences underplayed with period music, followed by TV news images, at which point the cycle repeats itself.

Karl's efforts to sabotage or exit the world of circles fail. His relationship with Lupo and Pepe is initiated in the hope of creating a democratic anarchy of information. By the end of the film all ideals, noble or otherwise, have dissolved and Karl is a prisoner of the common junkie's vicious circle. Karl must work for Lupo, Pepe, and the Soviets in order to fund his drug habit. He needs the drugs in order to hack, which means he must hack all the more to support his habit. Indeed, Karl's conviction that everything can be interpreted *in hindsight* by the number 23 is itself circular logic; he believes in this until his death.

Perhaps the most important circular structure in the film has to do with family histories and Oedipal itineraries. It follows a trajectory in which Karl increasingly becomes like his father—his negative role model and the figure against whom he rebelled. Even though Karl initiates a career as a journalist and thereby follows in his father's footsteps, his aim is clearly to combat the patriarch's project. At the school newspaper, Karl complains that the *Hannoversche Rundschau* vastly underestimated the number of protestors at the Brokdorf demonstration. He and his friends brazenly hawk their publication at his father's workplace. After the father demands that his son desist or else be sent to a boarding school, Karl calls him a hypocrite; Karl believes the freedom of the press is endangered, accuses his father of merely wanting the extra room for a girlfriend, and wishes him dead. When Koch senior dies shortly thereafter, Karl's obsession with the book *Illuminatus!* begins. His father had first given it to him thinking it was a harmless sci-fi fantasy, only later to fear its subversive impact on the impressionable youngster. Karl's interest is thus a postmortem rebellion against his father's wishes.

Karl begins to change not long after his father's death. When he invites his classmate Beate for a weekend on the North Sea coast, she declines; there is a demonstration that weekend and she needs to earn pocket change. Karl offers money from his inheritance and jokes about her political convictions. When Beate suggests that he has become like his father, Karl becomes angry. He dramatically hangs up a row of D-Mark notes on a clothes line and burns the money, maintaining it "only brings [him] bad luck." Nevertheless, Karl becomes involved in a financial spiral. After Karl appears in a Maiwald TV-news report on the new phenomenon of hacking, his computer friends accuse him of selling out. He responds by complaining that he has generously sponsored their hacking. Subsequently, his dependence on capital only increases. In one montage sequence after Sergej (the Soviet KGB officer) grants Karl, David, Lupo, and Pepe their first contract, the quartet celebrate in a West Berlin hotel pool with D-Marks floating through the air. Later, when Karl and David buy a massive computer system formerly used in a West German nuclear reactor in order to increase their hacking capability, the soundtrack reveals the protagonists' primal desire: a 1980s interpretation of the R&B chart "Money," with its programmatic refrain, "That's what I want!" Karl continues his quest for money and drugs, until his realization (which we hear in voice-over precisely halfway through the film) that things are out of control: "For a long time it hadn't been about dividing information equitably. Captain Hagbard's fight against the world conspiracy fell completely by the wayside. While I perhaps still thought I was working against the Illuminati, I had probably been part of their plan for a long time. Without realizing it, we had become guns-for-hire. Spies on the KGB's payroll."

Of course this voice-over, from a letter Karl wrote to David a day before his 23 May 1989 death, is retrospective. Until nearly the very end of Karl's stint as a hacker, he fails to realize how much he resembles his father. Neither the confrontation with Beate, nor his increasing dependence on money and things, nor even the irony of buying a computer from an atomic power plant give Karl reason to pause. It is only in the end, when Karl believes that his hacking into nuclear sites has caused the meltdown at Chernobyl, that the circle is completed and Karl breaks down. Chernobyl, at the end of Karl's hacking days, stands as a counterpart to Brokdorf, "the crap of [his father's] generation." Karl has transformed so radically that he believes he has become his father. Indeed, even after Karl's rehabilitation and assumption of a new identity, he ends up working for the West German government. Karl ends up as bourgeois as his father was, working for the establishment with two female subordinates who use a formal address. This is certainly not the anarchy of information that Karl Koch, alias Captain Hagbard, once had in mind.

Paranoia as Historical Principle

The Chernobyl incident is the climax of Karl's paranoia. Finding the power plant on his hacking list after hearing about the tragedy, he can only conclude he is responsible: "They're using my thoughts…. My father, Olof Palme, Tripoli. I thought it and then it happened." Karl takes politics and the course of history seriously and feels himself physically connected to these larger events. He is perturbed when a hanger-on does not know whether the just-murdered Olof Palme was the Finnish or Swedish prime minister. "This is important," he tells his visitors, before condescendingly recommending they smoke grass and shut up. Indeed, television news frequently accompanies the story of the errant hacker. Karl not only watches these images; he lives them. At one point Karl has a psychotic episode while traveling on the autobahn. He hears airplanes and imagines he is being attacked. After seeing a news story on the escalation of hostilities between the United States and Libya, Karl dreams about the American bombing there. A sound bridge of jet engines on television suggests Karl's corporeal relation to German history; indeed, his dreams take the form of TV images of night-vision bombings.

   In one sense, Karl's beliefs and actions mimic the work of a historian. As Dana Polan puts it, "paranoia is a historical activity."[8] The film depicts a particular way of ordering history and the pitfalls of selective vision and an excessive, retrospective hermeneutic. Karl's conception of the course of history, informed by *Illuminatus!*, always returns to the number 23; the world is doomed to repeat the past. Within this hermeneutical logic, there is a circularity of political events. Reagan's America engages in a tit-for-tat struggle with Ghaddafi's Libya, bombing civilian infrastructures in response to the explosion at the LaBelle discotheque. Karl sees Mozart, Goethe, Herder, and other icons of German cultural history as members of the Illuminati and thus conspiratorial agents. He believes that the Bavarian Adam Weishaupt, and not George Washington, was the first American president.

Of course, the number 23 is ubiquitous because Karl always looks for it. In a montage of a car ride to the tune of Iggy Pop's "The Passenger," Karl and David play the "23 game" as they drive through the suburbs of Lower Saxony. In a VW symbol they see the Roman numeral five— the sum of two and three—followed by the twenty-third letter of the alphabet. The mineral water Apollinaris and Camel cigarettes feature logos with the Illuminati pyramid. Advertisements for the perfume Chanel N°5 and the cigarette brand Ernte 23, likewise, confirm their numerology. Later, Karl and Lupo drive by the bombed-out LaBelle nightclub in West Berlin: the house number is "23." Schmid tantalizes the attentive viewer with the numerals "23" in a plethora of other places: on a packing crate, as a hotel room number, on the cigarettes Weber smokes, on billiard balls at the locksmith's, Maiwald's address ("5"), and even, across the filmmaker's oeuvre, as house addresses in his later films *Lichter* (*Distant Lights*, 2003), also starring Diehl, and *Requiem*.

Illuminatus! helps Karl explain and thus tame the otherwise seemingly arbitrary and terrible course of history: this is, according to scholars, the appeal of conspiracy theories for their believers. "The idea of conspiracy," as Timothy Melley notes, "offers an odd sort of comfort in an uncertain age: it makes sense of the inexplicable, accounting for events in a clear, if frightening, way."[9] Conspiracy theories and chaos theory constitute master narratives that attempt to organize the world into systems; they require a quasi-religious conviction, a sense that the conspiracy in question has almost supernatural powers. "Conspiracism," writes Daniel Pipes, "even claims priority over faith" and "resembles other 'isms,' in defining an outlook that can become an all-encompassing concern."[10] Furthermore, Pipes makes the claim for National Socialism as primarily a conspiracy theory that emphasized Judaism's threat to destroy the German "race." Aiming to replace Christianity, Nazism endeavored to claim truth in all areas of life, including mathematics. In this light, Einstein's theory of relativity represented a Jewish attempt to destroy German masculinity.[11] The nihilistic motto of the Illuminati ("Nothing is true, everything is allowed") includes a subtenet that resembles a parody of Marxist doctrine: "The history of the world is the history of the wars between secret societies."[12]

Conspiracism—including Karl's—mimics but ultimately perverts historical practice. Conspiracy theorists are every bit as thorough as their conventional historian counterparts. The two groups' methods, however, diverge dramatically. "Rather than piece together the past through the slow accumulation of facts," according to Pipes, conspiracy theorists "plunder legitimate historical studies to build huge edifices out of odd and unrelated elements."[13] Karl's "23 game" and his historical worldview resemble what David Bordwell calls "domestication,"—that is, "reaffirming existing conditions by applying the unknown to a master narrative."[14] His mistake in logic is that he confuses the likelihood that a chain of events would be connected if they were a function of a coordinated conspiracy with the probability that a conspiracy is at work if a series of events takes place.[15]

Karl's hermeneutical game leads to his destruction. The newspaper articles that he hangs on his wall of supposedly Illuminati-influenced events are certainly windows to larger political and cultural happenings inaccessible to a young man in Hannover. At the same time, they reflect the interior design of his mental prison. The film *23* is a parable about the human need for clarity via ideology and the concomitant madness of an untethered semiosis. As historian Hayden White observes, the increasingly all-encompassing reach of the media—and *23* plays against the backdrop of the internet—leads to "hermeneutic gymnastics" through which history becomes subject to the same "ambiguating" effects as the televised replays of crucial events in sporting contests. The drive for complete knowledge and clarification produces "wide-spread cognitive disorientation and despair."[16] Karl's paranoia is a symptom of *his* age in *this* age; a generational response to a certain moment in a certain culture.

The Space of the Paranoid Thriller

A film set in the 1980s, *23* opens with a classic song from the 1970s, Deep Purple's "Child in Time." The somewhat obscure lyrics warrant closer investigation:

> Sweet child in time you'll see the line
> The line that's drawn between the good and the bad
> See the blind man shooting at the world
> Bullets flying taking toll
> If you've been bad, Lord I bet you have
> And you've been hit by flying lead
> You'd better close your eyes and bow your head
> And wait for the ricochet.

The song's text intimates the film's central themes. On a literal level, Karl will later imagine himself being shot in the head. The Deep Purple number, furthermore, describes a figure deformed by history—much like Karl. He is lost to his time, caught between the fronts of a war in which he is an unwilling participant. Karl is overwhelmed by the events and anxieties of an apocalyptic era in which the end of the world (whether by nuclear annihilation, the extinction of forests, or other means) seems to be (only) a matter of time. Indeed, contemporary popular interpretations of "Child in Time" viewed it as an allegory of the Cold War; the song was especially popular in the underground East European civil rights movements, where it figured as an "unofficial anthem" of resistance.[17]

The musical motif of *23* from the 1970s is repeated throughout the film. Indeed, Schmid's film as a whole takes inspiration from the decade: it recalls the 1970s American paranoid thriller. To a large extent, this cycle's specificity lies in the internal location of threat to the community. Unlike the sci-fi films of the 1950s, for instance, which fixate their paranoia on the specter of Soviet communism or alien invasions descending onto ordinary lives, paranoid films of the post-Watergate era such as *The Parallax View* (1974), *Three Days of the Condor* (1975), *Marathon Man* (1976), and *All the President's Men* (1976) focus on the corruption of the US political system and the enemy within.[18] In a similar vein, *23* features cynical journalists and television producers, the German state (in the form of the Federal Criminal Bureau), spies from East and West, and petty thugs, all of whom are connected in a conspiracy. Karl is a character like Joseph Frady (Warren Beatty) in *The Parallax View*, Babe Levy (Dustin Hoffman) in *Marathon Man*, or Joe Turner (Robert Redford) in *Three Days of the Condor*. Similar to the journalist Frady, the graduate student (in history) Levy, and above all Turner, whose work for the CIA involves scrutinizing novels for hidden messages, Karl reads between the lines of fiction in order to decipher the world. A key line from *Three Days of the Condor* ("You can't trust anyone") echoes *23*'s subtitle, "Nothing is what it seems." Like the characters in American conspiracy films of the 1970s, wariness, suspicion, hypersensibility, and isolation mark Karl's personality. He is a paranoid, but his fears, like Turner's, are shown to be justified. These are characters who have a sharper vision than the "healthy" or normal response.[19] Karl, and perhaps Karl alone, is sensitive to the unsettling nature of historical change that underscores the film.

The paranoid thriller enjoyed a renaissance in later Hollywood films such as *In the Line of Fire* (1993), *The Pelican Brief* (1993), *Enemy of the State* (1998), *Snake Eyes* (1998), and *Wag the Dog* (1997). These productions, however, lacked the 1970s ideological perspective. Further examples in the sci-fi or psycho thriller vein—*The Game* (1997), *Pi* (1998), *Fight Club* (1999), *The Matrix* (1999) and its sequels—are solipsistic dramas that portray the existential fear of an entire loss of reality, rather than the disappointment in the nation's ideals and its political representatives, as the earlier cycle had. The films from the 1990s have less to do with political anxiety than a discontent regarding new media technologies and the fear that "reality" might no longer be real.[20] Thus, although *23* may come from the same historical moment as *The Matrix*, its historical project remains closer to that of *The Parallax View*. Even though its story revolves around the internet, *23* is ultimately based on a suspicion of the state's power and how political institutions abuse the internet's new technological possibilities.

In keeping with the 1970s productions, *23*'s construction of space— its geography, architecture, and set design—also reflects its historical paranoia. The title sequence, for example, provides a montage of newspaper clippings and photos in what we will later learn is Karl's room. George Washington, prominent names of German Illuminati, the score of a Bach cantata, the Pentagon, Olof Palme, Ronald Reagan's "Star Wars," the Tripoli bombings, police at the Brokdorf demonstrations: these are the evidence Karl has collected to prove the conspiracy. These traces provide an initial snapshot of 1980s West German history, and, simultaneously, anticipate the stations of Karl's subsequent descent. In each shot there is movement, whether a track or a zoom, and the dissolves connecting each shot create a sense of restlessness and semiotic overload. Director of Photography Klaus Eichhammer employs almost exclusively hand-held camera throughout the movie, providing the spectator with a jittery rendering of Karl's experience.[21] At the end of the film, the narrative returns to this room, which, as we learn in this second viewing, is the new apartment Karl has moved into after entering a witness protection program. It is precisely at this point and in this space—now accompanied by the non-diegetic chatter of voices rather than Deep Purple—that we learn that Karl has not been cured of his belief in the Illuminati. He has only learned to hide his obsession better.

Next to the unremarkable and lifeless trappings of other German genre pictures of the late 1990s such as *Knockin' On Heaven's Door* (1997), *Solo für Klarinette* (*Solo for Clarinet*, 1998), or *Bin ich schön?* (*Am I Beautiful?*, 1998), *23* offers an exceptional set design. Cluttered compositions in Karl's apartment and Lupo's living room display shrill curtains and furniture; Sergej's office, in East Berlin, is minimalist. In addition, a number of scenes display bizarrely stylized architectures. Of note here is especially the claustrophobic, oval-shaped chapel, a fitting setting for the funeral of Karl's father. Recalling the parabolic architecture of Félix Candela, the nave's distorted shapes and the high-key lighting correspond to Karl's alienation and final break with his family. In this scene, much like Alan J. Pakula's filmic spaces from his 1970s thrillers, "the architecture becomes monstrous, so that the individual becomes a foreign object."[22]

Muted colors mirror the story's evacuation of moral absolutes. As in Antonioni's *Il deserto rosso* (*Red Desert*, 1964), stylized color anticipates the threat of ecological disaster. The desaturated color scheme in *23* also implies a historical distance, stylistically augmenting the historicity of that which was in fact only ten years old. This strategy recalls that of Antonioni's film. "If *Red Desert* is a film about historical transformation and psychological change," film scholar Angela Dalle Vacche argues, "it is not surprising that Antonioni uses color to alter the nature of cinematic language, namely to paint the world anew according to abstract sensibility."[23] Also a film about historical transformation, *23* uses colors as signposts of this change and as psychological markers.

Figure 3.2: Monstrous architecture à la Félix Candela: the church funeral in *23*. Image courtesy of Claussen + Wöbke Filmproduktion.

The images are especially desaturated during times when Karl is under psychic stress, for example the opening (and closing) scenes at the Hannover City Hall, subjective hallucinations on the autobahn, and the unnaturally bright hues during his nervous breakdown.

Figure 3.3: Karl's breakdown in high-contrast hues in *23*. Image courtesy of Claussen + Wöbke Filmproduktion.

In addition to cinematography, set design, architecture, and color, *23*'s deployment of topography is essential to its paranoid project. Reviewers pointedly praised *23* for its specificity of place, a quality not evident in many contemporary domestic productions.[24] Unlike a film similar in subject matter, *War Games* (1983), *23* never adopts a nebulous, universal approach to space. In general, Hans-Christian Schmid's oeuvre stands out among young German directors for its careful attention to locality. Indeed, among contemporary directors working in the mainstream, only Marcus H. Rosenmüller, Christian Petzold, or Andreas Dresen are more attuned to the local sounds, colors, and feel of the German provinces. Originally trained as a documentarist, Schmid observed in an interview that "place is certainly a protagonist" in his work; he divides the world into "filmic and unfilmic spaces."[25]

In a nuanced and ambivalent manner, *23* negotiates geography. The action itself nervously alternates between Hannover and Berlin. The characters' attitude toward German spaces, furthermore, is conflicted. One scene, in which Pepe, Lupo, David, and Karl stand on a hill that looks over Hannover, is exemplary. Karl is close to a breakdown and David seeks an exit strategy so as not to ruin his future career chances; Lupo and Pepe try to dissuade them. In spite of Karl and David's complaints that Hannover is provincial and Lupo and Pepe's suggestion that, should anything go wrong, they might flee to the Soviet Union, Karl defends his home: "Moscow is even worse than Hannover." Indeed, in the last scene there is a metaphorical return to the German *Heimat*. Karl drives along a forest path, and the shot opens to an aerial view, suggesting that *23* is a kind of *Heimatfilm* that portrays a return to the German provinces.[26]

Figure 3.4: The final aerial shot and symbolic return to the German provinces at the conclusion of *23*. Image courtesy of Claussen + Wöbke Filmproduktion.

In many ways, Hannover would seem an implausible setting for a political thriller.[27] The film's unsettling effect hinges not on exotic locales, however, but rather on uncanny spaces. In his examination of the haunted house in literary Romanticism, Anthony Vidler says that uncanny spaces are "disquieting for the absolute normality of the setting, [their] *absence* of overt terror."[28] As both an aesthetic and psychological category, the uncanny, based on a response to space and an Oedipal imperative,[29] provides a useful rubric for understanding 23's mixture of (de)familiar(ized) spaces and generational conflict. Schmid's Hannover is, at once, secure and haunted.

Another important space in 23 is the internet. Still very much a novelty in contemporary productions such as *The Net* (1995), *You've Got Mail* (1998), and *The Matrix*, "cyberspace" functions in Schmid's film as a most suspicious topography. This view is not out of keeping with media historians who characterize the internet as the site of a peculiar paranoia. The medium, according to Wendy Chun, emerged through a particular stage of forces (namely, the US government's support of the internet as a military network and its decision in 1994 to privatize its backbone); contemporary discourse on the internet reduced political problems of state control and individual freedom to matters of technology.[30] The internet demonstrates a conflict of ownership: although the user produces and transmits data "freely," the servers and fiber optics by which this information travels belong to institutions and subject him or her to surveillance. Moreover, in terms of space, fiber-optic networks function on the ambiguous divide between physical and virtual locations, emphasizing "the physical necessity of location and the explosion of virtual locations" (26). The topography of cyberspace separates the users' body from their actions and thus "frees" human subjects from both their bodies and physical locations (37–38). In another way, as Lev Manovich contends, there is "no space in cyberspace"; the internet is perspectivally unmappable and unnavigable.[31] The internet enacts the uncanny's special relationships of exterior and interior, and actualizes Karl's ambiguity between the worlds of dream and reality.[32]

Faraway, So Close: The Historical Uncanny

Re-examining press responses to 23 enhances our appreciation of the film's particular retrospection. One reviewer noted how it transports the viewer into a world that "surprisingly already seems very far away," with its irreconcilably opposed positions on nuclear power plants and Pershing missiles.[33] A commentator for *Frankfurter Allgemeine Zeitung* remarked how the 1980s was an unfortunate decade: "If you could pick a time in the history of the republic not to grow up: the reasonable choice would be the 80s....At the same time that you learned about love and sex, you were warned about love and sex, because of a new, insidious virus." Whereas the generation of 1968 had read Marx and Marcuse, the generation to follow, unable to rebel further left than the parents, was drawn into the esotericism and paranoia of works like *Illuminatus!*[34] As one critic perceptively claimed about West Germans growing up in the 1980s, "a decade before, Karl might have bombed a department store and joined the RAF."[35] In another telling comment, Christiane Peitz noted how *23* underscores the distinction between Germany in the 1980s and late 1990s:

> Hans-Christian Schmid and his co-author Michael Gutmann have condensed Karl's biography into a time trip. With the sensitivity of archaeologists they unearth an epoch of the Federal Republic, which—only 10 years later—seems like a mythical past. The time before the fall of the wall was eschatological....Today, at the end of the 90s, the apocalypse is a public affair, more celebrated than feared. In the 80s it was a personal reality, an anxiety in our minds, which brought us together. That's why the apocalypse often provided a cozy atmosphere....We were at home with our hysteria.[36]

Tobias Kniebe expressed a similar sentiment. For him, the 1980s was a "time when evil was powerful and apocalypse still took its job seriously," a "great, strange time" that subsequently decayed like strontium-90. Of all the decades, opined Kniebe, the 1980s had the "shortest half-life":

> What happened to us, the children of the 80s? Evil has become more boring and less global and the end of the world isn't what it used to be. The girls from back then are today only afraid of getting old and if the rockets haven't been destroyed, then nobody knows their names anymore. The forests are still alive and *Der Spiegel* is printed in color. The Greens are in power and the nuclear power plants will probably be abolished, but nobody seems to be glad about it. Dad is buried. The wall is gone. Mother tends to the garden. Karl Koch didn't live to see the 90s. He was probably lucky.[37]

These commentators and Schmid's film attend to a vexing conundrum of historical experience: the closest reaches of history appear to be the strangest. This phenomenon features prominently in our daily lives: in popular culture nothing seems as out(dated) as the fashion, music, or interior design from the previous season, decade, or other cycle. At stake in this feeling are intertwined lines of proximity and distance, and of the familiar and the strange. Thus, the critics' notion of "a decade that has just passed but feels so far away"[38] might be called a "historical uncanny." In *23*, it certainly pertains to discourses regarding the loss of *Heimat*. As Peter Blickle writes:

> The idea of *Heimat* is based on an imaginary space of innocence projected onto real geographical sites. Whether this innocence is religious (paradise),

sexual (childhood), sociological (premodern, preindustrial), psychological (preconscious), philosophical (prerational, predialectical), or historical (pre-Holocaust) in character, in every case we find imageries of innocence laid over geographies of *Heimat*. The many *pre-* prefixes in the foregoing list point to a temporal dimension, a longing for an imaginary past, which affirms *Heimat*'s regressive tendencies.[39]

Indeed, the conception of *Heimat* at stake in 23 not only refers to vectors of space (provincial Hannover, isolated West Berlin), but also dimensions of time. In a circular return of the past that coincides with Karl's story and his paranoid take on history, we once again are faced with global threats—real or perceived—no longer of concern in the late 1990s when the film appeared. In short, a "historical uncanny" arises in reading these reviews of 23 ten years into the twenty-first century. Regarded with the hindsight of yet another decade, the comments of 23's reviewers betray how a cozy ennui gave way to less comforting postwall, pre-9/11 and climate change perspectives. The context of 23's reception was a unified German state with criss-crossed ideological lines: a coalition government of former 68ers which included no-longer radical Greens and the cigar-smoking Social Democrat, Gerhard Schröder. At this unique moment, Francis Fukuyama's thesis on the "end of history" had gained measurable credence.[40] The "clear-cut enemies" of Reagan, Breschnev, and Franz-Josef Strauß could be nostalgically mourned for the sense of purpose that had provided for a more united left.[41]

Just as the story of Karl Koch chronicles his awkward and ultimately fatal coming-of-age as it follows a circular pattern in which the son becomes the hated father, 23 speaks to the united Germany's growing pains and loss of innocence. There lies more behind the film's angst than just Y2K anxieties or millennial conspiracy theories. The belief in the Illuminati conspiracy as a guiding master narrative reveals both the vacuum of heroes in the 1980s—with the schizophrenic urgency to reject both the Nazi past *and* the Oedipal task to rebel against the 68er fathers—as well as the lack of political impetus in 1999 Germany's so-called "Fun Society."[42]

An unspoken disappointment about the aftermath of German unification haunts Schmid's film. This feeling was of a piece with the political ennui precipitated by the series of scandals in the late 1990s which brought about an end to the Kohl era. Although one cannot compare Kohl's loss of power after 16 years with the situation that led Alexander and Margarete Mitscherlich to diagnose a collective inability to mourn the loss of Hitler, Kohl was surely a father figure for Schmid's so-called "Generation Golf," the "children of Kohl and Commodore," for whom he had been the only chancellor.[43] The failure of both the conservative-nationalistic program and the utopian projects of the hippies, the Greens, and East European Socialism yielded in 1999 Germany, to paraphrase Norman Mailer, two attitudes beyond left and right: "apathy or paranoia."[44] The belief in conspiracy ultimately stems from a feeling of diminished human agency, a sense that individuals cannot effect meaningful social action; conspiratorial views function less as a defense of some clear political position than as a defense of autonomous individualism.[45] Paranoia, in this way, might be seen as a historiographical response to the challenges of 1999 Germany, but *23* chronicles this process: the transformation of utopian disappointment into what Hayden White speaks of as "cognitive disorientation and despair."

This general loss of faith helps us to understand the film's generic genealogy. Just as the 1970s American paranoid thriller responded to a series of historical disappointments from the Kennedy assassination to Watergate, *23* transposes a late-1990s cynicism and leftist nostalgia into the past in order to locate the beginning of the end. This transposition itself entails a curious renegotiation of a homegrown cycle of films; *23* recalls, namely, the New German Cinema's "case studies," such as *Abschied von gestern* (*Yesterday Girl*, 1966), *Katzelmacher* (1969), *Die verlorene Ehre der Katharina Blum* (*The Lost Honor of Katharina Blum*, 1975), and many others.[46] Like these productions, *23* is a narrative about a martyrdom, a biography of a life stunted by German history. Like *Das zweite Erwachen der Christa Klages* (*The Second Awakening of Christa Klages*, 1978) or *Die bleierne Zeit* (*Marianne and Juliane*, 1981), *23* is based on a real incident, lending the film a certain journalistic topicality. Thomas Elsaesser's description of the New German Cinema certainly seems applicable for *23*, when he argues that the family unit "is generally incomplete or asymmetrical in its power relations, and history in the New German Cinema is almost exclusively seen in the context of Fascism and its delayed aftermath: the radicalization and polarization of the 1960s culminating in the wave of urban terrorism in the early 1970s."[47] Accordingly, Elsaesser continues, the experience of society in these films occurs "from the vantage point of standing outside, alone and overwhelmed by personal impotence. Desire for change invariably involves rebellion which, as we shall see, is figured primarily as martyrdom or submission" (217).

The binary logic "martyrdom or submission" resonates with Karl's alternatives for his generation: conform or rebel. Nevertheless, although Karl the character feels profoundly alone and maintains a *Weltanschauung* similar to that of the heroes and heroines of the case studies, *23*'s stance toward its protagonist is quite different from that of the New German Cinema. As Elsaesser notes, the films of the New German Cinema feature a "mediated, highly coded depiction of history, society and the family from an emotionally coloured, even partisan perspective. It is a reaction to reality more than its description, which is why, perhaps too generally and simplistically, the New German Cinema is so often called 'subjective'" (215–16). Productions such as *Abschied von gestern* or *Die verlorene Ehre der Katharina Blum* align viewers with heroines in a way that encourages absolute sympathy. In these films, influenced by contemporary philosophies of collective psychology and the constructedness of subjectivity, the question of agency is absolute: the protagonists cannot expect better treatment because the game of history is rigged against them. Timothy Melley's notion of "agency panic" helps us understand this distinction. Agency panic, according to Melley, is "intense anxiety about the apparent loss of autonomy, the conviction that one's actions are being controlled by someone else or that one has been 'constructed' by powerful, external agents."[48] The New German Cinema historical films endorse an "all-or-nothing" notion of agency, viewing agency as "a property, parceled out *either* to individuals like oneself *or* to 'the system'" (10).

But 23 is more ambiguous. It exhibits a tension between, on the one hand, a highly organized network, and on the other, an individual who believes until almost the end that he can nevertheless manipulate this system to his own, personal favor. Karl does not consciously suffer from agency panic, the conviction that "one's actions are being controlled by someone else." Although Karl thinks that the Illuminati manipulate fate, his breakdown is precipitated by the belief that his thoughts and fantasies (whether Chernobyl, the Olof Palme murder, or his father's death) come true—in other words, that *he* is in control of history. Karl Koch desires both to be part of history *and* to exert a selective epistemological skepticism so that he might control his object of study. This, a feature of so-called "millennial historiography,"[49] departs from the New German Cinema's persuasion that the postwar subject is circumscribed by the Nazi past and the postwar socialization. Watching 23, the spectator is aware that although the protagonist is partially correct about his critique of the establishment, he is also disturbed. For that reason, Karl is a less sympathetic character than Anita G. or Katharina Blum, whose fates are absolutely determined by Germany's dark past and its fatal afterlife within the present. Among the "case studies" characters, Karl most resembles Fassbinder's ambiguous anti-heroes: cholerics like *Katzelmacher*'s Jorgos, curmudgeons such as Hans from *Händler der vier Jahreszeiten*, or melancholics epitomized by *Angst essen Seele auf*'s Ali. It is perhaps when we think of these complex, unreachable figures, victims of society who nonetheless share the guilt for their unhappiness, that we may understand the *Neue Zürcher Zeitung*'s comparison between 23 and the films of Fassbinder.

Although "the family is incomplete [and] asymmetrical in its power relations," very much like the New German Cinema, Oedipal strife in Schmid's postwall project is no longer absolute. The film depicts a character who rejects but subsequently assumes his father's role. Karl wants his father to die but then feels guilty in believing his thoughts were responsible for the parent's death. This layered, conflicted response reflects the aforementioned double-father constellation that plagues Karl Koch and (his contemporary) Hans-Christian Schmid's generation—the rejection of both the Nazis and the generation which rebelled against them. It evinces, moreover, Schmid's ambivalent relation to film history and the will of certain filmmakers from his generation to create a third-way cinema unlike both the New German Cinema and the ideologically contaminated films of the 1940s and 1950s. It is telling that Hanns Zischler, a favorite actor of Jean-Luc Godard who starred in several films by Peter Handke, Wim Wenders, and Rudolf Thome, plays the role of Karl Koch's father: such a casting choice both points to the generation of '68 as Oedipal target but, at the same time, references the New German Cinema and precludes his character's absolute vilification. This stance is symptomatic of a film that understands history not "exclusively in the context of the Fascism and its delayed aftermath," but rather as an archive of ambivalent traditions beyond good and evil.

Too often, looking back at the 68ers only takes into account their slogans or self-projections from 1968, without acknowledging their transformations over time, how age turned utopian ideals into pragmatic solutions. It is precisely these bent and criss-crossed biographies and constellations of the generation of 1968 that fascinate—but also disappoint—Schmid's generation. Returning to the examples of Gerhard Schröder, Otto Schily, and Joschka Fischer, it seems fitting that the historical cinema began proliferating on German screens shortly after their coming to power in 1998. Although the fall of the Berlin Wall and German unification were the most significant national events in the second half of the twentieth century, in many ways the early 1990s represented a status quo: the capital was still in Bonn and Helmut Kohl remained the federal chancellor. The real revolution became apparent after the September 1998 elections and the formation of the Social Democratic–Green coalition. For the first time in the history of the Federal Republic, the government changed completely on the grounds of the popular vote. The advent of Schröder, Schily, and Fischer signaled a changing of the ideological and generational guard, but also placed the former revolutionaries into a strange role. These upstarts, shaped by the protest movements of the 1970s and 1980s, had made the long awaited "march through the institutions" (the gradual revolution that would take place whence the 68ers took on key positions in government, culture, and education) once prophesized by the Socialist student leader Rudi Dutschke. And yet, one can only imagine what "Rudi the Red" might have thought, had he lived to see the results. In his youth, Gerhard Schröder spouted Communist slogans ("ownership is theft") as leader of the Young Social Democrats. As chancellor, he pushed through the "Hartz IV" reforms, which curbed unemployment and social welfare benefits, and resembled more the policies of Margaret Thatcher than the philosophy of Karl Marx. Schily, once a passionate defender of civil liberties and defense attorney for the RAF, proposed drastic anti-terrorism laws that allowed for a massive state surveillance apparatus. Fischer came of age as a radical, self-made man who lived in communes, earned his living as a taxi driver, and battled with police on the streets of Frankfurt. Nevertheless, it was during his turn as foreign minister that the German Army engaged in its first war mission since 1945. Schröder, Schily, Fischer, Hartz IV, and Afghanistan surely demonstrate a universal lesson about how young rebels become the Establishment. However, these ironies point even more so to the often twisted fate of modern Germany. Beginning in the 1968 protest movement and continuing in the terrorist splinter groups of the 1970s and the 1980s Green movement, for instance, the German Left's anti-American and anti-Israeli sentiments were in step with the nationalist-conservative project. Postwar German history was so troubling for its continuities, including politicians, judges, educators, or filmmakers whose vitae extended unbroken since the war. The postwall period has often been so curious for its abrupt turnarounds: former left-wing utopians or GDR functionaries who have become conservative ministers or anti-Semites.

Schmid's ambivalent perspective toward the 68ers' often bewildering metamorphoses and hypocritical contradictions characterizes several of the subsequent postwall period films that revisit the 1980s.[50] This attitude toward space is reflected in the films' reckonings with time: in each, the depicted past and contemporary present mingle in provocative and uncanny ways. As the first exercise in this vein, the enthusiastic press response to *23* was appropriate given the originality and novelty of Schmid's effort. The historical transposition of *23* serves as, if not the archetype, then certainly the prototype of postwall Germany's historical cinema.

Notes

1. "23," *Blickpunkt Film* 30–31 (1998): 32; Christiane Peitz, "Karl und wie er die Welt sah," *Die Zeit*, 14 January 1999; Michael Sennhauser, "Hacken in der Eiszeit," *Neue Zürcher Zeitung*, 29 January 1999.
2. See Eric Rentschler, "From New German Cinema to the Post-Wall Cinema of Consensus," in *Cinema and Nation*, ed. Mette Hjort and Scott MacKenzie (London: Routledge, 2000), 260–77; and Katja Nicodemus, "Film der neunziger Jahre. Neues Sein und altes Bewußtsein," in *Geschichte des deutschen Films*, eds. Wolfgang Jacobsen, Anton Kaes, and Hans Helmut Prinzler, 2nd rev. ed. (Weimar: Metzler, 2004), 319–56.
3. Tobias Kniebe, "Hannover kann sehr kalt sein," *Süddeutsche Zeitung*, 14 January 1999.
4. Merten Worthmann, "Ich bin schuld an Tschernobyl," *Berliner Zeitung*, 14 January 1999.
5. Dieter Strunz, "Der Tod des Hacker-Königs," *Berliner Morgenpost*, 14 January 1999.

6. E.g., *England!* (2000), *Happiness Is a Warm Gun* (2001), *Die Ritterinnen* (*Gallant Girls*, 2003), *Herr Lehmann* (*Berlin Blues*, 2003), *Am Tag als Bobby Ewing starb* (*On the Day Bobby Ewing Died*, 2005), and *Dorfpunks* (*Village Punks*, 2009).

7. The demonstrations against the runway, the so-called "Startbahn 18 West," mobilized thousands of environmental activists.

8. Dana Polan, *Power and Paranoia: History, Narrative, and the Narrative Cinema, 1940–1950* (New York: Columbia University Press, 1986), 13.

9. Timothy Melley, *Empire of Conspiracy: The Culture of Paranoia in Postwar America* (Ithaca, NY: Cornell University Press, 2000), 8.

10. Daniel Pipes, *Conspiracy: How the Paranoid Style Flourishes and Where It Comes From* (New York: Free Press, 1997), 22. See also Melley, *Empire of Conspiracy*, 8.

11. Pipes, *Conspiracy*, 23.

12. Robert Shea and Robert Anton Wilson, *The Illuminatus! Trilogy* (London: Raven, 1998).

13. Pipes, *Conspiracy*, 33.

14. David Bordwell, *Making Meaning: Inference and Rhetoric in the Interpretation of Cinema* (Cambridge, MA: Harvard University Press, 1989), 265.

15. This is, according to probability expert Leonard Mlodinow, a common fallacy among believers in conspiracies. See Leonard Mlodinow, *The Drunkard's Walk: How Randomness Rules Our Lives* (New York: Pantheon, 2008), 107.

16. Hayden White, "The Modernist Event," in *The Persistence of History: Cinema, Television, and the Modern Event*, ed. Vivian Sobchack (New York: Routledge, 1996), 23–24.

17. See http://www.filmstarts.eu/produkt/41469,23.html.

18. For more on the American cycle, see Ray Pratt, *Projecting Paranoia: Conspiratorial Visions in American Film* (Lawrence: University Press of Kansas, 2001), 113–36, and Gérard Naziri, *Paranoia im amerikanischen Kino: Die 70er Jahre und die Folgen* (Sankt Augustin: Gardez!, 2003), 16–17.

19. This is Freud's definition of paranoia. See Sigmund Freud, *Zur Psychopathologie des Alltagslebens* (Frankfurt: Fischer, 1987), 201.

20. Pratt, *Projecting Paranoia*, 236.

21. This hand-held style came into vogue via the American television series *NYPD Blue* (1993–2005) and films such as *Husband and Wives* (1992) and *Breaking the Waves* (1996). In fact, Schmid names these three works as reference points in the interview with Oliver Baumgarten, "Child in Time. Verfolgungswahn statt Verfolgungsjagd: *23*," *Schnitt* 13 (1999): 23–23 [sic]; here 23 [second page]. World-renowned Steadicam operator Jörg Widmer (*Schindler's List* [1993], *The Pianist* [2002], *Babel* [2006]) shot vital sequences for *23*. See Tom Beyer and Benjamin Heßler, "In der Schwebe," *Schnitt* 8 (1997): 18.

22. Naziri, *Paranoia im amerikanischen Kino*, 289.

23. Angela Dalle Vacche, *Cinema and Painting: How Art Is Used in Film* (London: Athlone, 1996), 44.

24. See, for example, Nicodemus, "Film der neunziger Jahre. Neues Sein und altes Bewußtsein," 328: "Apart from its derivative, pseudo-cool gesture, the German thriller suffered, like the comedy, from a deficit of reality that became more apparent the more ambitious the productions were. Nico Hoffmann's *Solo für Klarinette* (*Solo for Clarinet*, 1998) featured Götz George as a burnt-out police commissioner, who, deformed by violence, falls in love with a murder suspect. The rainy, bleak city through which this lone wolf moves is called Berlin, but it could just as well be Dortmund or Cologne, just like the American-style police station has very little in common with the dreary German versions."

25. Manfred Hermes, "Der Ort ist eine Hauptfigur," *taz*, 31 July 2003.

26. An important intertext for *23* is Andres Veiel's *Die Überlebenden* (*The Survivors*, 1996). Veiel's documentary, set in Swabia, addresses many of the same themes: father–son conflicts, the attempt to depart from the province, suicide, as well as idealistic

political engagement and its disappointments. In both films the protagonists are seen to be victims of German history. The two films even share a musical leitmotif, Deep Purple's "Child in Time." Indeed, asked what interested him about Karl Koch's life, Schmid essentially retold the project of *Die Überlebenden:* "The suicide made me curious. In many graduating classes, after ten years, two or three classmates are missing because of this reason. It's often the most sensitive, who aren't equipped against the harsh everyday life." See Katharina Dockhorn, "Am Computer bin ich Laie," *Neues Deutschland*, 14 January 1999.

27. Contemporary reviewers were quick to point this out. See, for instance, Tobias Kniebe, "Hannover kann sehr kalt sein," *Süddeutsche Zeitung*, 14 January 1999.
28. Anthony Vidler, "The Architecture of the Uncanny: The Unhomely Houses of the Romantic Sublime," *Assemblage* 3 (1987): 6–29; here 8.
29. Vidler, "The Architecture of the Uncanny," 12.
30. Wendy Hui Kyong Chun, *Control and Freedom: Power and Paranoia in the Age of Fiber Optics* (Cambridge, MA: MIT Press, 2006), 3, 6, 24–25 (hereafter cited in the text).
31. Lev Manovich, *The Language of New Media* (Cambridge, MA: MIT Press, 2001), 253.
32. Cf., for instance, the Romantics' descriptions of a storm outside that makes one even more mindful of the snugness within. See Vidler, "The Architecture of the Uncanny," 14.
33. Rainer Braun, "Dem Hacker auf der Spur," *Märkische Allgemeine*, 14 January 1999.
34. Bertram Eisenhauer, "Jugend forscht für die Weltverschwörung," *Frankfurter Allgemeine Zeitung*, 20 January 1999.
35. Thomas Klingenmaier, "Das Mosaik der Welt," *Stuttgarter Zeitung*, 13 January 1999.
36. Christiane Peitz, "Karl und wie er die Welt sah," *Die Zeit*, 14 January 1999.
37. Tobias Kniebe, "Hannover kann sehr kalt sein," *Süddeutsche Zeitung*, 14 January 1999.
38. Bertram Eisenhauer, "Jugend forscht für die Weltverschwörung," *Frankfurter Allgemeine Zeitung*, 20 January 1999.
39. Peter Blickle, *Heimat: A Critical Theory of the German Idea of Homeland* (Rochester: Camden House, 2002), 130.
40. Francis Fukuyama, *The End of History and the Last Man* (New York: Free Press, 1992).
41. See Schmid's own mourning of the "clear-cut enemies" Strauß and Reagan in Katharina Dockhorn, "Am Computer bin ich Laie," *Neues Deutschland*, 14 January 1999, or the interview "Child in Time. Verfolgungswahn statt Verfolgungsjagd: 23," *Schnitt* 13 (1999): 23–23 [sic]; here 23 [second page].
42. The term *Spaßgesellschaft*, used to describe the hedonism and consumerism in postwall Germany preceding the dot-com bust, was bandied about in the federal and state elections around the turn of the twenty-first century. Gerhard Schulze more soberly diagnosed 1990s Germany as a superficial "society of experience." See Gerhard Schulze, *Die Erlebnisgesellschaft: Kultursoziologie der Gegenwart* (Frankfurt: Campus, 1992).
43. See Alexander Mitscherlich and Margarete Mitscherlich, *The Inability to Mourn: Principles of Collective Behavior*, trans. Beverly R. Placzek (New York: Grove Press, 1975). For more on the peculiarity of Schmid's generation, see Philipp Bühler, "Geheimziffer 23, Quersumme 5," *taz*, 14 January 1999.
44. Norman Mailer, "Footfalls in the Crypt," *Vanity Fair*, February 1992, 124–29, 171; here 129.
45. See Melley, *Empire of Conspiracy*, 11.
46. For example: *Händler der vier Jahreszeiten* (*Merchant of Four Seasons*, 1972), *Alice in den Städten* (*Alice in the Cities*, 1974), *Angst essen Seele auf* (*Ali: Fear Eats the Soul*, 1974), *Jeder für sich und Gott gegen alle* (*The Enigma of Kaspar Hauser*, 1974), *Im Lauf der Zeit* (*Kings of the Road*, 1976), *Stroszek* (1977), and *Messer im Kopf* (*Knife in the Head*, 1978).
47. See Thomas Elsaesser, *New German Cinema: A History* (London: British Film Institute, 1989), 216 (hereafter cited in the text).
48. Melley, *Empire of Conspiracy*, vii (hereafter cited in the text).

49. This double role constitutes a version of what Vivian Sobchack calls the new, "millennial stance to history" in "Introduction: History Happens," in *The Persistence of History: Cinema, Television, and the Modern Event*, ed. Vivian Sobchack (New York: Routledge, 1996), 5.

50. Among them are distinct differences in sensibility: *Kleinruppin Forever* and *Am Tag als Bobby Ewing starb* maintain a more uncritical nostalgia for the decade, whereas *England!* and *Happiness is a Warm Gun* share 23's jaded and paranoid edge. All, however, plot a return to the *Heimat*, whether it be the lakes of the northern GDR in *Kleinruppin Forever*, the hippie heath in *Am Tag als Bobby Ewing starb* and *Dorfpunks*, *England!*'s Ukrainian plains and British waters, the utopian sunflower fields in *Happiness is a Warm Gun*, or 23's concluding aerial of the Lower Saxon province.

Chapter 4

"Ostalgie," Historical Ownership, and Material Authenticity
Good Bye, Lenin! and *Das Leben der Anderen*

On 9 February 2003, one year after *Baader* (2002) flopped at the Berlinale, *Good Bye, Lenin!* premiered at the festival to great acclaim. Four days later, Wolfgang Becker's film about a young man who deceives his frail mother into believing the GDR still exists found general cinematic release in Germany, where it would become a huge box-office success. American-level advertising saturation, festival coverage, and word of mouth led 360,000 Germans to the cinema in its first four days; more than six million people had seen the film by the end of the year.[1]

Good Bye, Lenin! continued Becker's career-long preoccupation with the end of childhood and the disintegration of the family.[2] In interviews before and during *Good Bye, Lenin!*'s release, Becker emphasized the film's generic quality, asserting that "the fall of the wall is only the background" to the mother-son love story.[3] This claim belies the reception as a film of national and historical importance. *Good Bye, Lenin!* was used in school history lessons, and Brandenburg's cultural minister Steffen Reiche sought to make it mandatory viewing for all of the state's schoolchildren.[4] The screenwriters discussed it with pupils from East and West. After a special screening for the Bundestag, which reportedly attracted between 180 and 250 politicians, MPs staked out positions in television interviews about the effectiveness of the film's memory politics. One conservative MP admitted crying; one former GDR civil-rights activist and representative for the Green Party/Alliance '90 lashed out at the film for turning the GDR into an "operetta-state."[5]

German critics were in general skeptical about the film's artistic merits; only the populist right and dogmatic left seemed not to have any reservations.[6] Internationally, French, British, and Italian reviews were surprisingly generous in their appraisals, and the film scored both at European box offices and at the European Film Awards. During the Berlin Film Festival, producer Stefan Arndt made sales in thirteen territories, including the United States, Britain, and France; two months later the film was under contract in seventy countries. For journalists this was a sign that "very German" films could achieve foreign success.[7]

Commentators spent more time discussing broader cultural questions and identity politics than the aesthetics of the film itself. The primary issue was whether co-screenwriters Wolfgang Becker and Bernd Lichtenberg, who both hail from West Germany, were "allowed" to write the definitive pop-cultural chapter on the *Wende* to be taught in schools and prosthetically remembered. It had been controversial when Thomas Brussig and Leander Haußmann made *Sonnenallee* (*Sun Alley*, 1999), a farcical tale about coming of age in 1970s East Berlin. "Help e.V.," an organization dedicated to supporting victims of violence, cited Paragraph 194 of the German penal code in their suit against the filmmakers ("Insult to the members of a group persecuted under totalitarian rule").[8] Because Brussig and Haußmann were both born in the GDR, however, they enjoyed a certain credibility. In the case of *Good Bye, Lenin!*, prominent Eastern critics had serious objections to the prospect of Westerners telling the story of the GDR. East German writer Jana Hensel compared Lichtenberg to Karl May, the nineteenth-century bestselling author of cowboy-and-Indian novels who had never been to America. She rejected the film's image of the GDR as an object of speculation; according to her, the project wasted most of its energy on authentic match sticks.[9] In his book *Mein kurzer Sommer der Ostalgie* (My Short Summer of *Ostalgie*), Christian Eger chastised *Good Bye, Lenin!* as another "product" that allowed the GDR to live in its Western mirror-image: "This Sauerländer's film … is just as cowardly and full of clichés and lies as all the others that want to touch the GDR without grasping it …. The harmless humor is a means of distanciation from the people who lived [in the GDR]. This is no accident. This society is afraid of the GDR."[10]

The objections of these Eastern critics derived from a sense of historical ownership: how dare *they* tell *my* history? In many ways the question echoed the discourse regarding the January 1979 West German broadcast of *Holocaust* and the subsequent 1984 airing of Edgar Reitz's *Heimat*. The American miniseries had opened up a widespread public debate on the German people's complicity in the wartime deportation and genocide of Jews, and Reitz's film aimed to respond to Hollywood's "expropriation of [German] history" with history "Made in Germany."[11] *Good Bye, Lenin!*'s reception reveals that in 2003 there existed no collective German understanding of the GDR's history and makes it clear that a distinct Eastern identity was claimed by the former GDR citizens.[12] The "validity" of this feeling did not go unchallenged. In the pages of *Merkur*, Jens Bisky launched a sharp counterattack on a "special" Eastern identity and questioned East Germans' ability to tell their own history better than West Germans: "It is one of the life-long East German illusions that every GDR citizen knew his country and because of his heritage alone must be an uncontestable expert in German socialism."[13]

Another commentator noted the irony of the film's cursory attention to political oppression in the GDR. Today's filmmakers from Cologne have the same sanitized images of East Germany as did the Communist censors from back then: Trabant automobiles and *Ampelmännchen* (the East German pedestrian traffic lights).[14]

Good Bye, Lenin! satisfied a broader cultural desire to relive the GDR in the safe space of material culture. Wolfgang Becker's film became the public face and acme of a so-called *Ostalgie* (nostalgia for the Eastern past) in German popular culture. The wave had given rise to multiple features.[15] *Ostalgie* was not restricted to cinema, however. Television series such as "Die DDR-Show," "Die Ostalgie-Show," "Ein Kessel DDR," and "Die Ultimative Ost-Show" sprouted on various private and public channels, and allowed former GDR celebrities to remember the old days and quiz others on their memories. Even the theater ("Sonnenallee, The Musical") became a site to reminisce.

Ostalgie became a marketing strategy and a fashion statement.[16] The Berlin Tourism Bureau offered an Ostalgie-Tour, on foot or in the form of a "Trabi-Safari." Numerous secondhand shops in East Berlin enabled young professionals to outfit their apartments in the style that many GDR burghers had discarded a decade earlier. Bars such as the "Klub der Republik" in Prenzlauer Berg or "Ostzone" in Mitte self-consciously outfitted themselves with old signs and symbols of the GDR. A wave of memoirs including Hensel's *Zonenkinder,*[17] but also low-brow East German joke books and cookbooks (*DDR Getränkebuch, DDR Backbuch, Deutsche Delikatessen Republik*) lined store shelves. Graying East-rockers Dirk Michaelis, IC, Dirk Zöllner, and Die Puhdys made comeback tours. Trabant cars became highly regarded vintage vehicles. Curators rushed to present museum exhibitions on "Art in the GDR" (Neue Nationalgalerie, 2003) and GDR Design; the latter created a potentially uncanny situation for East Germans, who might have seen the same articles in their own living rooms. There were *Ostalgie* board games, *Ostalgie* parties, and plans for *Ostalgie* theme parks. The internet became another virtual space of fantasy GDR and the phenomenon spread worldwide, garnering international media attention.[18]

Good Bye, Lenin! came to be considered as the archetypal *Ostalgie* film against the wishes of its director, who insisted in interviews that he had no interest in the "despicable *Ostalgie*-shit."[19] Indeed, the story of the film's conception and production attempted to diffuse the East–West identity politics that would come to dominate the film's reception. Becker and Lichtenberg emphasized their extensive historical research, the amount of archival materials viewed, the special researchers employed, and the number of Easterners interviewed. Although cast members Katrin Saß and Michael Gwisdek—who both hailed from the former GDR—had acted in DEFA films, most of the other actors played against their personal histories. Easterners Florian Lukas and

Alexander Beyer, for example, performed as clueless Westerners. Daniel Brühl received training from a vocal coach to rid himself of his Cologne accent and listened to CDs of Young Pioneer songs to gain a sense of what it might have been like to grow up on the other side of the wall.[20] The film's comedy has an even distribution of *Ossi-Wessi* gags to satisfy both demographics. Post-screening interviews revealed that spectators laughed at very different places: the Westerners at IKEA "Billy" bookcases and the Easterners at special GDR brand names and the blunders of Ariane's Western boyfriend.[21]

The official story behind the making of *Good Bye, Lenin!* positions the production as a family drama without Eastern or Western bias; the film aims to erase bilateral difference. *Good Bye, Lenin!* conjoins national history and the fictional story of the Kerner family from a youthful, retrospective viewpoint in order to stage a coming-of-age for Germany, thirteen years after the unification in a way that incorporates *Forrest Gump* (1994), another mythology of intranational harmony. Its multilayered temporalities and journey through film history present an Eastern past that is subject to human and media manipulation, only in the end to retreat from the implications of such cynical self-reflexivity. *Good Bye, Lenin!* and its supposed opposite, the later *Das Leben der Anderen* (*The Lives of Others*, 2006), are ultimately—despite all of their obvious aesthetic differences—European "quality films" that smoothe over the historical trauma of unification by depicting the nation as a cabinet of mass cultural curiosities or a laboratory of universal material "authenticity," respectively.

Youthful Subjectivity

The story focuses on the Kerners: elementary schoolteacher Christiane (Katrin Saß), doctor Robert, thirteen-year-old Ariane, and eleven-year-old Alex (Daniel Brühl). The family has an idyllic East German existence until 26 August 1978. On that day Robert Kerner disappears to the capitalist West. Traumatized by this event, Christiane becomes a patient in a mental hospital. She recovers and thereafter channels her energy into socialist utopianism.

Eleven years later, Christiane watches her son being arrested for participating in a pro-democracy demonstration and falls into a coma. She sleeps through the fall of the Berlin Wall and misses the drastic political changes that come after the demise of the GDR. She finally awakes in the summer of 1990. The doctors warn Alex that upsetting Christiane in any way might prove fatal. He decides to attend to her recovery at home and pretend that the GDR still exists. In their 79m² high-rise apartment near Alexanderplatz, socialism lives on: Alex salvages the old furniture that had been gleefully tossed in the wake of the *Wende* and fills old jars and bottles with the new Western food and drink that have completely replaced the old Eastern brands in the supermarkets. Sister Ariane and new girlfriend Lara initially play along. As clues slip by that a new order has arrived, Alex resorts to more desperate measures. He hires neighbors to visit his mother and act as if the GDR still exists. Schoolboys come by and sing Young Pioneer tunes. When his mother requests a television to pass the time, Alex and his colleague Denis produce fake news broadcasts. Alex's television programs become exercises in damage control, direct responses to slip-ups in the charade. When a Coca-Cola banner appears outside his mother's window, Alex and Denis produce a news report claiming that the soft drink was actually invented in the East. After Christiane leaves the apartment and sees the large number of Westerners in the neighborhood, the amateur filmmakers present a program relating how Erich Honecker has allowed thousands of capitalism-weary Westeners into the country. In this alternative history, the fall of the Berlin Wall becomes socialism's final victory rather than its demise. Alex admits that his nostalgic image of the GDR depicts the imaginary country of his dreams.

By the time Robert Kerner returns, Christiane has confessed that she has been lying all along. The entire family had intended to flee East Germany; her commitment to socialism thereafter was only a sham meant to prevent the state from removing the children. Christiane dies before experiencing the political unification of Germany, although she does discover her son's efforts to spare her the truth.

The characters offer an array of attitudes toward the GDR and the newly augmented Federal Republic. The Kerner's older neighbors, Herr Ganske, Frau Schaefer, and Herr Mehlert, wish the socialist state back, even if they are not convinced socialists. These figures envy Christiane Kerner's blissful ignorance and willingly play along with Alex's charade: the West has only brought ruin to their lives. On the other extreme is Alex's sister. Immediately after the *Wende*, she ceases her university studies to work at a Burger King drive-through, where she promptly takes up with Rainer. She is skeptical of Alex's attempts to resurrect the GDR and ridicules the old state's material culture. When Alex prompts his sister to wear an old pullover, Ariane says to her baby, "Look! This is the crap that we wore back then." The Westerner Rainer is an almost colonial figure: he moves to the East, takes an Eastern girlfriend, and buys a Trabi. Alex stands somewhere in between. Although he clearly enjoys the new times and expanded possibilities, he maintains an affection for the old GDR. He chooses the Russian Lara for a partner, first kissing her after remembering the old party slogan "we solve problems by marching forward." He adamantly criticizes the currency union and maintains his special Eastern identity ("This was *your* money"; "I come from another land.") The entire game with his mother, moreover, is an attempt to preserve—or create for the first time—an idyllic childhood state. He still believes in the rectitude of socialism, but does not think that the GDR succeeded in transforming Marxist theory into socialist practice.

Good Bye, Lenin! is told from Alex's perspective. His youthful fix is vital to the overall nostalgic stance, and differentiates it from a series of other historical films about the GDR which see things through the prism of Christiane Kerner's generation.[22] Examining *Good Bye, Lenin!*'s historical narration provides insight into its representation of the GDR.

Alex's story hinges on the coincidence and tension between public German history and the private memories of his family. Robert Kerner leaves home on the same day that the "GDR was on world level," with Sigmund Jähn, the astronaut, appearing on television from outer space. The celebrations for the GDR's fortieth anniversary and the democracy movement's demonstrations on that night coincide with Christiane Kerner's heart attack. This is also the evening that Alex—choking on an apple while chanting "Freedom of the press!"—first meets his love interest Lara. Similarly, the signing of the *Staatsvertrag* on 22 June 1990 is the day of Alex and Lara's first kiss as well as the day on which Christiane Kerner awakes from her coma. Mother Kerner's ambulance ride home is accompanied by the radio announcement of the currency union. Christiane dies, Alex's voice-over tell us, three days after the unification of the two Germanies. In sum, all important happenings in the Kerner private sphere parallel events of national import.

This public/private interplay is introduced in the title sequence designed by Darius Ghanai.[23] The opening intercuts old GDR postcards (Ghanai collected them at East Berlin flea markets) with the staged Kerner family home movies. We see father Kerner shooting an 8mm (actually 16mm) film of Alex and Ariane carrying on at the family's summer cottage; the scene then shifts to Alex in front of Alexanderplatz with a cosmonaut T-shirt, the entire image superimposed by a zooming-in digital hammer and sickle. The film wipes to a zoom out from a postcard of the Palast der Republik and then again to soccer play at the *Datsche*, wiping once again to a zoom out from a postcard of the Haus des Lehrers. This pattern of alternation continues with a series of party symbols and state iconography (the World Time Clock at Alexanderplatz, Karl-Marx-Allee, Kino International, a bust of Lenin, the SED logo, commemorative cosmonaut stamps). The editing brings together official utopian designs and childhood mementos.

Alex's voice-over narration is the chief link between public history and the story of the Kerners. Throughout the film, in the numerous montage sequences of documentary footage from the end of the GDR, personal memory always brackets public history. Phrases such as "Mother slept through…," "Mother's sleep made her miss…," "Mother's deep unconsciousness made her unable to…, "Her sleep spared her...," introduce the voice-over commentaries that accompany images of Erich Honecker's resignation, the fall of the Berlin Wall, or the first free elections in the GDR.

Alex's voice-over often creates an ironic counterpoint to what we see. Take, for instance, the first shot of 1989: the camera tilts down a high-rise apartment building adorned with communist and GDR flags to Alex sitting on a park bench, drinking a beer. Various shots of an empty East Berlin being decorated with flags and insignias follow. One of these captures the inebriated Alex slouching on a bench; in the background a banner reads, "The human being stands in the center of the socialist society." Alex's off-screen voice comments: "The GDR turned forty. I had the day off from the TV-repair company 'Adolf Hennecke' and felt at the pinnacle of my masculine charisma." Clearly, text, image, voice-over, and perhaps the spectator's own historical knowledge of the parade are not in synch.

Alex's account of the political events which transpire in the coming days and months functions similarly. The voice-over describes the parade of the National People's Army on the GDR's fortieth anniversary as "the last performance" of an "over-dimensional rifle club." Later that evening a violently dispersed demonstration protesting for democracy

Figure 4.1: Alex at "the pinnacle of [his] masculine charisma" in *Good Bye, Lenin!* Image courtesy of X Filme.

Figure 4.2: Text, image, and voice-over out of sync before the GDR's 40th anniversary in *Good Bye, Lenin!* Image courtesy of X Filme.

and freedom of the press is characterized as an "evening stroll." To the footage of Helmut Kohl and Willy Brandt's discordant rendition of the German national anthem, Alex adds: "[Mother] slept through the classical concert in front of Schöneberg City Hall." The ironic voice-over provides a counterperspective to the authoritative documentary footage of well-known political events. Above all, the voice-over issues from a different temporality than the images; Alex's commentary is clearly articulated from a much later perspective. His off-camera voice knows that the GDR's fortieth anniversary is indeed a last picture show.

How is one to understand the film's retrospective subjectivity? Of course, as theorist Sarah Kozloff notes, the addition of a spoken narration track always increases a film's opportunity to manipulate chronology.[24] Traditionally, the most common contrast is between a character's youthful self and mature present, a rule that exceptional voice-over examples (e.g., *Badlands* [1973]) confirm. In Becker's film, Alex's off-screen voice provides a mature, nostalgic view of his mother's last days, suggesting he has "grown up." With the benefit of hindsight, a wiser Alex can identify his past follies and laugh them away.

In a film that so studiously connects private memory and national history, however, much more is at stake. The implication is that not just Alex, but the whole nation "knows better" in the meanwhile. The first-person narration provides a direct line of communication to a 2003 German audience that can no longer look back to the memories of November 1989 with rosy eyes. In belittling the GDR civil rights movement as "an evening stroll for the right of borderless strolling," and responding to Kohl and Brandt's patriotic gesture with a snide critique, the voice-over speaks from a future position in which any revolutionary élan has faded and the problems of unification have long become apparent. These interpretations are a historiographical universe away from, for instance, the deadly serious voice-over to well-known footage of the Berlin Wall being built in *Das Versprechen* (*The Promise*, 1995). Margarethe von Trotta's film addresses a German audience which is still mourning the years of division, still patriotic about the fall of the Berlin Wall, and still hopeful about the unified future. Alex and *Good Bye, Lenin!* look to different stages of the German past (1978, 1989/1990), acknowledging the *Gemütlichkeit* and tragedy of 1978 East Germany and the euphoria as well as problems of the *Wendezeit*, but always through the sober and more edified lens of the early 2000s Federal Republic. In *Good Bye, Lenin!*'s narration, a "grown-up" present nudges out the past. Just as Alex has matured since his mother's death, so has—or, better, *should*—Germany come of age and come to grips with the political events of the late twentieth century.

Manipulable Temporalities: The Quotation Film

Placing the Kerner story within a larger national history is an economical method of marking narrative time; in the process, the documentary footage of well-known historical events serves as an orientating "clock" for the spectator. The film is resolutely self-conscious about its examination of time. It features numerous shots of clocks (for example, in the hospital scenes, or the World Time Clock in time lapse), calendars (e.g., the nurses' April 1990 schedule), and dated newspapers.

In general, time in *Good Bye, Lenin!* functions as an unstable and manipulable property. Within the story itself, it is subject to human agency. Alex both attempts to reverse or arrest time (hoping to conserve the old GDR in the apartment) as well as to speed it up: he rips pages off the wall calendar to make it appear that the celebrations for German unification (2–3 October) are actually the forty-first anniversary of the GDR (7 October). Alex's manipulation of television involves a series of formal and self-reflexive touches. When Alex redecorates the family apartment after his mother expresses her wish to come home, for example, Becker renders the scene in fast motion. Similarly, once Alex is employed by a new Western satellite company or rushes to his girlfriend's squatted apartment in Prenzlauer Berg, the "new times" find expression in quick fast-motion shots. Editing functions as another means of reconfiguring time. The montage sequences of largely documentary footage, narrating German history in compressed form, are the most prominent examples.[25] Furthermore, scenes (such as Alex's bedside vigil for his mother) are telegraphed in a collection of "waiting" shots.

A further temporal layer in *Good Bye, Lenin!* resides in the numerous film historical quotations. The plot certainly takes major cues from *Situation Helpless But Not Serious* (1965), in which an elderly German refuses to tell American soldiers hiding in his basement that World War II has ended, as well as Emir Kusturica's more recent Emir Kusturica's more recent *Podzemlje* (*Underground*, 1995). In the latter film, a profiteer makes workers in a Belgrade munitions factory believe that World War II has continued for more than fifty years. Some critics noted that Alex's bedside manner recalled Pedro Almodóvar's contemporary arthouse hit *Hable con ella* (*Talk to Her*, 2002), specifically its scenes about caring for women in comas and the problems of communicating with them.

Lichtenberg's screenplay also reverses the plot of *One, Two, Three* (1961). In that film MacNamara, the head of Germany's Coca-Cola division, must sustain an elaborate charade so that his boss will not find out that his daughter has married a communist. Becker makes the connection transparent by shooting at the very same Coca-Cola building in Berlin-Lichterfelde that Billy Wilder used for his film. The X-Films co-founder has gone on the record to say he lifted the montage sequence of nurses' legs at the hospital from Truffaut's *L'Homme qui aimait les femmes* (*The Man Who Loved Women*, 1977). Alex, after realizing that the family's Eastern marks are worthless, describes himself as a submarine captain much in the manner of *Das Boot* (1981): "I felt like the commander of a U-boat in the North Sea fleet whose battle-scarred steel skin was springing a leak. Just as soon as I had repaired a leak, a new one broke out." The Lenin statue scene recalls the opening sequence from *La Dolce Vita* (1960), in which the camera follows a helicopter transporting a statue of Jesus over the city of Rome. The sequence functions, similar to the corresponding scene's role in Becker's film, as a symbol for the uprooting and loss of a system of utopian values (Catholicism). The post-communist epic *Ulysses' Gaze* (1995), similarly, captures a dismantled giant Lenin statue on a ship floating down the Danube.[26] Furthermore, the East–West direction of an airplane over the Charité Hospital recalls an almost exact shot in *Die Beunruhigung* (*Apprehension*, 1982), where an airplane's westward trajectory maps an atlas of desire.

Employing two cameo appearances of Jürgen Vogel, Becker alludes twice to his own film, *Das Leben ist eine Baustelle* (*Life Is All You Get*, 1997). The first comes in the prison scene, just as Alex is released to visit his mother in the hospital. Vogel stands among the arrested demonstrators, which links his arrest to Becker's earlier film. The second comes when Alex searches the supermarket aisles, newly restocked with Western goods, for the old Eastern products; Vogel appears in his chicken costume from *Das Leben ist eine Baustelle*. The intersection of these two characters—similar to Kieslowski's *Rouge* (*Red*, 1994) or fellow X-Film colleague Tom Tykwer's *Lola rennt* (*Run Lola Run*, 1998), for example—makes it clear that the events are part of a film universe. It orients the spectator with an illusion of simultaneity. Casting Katrin Saß recalls her DEFA roles as a suffering mother, for instance, in Herrmann Zschoche's *Bürgschaft für ein Jahr* (*Bond for One Year*, 1981). In many ways her biography and personal battle with alcoholism mirror the film's interrogation of daily existence in the GDR. The fast-motion scene where Alex and Denis reconstruct the GDR in the apartment, accompanied by the William Tell Overture, clearly defers to a scene from *A Clockwork Orange* (1971). In Stanley Kubrick's film, the protagonist Alex undergoes a rehabilitation experiment in which he is bound to a cinema seat and compelled to watch graphic scenes of violence. In *Good Bye, Lenin!*, Alex subjects his mother to a similar arrangement. He produces his *Aktuelle Kamera* for an audience of one, and models the family's *Plattenbau*-style apartment into a GDR Plato's cave. Finally, in one crucial scene, Denis shows Alex how he has quoted *2001: A Space Odyssey* (1968) on a wedding video: a bouquet flies through the air in the same manner as the bone in Kubrick's famous film. Alex falls asleep during the presentation of the wedding video, but when Denis asks him, "Did you recognize [which film it derives from]?," he also addresses the audience: Becker's feature challenges the viewer to recognize film historical quotations and references. In the final version of *Good Bye, Lenin!* Denis only mentions *2001*; the original script had him discussing the plot points of *The Matrix* (1999), *The Truman Show* (1998), and *Lola rennt*.[27]

Good Bye, Lenin! is certainly not the first "quotation film." Robert Stam describes how nouvelle vague directors pitted "antipathetic codes against one another in a single text ... provok[ing] a collision of conventions in a veritable war of conflicting rhetorics, thus actuating a complex spectatorial response ... a cohabitation of languages."[28] *Good Bye, Lenin!*'s intertextual archive surely exhibits a "collision of conventions" and rhetorics; its references cohabit diverse periods and traditions which include DEFA, *nouvelle vague*, Fellini, Wilder, Angelopoulos, Kusturica, *The Truman Show*, 1960s Hollywood genre cinema, and *The Matrix*. Furthermore, *Good Bye, Lenin!* is one of cinema's many quotation films from around the turn of the twenty-first century. One need not go further back than *Lola rennt* to find another German cinematic endeavor well aware of its predecessors. Nevertheless, the idea of a historical film, concerned with East–West German tensions (which in 2003 were a particularly serious matter), which abounds with such playfulness raises serious questions.

The allusions superimpose yet another layer of temporality, that of film history, in addition to that of public history and private memory.

With a wealth of diverse quotations, Becker utilizes cinema as a time-travel machine that can access multiple traditions simultaneously. Film history in *Good Bye, Lenin!*—just like the youthful, retrospective historical narration—is presented as something readily subject to manipulation. Just as film history can be easily accessed and refigured—regardless of its status as popular or art cinema, or of its country of origin—so too, *Good Bye, Lenin!* seems to suggest, can history be successfully overcome. This relationship to the past resembles what Svetlana Boym speaks of as conservative and "restorative" nostalgia. This mode of remembrance seeks "to conquer and spatialize time."[29] *Good Bye, Lenin!*, in short, endeavors to re-master film history in its own image.

A Self-Reflexive Retrospection

Good Bye, Lenin!'s numerous allusions and references point to its high degree of self-consciousness. Indeed, the scene in which Denis screens the *2001* wedding video calls attention to the workings of the film as a whole. Denis uses Western technology to raid the GDR's TV archives, rewinding, fast forwarding, editing, and deleting. Alex collects sparkling wine bottles and carrot jars from the old GDR and fills them with Western products—in that way, like Denis, attempting to dupe mother Kerner into believing the GDR still exists. Becker assembles television clips, digitally deletes anachronisms in filmed footage, raids secondhand stores for props, costumes, and other Eastern material objects—all to preserve a fantasy for the film's viewer. Both in the film's fiction and in its production, history becomes a patchwork of the public and private subject to the mutable laws of rewinds and splice edits.

Commentators have attempted to redeem the *Ostalgie* films by drawing attention to their self-aware modes of address. Paul Cooke has written how *Sonnenallee* "performs *Ostalgie*" in the way that its "intricate network of Eastern and Western cultural references … forces the East German spectator to reflect upon, and ultimately reject, any manifestations of *Ostalgie* which would ostensibly call for a return to the GDR."[30] Anthony Enns concurs: "Rather than dehistoricizing and depoliticizing the GDR's past," he concludes, "the *Ostalgie* phenomenon seems to employ nostalgia more often as a critical tool to promote and enable an active engagement with the present."[31] Seán Allan divides the *Ostalgie* films into two periods. The first encompasses the early unification comedies (*Go Trabi Go* [1991], *Go Trabi Go 2* [1992], *Wir können auch anders* [1993]), which "offer a crude and distorted picture of the GDR."[32] The second era begins with *Sonnenallee* and *Good Bye, Lenin!*, which, to his mind, "make an important contribution to the normalization of German–German relations."[33] According to Allan, *Good Bye, Lenin!* "prompts the viewer to reflect on the complex relationship between history, memory, and fiction."[34] Allan notes how these two later *Ostalgie* films self-reflexively depict the invention of history and memory. Alex fakes the episodes of *Aktuelle Kamera*; in *Sonnenallee*, the pimply protagonist Micha counterfeits years of diaries in order to win the attention of an East Berlin belle. Allan might have also mentioned *Drei Stern Rot* (*Three Star Red*, 2002), which features the metatextual conceit of a former border guard traumatically recalling the past after playing himself in an *Ostalgie* film.

There is no question that the later *Ostalgie* productions are much more sophisticated in their formal approach, narrative structure, and mode of address. The matter of whether their self-reflexivity necessarily constitutes subversiveness or a critical engagement with history is far from obvious, however. As Robert Stam writes, film theorists of the late 1960s and 1970s often equated self-reflexivity with progressive politics. Especially film theory's Althusser fraction came to regard reflexivity as a political obligation.[35] Nicholas Garnham, for example, wrote that "[The television documentary's] total artificiality must constantly be stressed. It must be seen as part of a process and not as a commodity." Peter Wollen argued that films that foreground the apparatus are "revolutionary" because they make "the mechanics of the film/text visible and explicit."[36] For Stam, self-conscious films may well "cast suspicion on the central premise of illusionistic narrative."[37] Reflexive works "break with art as enchantment and call attention to their own factitiousness as textual constructs" (1). However, as Stam warns, the equation of reflexivity with progressive politics can be problematic. The reflexivity of commercial television or "*Singin' in the Rain* has little to do with leftist politics" (16). In fact, many of the techniques that are called reflexive in Godard films are also found on television, but, "rather than trigger 'alienation effects,' commercial television often simply alienates" (16). According to Stam, television advertisements' self-referential humor only "signals to the spectator that the commercial is not to be taken seriously, and this relaxed state of expectation renders the viewer more permeable to its message" (16). Rather than "de-mystifying the product or exposing hidden codes," this self-referentiality simply "conceals the deadly seriousness of the commercial—the fact that it is after the spectator's money" (16). Although "authentic reflexivity" may elicit an active spectatorship rather than passive consumption, much reflexivity in television and commercial filmmaking "is as narcotic and culinary as the bourgeois theatre that Brecht denounced" (16–17).

Even if *Good Bye, Lenin!* acknowledges history as a hodgepodge of manipulable discourses, it retreats from the implication of its own self-consciousness. In an interview, Becker emphasized the film's meta-commentary and his desire to create a "fabrication within a fabrication."[38] Nevertheless, it becomes clear that his subsequent quotation of Godard—that film is "a lie, twenty-four frames per second"—is unironic, for he continues to say that the "viewer's loss of belief in fiction is the worst." Uninterested in the historiographical dimensions of exposing the artificiality of the medium, the director sought to create a more perfect illusion, a "felt," affective history: "[*Good Bye, Lenin!*] is no history lesson: [I] had a lot more fun faking history."[39]

Indeed, the flurry of references that Cooke and Allan praise seem more like the "timelessness of objects" that Brecht criticized in bourgeois theater. The allusions constitute a game of "did you recognize it?," a quiz show on the level of the *Ostalgie* television programs, rather than a serious attempt to mobilize film history. Jane Feuer's analysis of the "conservative" or "constructive" reflexivity of late Hollywood musicals seems to be a more pertinent way to regard *Good Bye, Lenin!* Feuer describes how the genre's 1950s incarnations borrow from earlier sources less for the purpose of demystification, than "merely because they have nothing new to say," thereby reaffirming their continuity and deference.[40] Indeed, like the late Hollywood musical, self-reflexivity in the late *Ostalgie* film is more a question of fashion or even a *sine qua non* of the genre in its current evolution, than any true subversion. When *Sonnenallee*'s Micha finds Winfried Glatzleder (Paul from *Die Legende von Paul und Paula* [*The Legend of Paul and Paula*, 1973]) in Miriam's apartment building, accompanied by Die Puhdys' theme song, the *Ostalgie* film reduces the East German production's social critique to mere entertainment.[41] As Jennifer M. Kapczynski writes, "despite Becker's efforts to problematize *Ostalgie* as both a 'canned' product of Western marketing, he undermines his own critique through a decidedly *ostalgic* mode of filmmaking."[42]

History Lessons from Robert Zemeckis

With a narrative about rewriting the past to serve present needs, *Good Bye, Lenin!* performs this function itself. In so doing it resembles and indeed transposes the workings of a Hollywood production concerned with the politics of national identity: Robert Zemeckis's *Forrest Gump*. It is considered that *Good Bye, Lenin!*'s historical project resounds with *Forrest Gump*'s in three crucial ways.

First, both productions code a woman's body as a destructive site of national history. The type of diseases from which these women suffer reveals the peculiarities of each film's historiography. In *Forrest Gump*, Jenny dies of a thinly veiled HIV-like virus. AIDS was, at the time of the film's production, a disease linked with a very specific historicity and lifestyle. Jenny dies, the film implies, because of her "excessive" way of life and as a result of her utopian beliefs in 1960s leftist politics. In *Forrest Gump*'s logic, Jenny must perish in order to liberate history from the threatening political, cultural, and sexual ideologies of the

1960s and 1970s.[43] In *Good Bye, Lenin!*, Christiane Kerner suffers two breakdowns: the first after her husband Robert leaves the GDR and the second after she witnesses her son's arrest. The result of the second breakdown is, in her doctor's words, "amnesia…a mixture of long and short memory, misrecognition." Staging a story from the perspective of a son about his mother's inability to order memory suggests that it is the younger generation—one that is more readily able to integrate into the new Westernized capitalist order—whose version of history is to be trusted. Just as Jenny—a victim of 1960s and 1970s leftist "excess"— must die in *Forrest Gump*, Christiane Kerner's amnesia and death wipe the slate clean for a nation previously troubled by competing ideologies and geographical divisions.

Second, Robert Zemeckis's film and *Good Bye, Lenin!* merge a fictive private memory and a national narrative. Both films, for example, mix documentary and fiction footage. In *Forrest Gump*, the title character is sutured into archive footage of John F. Kennedy, Lyndon B. Johnson, and John Lennon. *Good Bye, Lenin!* also uses this technology, such as when Christiane Kerner accepts a government prize in a news story that young Alex watches, or within the story itself, when Denis inserts Sigmund Jähn into a GDR television piece on Erich Honecker. In each case, the documentary footage is digitally retouched so that it seamlessly fits into the overall aesthetic. The audience is not supposed to know what is archive material and what has been shot for the film; Becker was decidedly pleased that audiences thought that he had actually restaged the National People's Army parade.[44] The goal of both productions is to create an illusion of seamlessness between news footage and the reenactments, as well as between the national history and the fictional narrative.

Both Gump and Alex mediate between public and private; as narrators they create and chronicle history. The two films overlay the half-documentary, half-staged footage with a naïve (*Forrest Gump*) or cynical (*Good Bye, Lenin!*) voice-over commentary. For example, Gump describes his ancestor who "started up a club called the Ku Klux Klan … [who] liked to dress up in white sheets, and act like a bunch of ghosts or spooks or something." The soundtrack accompanies Tom Hanks's face in a faux period photograph. The supposed Gump ancestor rides away in mock archival footage in the manner of D.W. Griffith. (Zemeckis's production is every bit as self-consciously aware of film history as Becker's.) The title figure's feeblemindedness makes his historical ignorance endearing to the audience and prompts "reconciliation, a healing acceptance" of the trauma experienced by Americans in the 1960s and 1970s.[45] In *Good Bye, Lenin!*, the cheeky voice-over likewise flatters the viewer into believing he or she is not a voyeur, but rather a confidante. Alex's reference to the National People's Army as an "overdimensional rifle club" resonates with the narrative overdub used by Zemeckis. In this regard, the 7 October 1989 demonstration scene in *Good Bye, Lenin!* is exemplary. In Alex's retrospective narration this milestone in the East German democracy movement—in which scores of protestors were savagely beaten by the police and Stasi—is cast off as an "evening stroll for the right of borderless strolling," and we see him nonchalantly eating an apple while chanting for freedom of the press.

In both films, casting amplifies this illusion of being a "confidante." Although Tom Hanks had won an Academy Award for his serious turn in *Philadelphia* (1993), in 1994 he was still best known as a neighborly "regular Joe" from a host of slapstick, youth, and romantic comedies, for example, the TV series *Bosom Buddies* and films such as *Bachelor Party* (1984), *Splash* (1984), *The Money Pit* (1986), *The 'Burbs* (1989), *Turner & Hooch* (1989), and *Sleepless in Seattle* (1993). Hanks's greatest success from the 1980s, *Big* (1988), perhaps best illustrates his contemporary innocent and boyish appeal.

Daniel Brühl's career began with radio plays and dubbing work, including several early Jackie Chan films. Several of his subsequent roles prominently employ his voice-over, for example *Nichts bereuen* (*No Regrets*, 2001), *Das weiße Rauschen* (*The White Sound*, 2001), and *Vaya con Dios* (2002). Arguably, no other German actor was more associated with the youth-film wave. Brühl starred in a host of coming-of-age films (*Schule* [*No More School*, 2000], *Nichts bereuen*, *Elefantenherz* [2002], *Was nützt die Liebe in Gedanken* [*Love in Thoughts*, 2004], *Die fetten Jahre sind vorbei* [*The Edukators*, 2004]). He won the Berlin Film Festival's "Shooting Star" Award the year that *Good Bye, Lenin!* premiered there. Like Forrest Gump, Alex has a historical point of view that is "forever young." This youthful subjectivity, along with a safely retrospective point of view, free Alex from the traumatic implications of historical events.

Finally, both films attempt to resolve intranational divisions. Most cinematic representations of the American military involvement in Vietnam (e.g., *Platoon* [1986] or *Apocalypse Now* [1979]) depict segregation and racial tension among the American troops. In *Forrest Gump*, however, the title character's best friend during his tour of duty in East Asia is the African-American infantryman Bubba. In the story's frame, furthermore, Gump narrates his series of flashbacks to both blacks and whites who share his park bench. In general, Gump's presence—both in the archival images of important historical events as well as in the speaking present—furthers a reconciliation among the races.[46]

Similarly, *Good Bye, Lenin!* seeks to smooth over East–West tensions. Although it presents a measured critique of the West, the comedy always brackets historical trauma. Alex pokes fun at the Westernization of the family apartment that Ariane's boyfriend undertakes, as well as the latter's preference for Indian culture. Among the Easterners, *Good Bye, Lenin!* includes characters who are losers of history and nonetheless jolly curmudgeons: for instance, Alex's jocularly disgruntled neighbors and Klapprath's alcoholic slapstick. Although Herr Ganske's joblessness surely brought to mind Germany's record unemployment in 2003 and the specter of the Hartz IV reforms, the film discounts the senior citizen's problems as the grumblings of a senile dreamer. In general, the film's juxtaposition of official history and personal fiction either displaces the latter or highlights the sillier moments of the former. One thinks especially of the montage sequences that show *Ossis* fascinated by Beate Uhse porn shops or the eccentric postwall East Berlin club scene replete with body painting and inflatable condoms. When the film broaches the serious problem of doctors leaving East Berlin for the West, a comic touch deflates any possible critique: the physician strikes Alex on the chest in order to demonstrate a revival technique. After Alex loses the family's savings due to the bureaucratic rules of the currency union, the sequence concludes with him throwing the money and literally monkeying around. The historical problem of Western firms exploiting naïve Eastern consumers, likewise, finds expression in the film when Alex's satellite firm profits from World Cup patriotism in order to rack up sales. But any critical weight evaporates in a montage of provincial bumpkins with heavy regional accents.

Ultimately, East–West hostility yields to East–West harmony. The friendship between *Ossi* Alex and *Wessi* Denis mirrors the white/black liaison of Forrest and Bubba. The videos for mother Kerner are described as an "East–West co-production" and the two bond over the World Cup team. Alex "unites" East and West by employing a faux socialist vocabulary to describe the (West German) national squad's progress: "The German team convinced by over-fulfilling their plan [*Planübererfüllung*]." Parallel to public history's "all-German treaties" [*gesamtdeutsche Verträge*] comes Ariane and Rainer's "all-German baby" [*gesamtdeutsches Baby*]. It must be emphasized that although a smattering of similar East–West relationships did exist in immediate postwall Germany, the film presents a decidedly rare exception.[47] Alex's faked history of the unification depicts a conciliatory, unified nation in which historical wrongs have been corrected. Coca-Cola becomes a victory for Eastern socialism, the neighbor brings back a Bavarian woman after a holiday in Hungary, and Western refugees flood East Berlin. *Good Bye, Lenin!* completes the socialist project in a virtual history in order for its reality to be put to rest and forgotten. Although admitting the problems of the *Wende*, the film hardly suggests that Easterners were so conned that they should reject the Federal Republic or revolt. Precisely by showing the failure of these utopian dreams in an allegorical mode, its message corresponds to Helmut Kohl's slogan: "The train has already left" [*Der Zug ist schon abgefahren*]. *Good Bye, Lenin!* takes leave, not of Lenin, Stalin, or Honecker, but rather of the hopes of German intellectuals such as Günter Grass, Christa Wolf, and Stefan Heym.

Good Bye, Lenin! is a time-travel film and a virtual history that looks at 1989/90 from the vantage point of 2003. This is a common strategy of historical films about the GDR, for example, *Küss mich, Genosse! (Kiss Me, Comrade!*, 2007). This TV-movie literalizes the retrospective logic by staging the *Back to the Future* (1985) plot as an East/West German dramedy: in the 1974 World Cup the GDR wins a match against the FRG and it is precisely during Jürgen Sparwasser's goal that the protagonist Jenny is conceived by her East German father and West German mother. In 2006, a freak accident transports Jenny back to 1974, where she must bring her parents together for their one-night-stand in order to ensure her future existence. *Kleinruppin Forever* (2004) is another example. It portrays two separated identical twins—one who grew up in the West, one in the East—who trade places. The film utilizes a nostalgic, retrospective logic for the pre-unification GDR. Although the film is set in 1985, it implies a twenty-first century spectatorship: the film's last line—"Let's go to Venice"—would be cruel were it not for this additional layer of memory. Similar to how Elena Gorfinkel describes the retrospective logic of "social issue" historical films such as *Far From Heaven* (2002), these German films insert "the historically and socially possible into the film historically impossible."[48]

As Thomas Elsaesser and Warren Buckland argue, there are at least two ways to interpret the implications of time-travel films: "One is to say that history is only a discourse or a set of representations which we can make or fake, rewrite and alter....The other is to say that since we cannot change anything about our past, we might as well learn to love that which we don't like about our past."[49] Both strategies are at work in *Good Bye, Lenin!* On the one hand, the film questions the belief that history can be told in a truthful, straightforward fashion. On the other, it urges us to realize that Alex's lies were well intended and that the course of events has turned out for the best. *Good Bye, Lenin!*'s melodrama hinges ultimately on the *good intentions* that motivate Alex to lie and falsify history. Given the intimate relationship between family story and political history, the film implies that the lies of Kohl, Honecker, and the *Aktuelle Kamera* were equally justified.

Alex and the film itself do not conserve the GDR in the past tense; they imagine it in the past subjunctive mood. Both entertain counterfactual history, best summed up in Alex's voice-over admission: "The GDR that I created for my mother became more and more the GDR for which I would have wished." The film imagines the fantasy of a third-way socialism that leftist intellectuals proposed in the wake of the *Wende*, a socialism under which no one will want to leave. Here, however, the citizen is a patient bound to her bed. Furthermore, the constant irony of the temporally alienated voice-over narrator, coupled with the editing, discourages any concrete political stance. Helmut Kohl looks just as clueless as Erich Honecker.[50] The implied lesson is that retrospection does not necessarily make for enhanced historical awareness. "The country, which my mother left ... [was] a country that in reality had never existed." Viewed in retrospect, the history of the GDR becomes a Rip Van Winkle fantasy.

The Eastern Past as Fairy-Tale Fantasy: *Das Leben der Anderen*

On 15 March 2006, nearly exactly three years after the premiere of *Good Bye, Lenin!*, Florian Henckel von Donnersmarck's *Das Leben der Anderen* opened in German cinemas. The story takes place in 1984 and revolves around the fictional Stasi agent Gerd Wiesler, who is charged with spying on the writer Georg Dreyman and his actress wife, Christa-Maria Sieland. Although ideologically committed to the GDR, Wiesler finds himself sympathizing with Dreyman and, ignoring grave personal and professional danger, abets the playwright's efforts to smuggle an article critical of the government to the West.

For commentators put off by *Sonnenallee*'s satirical touches and *Good Bye, Lenin!*'s farcical moments, Cologne-born von Donnersmarck's feature marked a breakthrough. The film, by all appearances, made good on critics' wishes for serious treatments of the GDR's dark side.[51] The title of the review in *Der Spiegel* reflected this new enthusiasm: "Stasi without Spree Forest Pickle."[52] Many commentators were ecstatic, and the film went on to win the 2007 Academy Award for Best Foreign Language Film. Although *Das Leben der Anderen* was von Donnersmarck's first film to span more than a half hour, he immediately became a hot commodity in Hollywood and, able to choose between hosts of offers, selected *The Tourist* (2010), a thriller starring Angelina Jolie and Johnny Depp, as his sophomore project.

Despite the notion promoted in the media that the film's serious regard of the Stasi was new, there had indeed been earnest cinematic treatments of the *Staatssicherheit*. Several of these projects premiered in the first years after the unification.[53] *Der Tangospieler* (*The Tango Player*, 1991), Roland Gräf's adaptation of the Christoph Hein novel, tells the tragically absurd story of a historian, who, while moonlighting as a pianist, inadvertently plays a song that "endangers the state." He spends nearly two years in jail for this offense; his life after his release is marked by isolation, frustration, and then complicity with government agents. Other key projects included Michael Gwisdek's *Abschied von Agnes* (*Farewell to Agnes*, 1993), a psychothriller that chronicles the symbiotic relationship between a widower, Heiner, and a former Stasi agent, Stephan.

Of course, the press's enthusiasm for *Das Leben der Anderen* did not reflect any absolute novelty of feature films about the Stasi; it reflected their "quality." *Der Tangospieler*, *Abschied von Agnes*, and others were small-scale productions that found resonance with very modest audiences. The acclaim for von Donnersmarck's film derived, in the first instance, from the desire for a production of a certain generic appeal. The popularity of *Das Leben der Anderen* in Germany (over 1.5 million admissions in its first nine months of release)[54] can be explained by a whole host of factors. Von Donnersmarck's debut evinced an epic scope and high production values. As the producers explained in their DVD interview, they always began by inviting the "very best cast and crew" to join the production, whether Germany's top casting agent Simone Bär, veteran actors Ulrich Mühe, Sebastian Koch, Ulrich Tukur, and Martina Gedeck, or composer Gabriel Yared, whose credits included *The English Patient* (1996), *The Talented Mr. Ripley* (1999), and *Cold Mountain* (2003). With muted colors in the set design, post-production desaturation, and the fact that the majority of scenes take place at night, the filmmakers created a claustrophobic but not unattractive East Berlin in 1984, one that situated their tale of GDR hypocrisy and surveillance in the aesthetic of *The Conversation* (1974) and, as scholar Jaimey Fisher has elaborated, the generic hybrid of the historical melodrama and police thriller.[55]

The story attends to classical trajectories and characterization. For instance, supporting player Thomas Thieme plays government minister Bruno Hempf as an undynamic and purely evil character. These traits are brought to bear in very few, but visually (and morally) stunning scenes, such as when, at the cast party for Dreyman's play, Hempf slovenly chews on a chocolate pastry while casually discussing the destruction of a director's career. His evil is unambiguous, unmistakable, and overdrawn, like a figure from a Grosz drawing. In a later scene, the fat apparatchik lures Sieland into the back of his plush chauffeured limousine and, wheezing heavily, brutishly gropes and then rapes her. The episode recalls contemporary Hollywood images of villainy, such as the lecherous priest in Clint Eastwood's *Mystic River* (2003).

The static characterization of Hempf is meant to contrast with the criss-crossed metamorphoses of the two main figures. Dreyman, who begins as an idealistic but naïve conformist gradually finds his critical voice, while the similarly utopian but dogmatic Wiesler defies his bosses when he realizes that their intentions for spying on Dreyman have more to do with career advancement (Grubitz) and sexual gluttony (Hempf) than with the victory of socialism. Perhaps even more so than *Good Bye, Lenin!*, coincidences and layers of dramatic irony are built into the screenplay and visualized in the mise en scène and editing. Sieland dies in a melodramatic *pietà* pose, which echoes her very first appearance, in which she falls to the ground on stage. Graphic matches and parallel camera movements make the similarities between the seeming antagonists Dreyman and Wiesler manifest. Dreyman believes that Sieland was his "guardian angel" rather than his traitor until, years after unification, he looks into his Stasi file. At the very end, his research reveals that the truth was the opposite: agent HGW XX/7, Wiesler, was both his initial oppressor and final savior. The emotional power of these ironies and coincidences works—as suspense always does—on discrepancies of knowledge between characters and, above all, between characters and the viewer: well before Dreyman, we know the truth about Sieland and Wiesler, and we respond to their respective demises accordingly. To this end, parallel editing, like in *The Conversation*, is used frequently to progress the narrative and make ironies explicit. This strategy is anticipated already in the opening, in which an interrogation conducted by Gerd Wiesler is intercut with a lecture on interrogation that Wiesler gives to cadets at the Stasi academy.[56]

Neo-Aristotelian narratology and Hollywood screenwriting manuals have a concise name for the characterization and narrative arc present in *Das Leben der Anderen*: they call it the "reform plot" or "redemption plot." For literary critic Norman Friedman, this trajectory depicts a character who is initially deceived into doing evil until he finds his way to the "just and proper path." This course of events provides pleasure for the reader, who experiences "a sense of confirmed and righteous satisfaction when [the protagonist] makes the proper choice."[57] Hollywood script guru Robert McKee identifies the redemption plot with films such as *The Hustler* (1961), *Drugstore Cowboy* (1989), and *Schindler's List* (1993), which hinge on "a moral change within the protagonist from bad to good."[58] Both Friedman and McKee agree that narratives deploying the redemption plot must be character-driven with nuanced characterization. Stories, as seen in the arc of Wiesler in *Das Leben der Anderen*, turn on the realization of the "ruinous nature of [the protagonist's] obsession," which provides an ironic conclusion: "the protagonist sacrifices his dream (positive), a value that has become a soul-corrupting fixation (negative), to gain an honest, sane, balanced life (positive)."[59] This potent formula has elicited heavyweight Hollywood performances, and McKee offers a list of examples to prove that it is a "magnet" for Academy Awards.

Daniela Berghahn, drawing on McKee as well as David Bathrick's Brechtian analysis of Holocaust films such *La vita è bella* (*Life is Beautiful*, 1997) and *The Pianist* (2002) as *Greuelmärchen* (horror fairy tales), argues that *Das Leben der Anderen* can be read productively as a *Schindler's List* of the GDR.[60] Both films single out a morally ambiguous man, and transform him into the "good" German or Stasi officer; both projects conclude with expressions of gratitude from the victims. In *Schindler's List*, this takes the form of documentary footage of "Schindler's Jews" paying respect at Oskar Schindler's grave. Dreyman, at the end of *Das Leben der Anderen*, dedicates his book to Wiesler, "with gratitude."

The reality of an Oscar-ready redemption tale of a Stasi man put off many commentators, however. Whereas the story of Schindler—as improbable and exceptional as it was and however much it was dramatized by Spielberg for the big screen—was a matter of fact, there has been no single recorded example of Stasi sedition of the scale that von Donnersmarck's film imagines. The idea that a Stasi officer would put his career and perhaps even his freedom or life in jeopardy for one of his targets was too unbelievable for Timothy Garton Ash, the British historian who had lived in the GDR while writing a book that resulted in him amassing a not insignificant Stasi file. The transformation of villain to hero (and then to victim) was too quick, and his recuperation too facile: "So Wiesler did one good thing, to set against the countless bad ones he had done before. But to leap from this to the notion that he was 'a good man' is an artistic exaggeration—a *Verdichtung*—too far."[61] In a critical reckoning with the film, Ash pointed out weaknesses in the language, dress, and behavior of the Stasi and other characters; Dreyman, in Ash's estimation, "dresses, walks, and talks like a West German intellectual from Schwabing." These inaccuracies smack of "the vocabulary of the uprooted German aristocracy among whom the director and writer Florian Henckel von Donnersmarck grew up—both of his parents fled from the eastern parts of the Reich at the end of the Second World War—[rather] than that of the real East Germany in 1984." In the words of Eastern filmmaker Andreas Dresen, *Das Leben der Anderen* "has as much in common with the GDR as Hollywood has with Hoyerswerda."[62]

Of course, as later academic commentators have pointed out,[63] these objections are based more or less on the "fidelity" thesis that period films should reflect the historical record as closely as possible; Ash and Dresen's articles are more interesting as artifacts of the film's reception than as actual interpretations. They reveal how sensitive the issues of "authenticity" and "ownership" were in the case of the GDR's dark past. In fact, the filmmakers calculated these potential criticisms into their production and promotion of the film. As a preemptive strategy, the marketing of *Das Leben der Anderen* heavily emphasized its historical authenticity; von Donnersmarck went on the talk show *Johannes B. Kerner* and spoke of years of research, interviews with Stasi members and their victims, and trips he took with the principal actors to remote parts of the former GDR. In the press kit and later in the DVD extras, the filmmakers distanced themselves from the *Ostalgie* wave—a refrain that echoed Becker's comments about *Good Bye, Lenin!*—and the director emphasized that, although he grew up in the West, his mother originally came from Magdeburg and his father's blue-blood family had their lands in the formerly German territories of Silesia. Much like the functions of Michael Gwisdek and Kathrin Saß in *Good Bye Lenin!*, the casting of Ulrich Mühe, an actor who was subject to surveillance in the GDR, added to the production's "credibility."

Despite these efforts and for all of the aesthetic differences to *Good Bye, Lenin!*, von Donnersmarck's film is another counter-factual history, a fantasy about what a resistance fighter might have looked like in the GDR, if there had been one. Although the film's colors and tone are much darker than the crudest *Ostalgie*, it too offers larger-than-life characters, a world of intrigue and rebellion, and a comforting fairy tale about the universal goodness of humanity. *Das Leben der Anderen* subscribes to the idea that everyone, even the most deluded, can change. The screenplay takes pains to make this message explicit; it is Hempf's derogatory exegesis of Dreyman's work: "That's what we all love about your plays: your belief that people can change. Dreyman, no matter how often you write that in your plays, people do not change." In *Das Leben der Anderen* the revelation that Dreyman was under perpetual surveillance but that his oppressor had also protected him enables the playwright to begin working again, and ends his years of mourning over Sieland. In retrospect, Sieland's death—not out of keeping with those of Jenny in *Forrest Gump* and Christiane in *Good Bye, Lenin!*—hinders any uncomfortable recriminations about the past, and encourages reconciliation.[64] It becomes the occasion that Dreyman can forgive, the occasion for perpetrator and victim to resolve any past differences and unite.

Historical Authenticity for Authentic History

Das Leben der Anderen and *Good Bye, Lenin!*'s tales of benevolent falsification place them in a tradition with *Jakob der Lügner* (*Jacob the Liar*, 1975) and *La vita è bella*. The link to the latter film transcends mere theme, however. Together with productions such as *The English* and *Il Postino* (*The Postman*, 1994), they figure in a wave of Oscar-worthy, ready-for-export European "quality films." These pictures combine relatively high production values and involve family or romance stories set on the brink of traumatic national history. Indeed, in interviews Becker often drew positive parallels between his film and the German-Jewish love story *Aimée & Jaguar* (1999). According to Becker, both his and Max Färberböck's films show that even during dictatorships one finds beautiful moments.[65]

Some film critics have taken this mode of filmmaking to task. Elvis Mitchell, writing in *The New York Times*, called *Good Bye, Lenin!* a "flabby, dramatic version of the first *Austin Powers* movie, another exercise in living anachronism as storytelling device."[66] Tobias Kniebe quipped that these "terrible, especially-worthwhile films" are "calibrated to the cultural level of a week-long student trip."[67] These journalistic condemnations may well be exaggerated and insofar unfair. Nonetheless, they are correct in their claims that these films provide domestic confirmations of national identity as well as foreign advertisements of that same sentiment.[68] This second part was a point that the American columnist Anthony Lane made in his review of *Das Leben der Anderen*. Paraphrasing the last line of the screenplay, he claimed that the film is "for us," that is: non-German, middle-class Westerners, *New Yorker* readers, and eager tourists of a terrible history.[69]

The stylistic link among these films, moreover, is their preoccupation with "authenticity." *Good Bye, Lenin!* is exemplary in the way it compensates for a historical vacuum (implied by the story and mirrored by the film's form) and fetishizes Eastern material culture. Like *Forrest Gump* as well as the European historical "quality films," *Good Bye, Lenin!* defines nation as a collection of mass cultural artifacts and experiences divorced from the period's traumatic political realities.[70] This is what *Good Bye, Lenin!*—despite its witty voice-over, sophisticated narrative, and subtle self-reflexivity—has in common with the "despicable *Ostalgie*-shit" so much disparaged by Becker: a fascination with peculiar linguistic forms, brand names, and an obligatory ensemble of architectures, clothes, and haircuts. The GDR becomes a shop of commodity items. *Good Bye, Lenin!* revolves around preservation, both in its story and the film itself—not to mention its most prominent material object, preserves. In the displays of the jangle bell-bottom jeans and the "multifunctional table" in *Sonnenallee*, or the Mokka-Fix coffee and Spreewald [Spree Forest] pickles in *Good Bye, Lenin!*, these films typically foreground these objects as gags, only to forget them. Taken together (for individually, they are meaningless), these remnants of the GDR function as props meant to create a seamless illusion of authenticity.

A scholarly debate has arisen regarding the role of consumer goods in *Good Bye, Lenin!* and other historical films which depict the Eastern past. Nick Hodgin contrasts *Good Bye, Lenin!* and *Berlin Is in Germany* with earlier period films about the GDR and unification, and concludes that the more recent productions "invoke the East German state in order to bid it a final farewell."[71] Becker's film offers a third-way representation of the GDR as a "location of idealism and even achievement without ever straying too far from its much-publicized iniquities, a dualism that is one of its defining characteristics" (36). Rather than *Sonnenallee*'s fetishization of GDR goods, *Good Bye, Lenin!* offers an archaeology of material objects as "consumer relics of an inferior past, the clumsy packaging and unlovely labels appearing all the more drab next to the rows of shiny, new western products" (41). As a whole, the film gestures toward the serious problems of unification faced by Easterners "without actually engaging with those issues, seemingly unable or unwilling to flesh out the bones of its social critique" (42).

More sympathetic to the productions, Michael D. Richardson has argued that *Sonnenallee* and *Good Bye, Lenin!* offer two levels of "consumption." First, the stories revolve around the vital role that "Western consumer goods and their less-appealing Eastern counterparts played in the daily lives of East Germans."[72] Second, there is the consumption, in the present, of *Ostalgie* itself, that is, the retro-fashion of GDR material goods. Noting the significant role played by consumer goods in the development of East German identity during the existence of the GDR, Richardson argues that the representations of objects in *Sonnenallee* and *Good Bye, Lenin!* do not idealize the past but rather "recuperate East German identities and undermine the existing historical understanding regarding everyday life in the GDR."[73]

Richardson's point about the role of consumerism in the GDR is well taken; indeed, other commentators have convincingly elaborated how the scarcity of products and the care with which Easterners repaired and cared for them entailed intimate connections with them, "product biographies."[74] However, Richardson uses this fact to argue, in the vein of Allan and Enns, that the films encourage "critical reflection" and posit "a multitude of historical narratives" because of their humor, their self-reflexivity, and their foregrounding of "temporal and spatial difference."[75]

The debate about consumer goods in the GDR fiction films has largely revolved around their symbolic value to stand in for subjective viewpoints. For Richardson, Allan, Enns, and others, they represent a positive *Trotzidentität*, that is, Easterners' attitude of defiance toward Western products, a protest against what was sometimes considered a "colonization" or "annexation" of their culture by the West, and a recuperation of a perceived special Eastern identity.[76]

Other commentators such as Berghahn—myself among them— maintain that these gestures toward a "special Eastern identity" are empty symbols: they recognize unique Eastern consumer items in order to classify them as an intermediary in the progress toward an inevitable unified state and consumer culture, an adolescent stage that parallels Alex's retrospective youthful subjectivity. As Anna Saunders writes, *Good Bye, Lenin!*'s *Trotzidentität* should not be seen as antithetical to the project of national harmony: "Rather than representing an anti-western stance, [*Ostalgie*] is instead an attempt to write the validity of a range of east German experiences and memories into the normality of an all-German present, where they may find a place alongside those of the west."[77]

The *Ostalgie* films raise the *Ausstatter*, the production designer, to the role of auteur. *Good Bye, Lenin!*'s set designer, Lothar Holler, worked on about half of the GDR historical fictions: *Sonnenallee*, *Der Zimmerspringbrunnen* (*The Room Fountain*, 2001), *Good Bye, Lenin!*, and *NVA* (2005). However, the "auteur" label is misleading, since Holler's central function involved scouting for period props in antique shops. The production designer, who was interviewed nearly as often as

Wolfgang Becker, Daniel Brühl, and Katrin Saß, compared his work to that of a forensic scientist: "My set design is only partially related to reality. It's about working with signs that everybody understands…a larger-than-life [*überzeichnete*] world."[78] Holler reported the extreme difficulties in finding authentic match sticks and other smaller props. Alex, one might say, dramatizes Holler's role, enacting how difficult it is to find scarce GDR material objects. *Good Bye, Lenin!* can be read as a parable about the vicissitudes of shooting an *Ostalgie* film more than ten years after unification.

There are national implications to this emphasis on authenticity. In a group of films that weighs material goods much as Wuschel does in *Sonnenallee* (a Rolling Stones album is worth more than his own life), these accessories stand as signifiers of the GDR's socialist practice for *West* Germans and, as a body, create an exhibition of Eastern curiosities. After all, what a Western viewer sees as silly getup might be déjà-vu for the Easterner.[79] A pan-German national identity is made possible by devaluing the differences between communism and capitalism. The message the film sends to Westerners—the ultimate addressees—is that the East too was just as enthusiastic about its own consumer culture; only the brand names were different. Since, as Homi Bhabha writes, "the living principle of the people is that continual process by which national life is redeemed …. The scraps, rags, and patches of daily life must be repeatedly turned into the signs of a national culture,"[80] the film acts to turn the East–West "us–them" situation into a "we." The materialization of the Eastern experience fosters a universality; this experience becomes both compatible with that in the West and palatable to Western sensibilities. Thus, the paradox of *Ostalgie*'s obsession for historical authenticity—finding precisely the correct match sticks and pickles—is that the closer the film attends to the authenticity of Eastern material objects, the more perfectly the film promotes a Western perspective.[81] This is *Good Bye, Lenin!*'s ultimate self-reflexive irony. Its attitude to historical re-creation moves in two contradictory directions: on one hand, it discards the grand narratives of authentic history as subject to manipulation and yet, on the other, it seeks extreme historical authenticity as the form to tell that very story. In the film's formal workings—just as in the mother-son love-lie story—one layer of deception is uncovered, but another remains.

In fact, one serious confrontation with the Eastern past as mother-son story—albeit from an unabashedly idiosyncratic Western perspective—had already premiered on German screens: Oskar Roehler's *Die Unberührbare* (*No Place to Go*, 2000). Like *Good Bye, Lenin!*, Roehler's film extends a problem with time into one of space and material culture. But whereas the high-rise apartment building in Becker's film functions as colorful 79m² utopia, a GDR *Heimatmuseum* that offers a cozy shelter from the present, in *Die Unberührbare* East German architecture appears as a marker of sprawling deterioration. These two *Wende* films bear out both the postive and negative implications of architecture theorist Dieter Hoffmann-Axthelm's maxim that "locality is the opposite of utopia."[82]

Notes

1. Its opening-week box-office surpassed even the contemporaneous *Harry Potter* and *Lord of the Rings* sequels; its third-place ranking in Germany for the year outpaced *Pirates of the Caribbean: The Curse of the Black Pearl* (2003) and *The Matrix Reloaded* (2003). See the German Federal Film Board statistics (http://www.ffa.de) as well as Nicole Dolif, "Lenin lässt die Kinokassen klingeln," *Die Welt*, 18 February 2003. See also Matthias Dell, "Sandmann, lieber Sandmann," *Freitag*, 28 February 2003. A few months later, *Good Bye, Lenin!* won by far the most awards at the German Film Prize ceremony. See Michael Althen, "Systemsieg," *Frankfurter Allgemeine Zeitung*, 10 June 2003.

2. See, for example, *Schmetterlinge* (*Butterflies*, 1988), *Kinderspiele* (*Child's Play*, 1992), *Das Leben ist eine Baustelle* (*Life Is All You Get*, 1997). See Claudia Schwartz, "Die persönliche Biographie lenkt den Blick," *Neue Zürchner Zeitung*, 21 February 2003, as well as Franz Ulrich and Dominik Slappnig, "Hast 'ne Idee? Gespräch mit Wolfgang Becker," *Zoom: Zeitschrift für Film*, September 1993, 33–34.

3. See Christiane Peitz, "Gefühlte Geschichte," *Tagesspiegel*, 2 February 2003; Caroline M. Buck, "Eine Mutter-Sohn-Geschichte," *Neues Deutschland*, 13 February 2003; Julian Hanich, "Die DDR soll leben," *Tagesspiegel*, 28 October 2001; Markus Tschiedert, "Bitte einmal ohrfeigen," *Hamburger Abendblatt*, 13 February 2003; and Dina Iordanova, "East of Eden," *Sight and Sound*, August 2003, 26–28.

4. By the end of 2003, Germany's Federal Agency for Civic Education (Bundeszentrale für politische Bildung) had compiled a 24-page booklet for teachers to use the film in history classes: "*Good Bye, Lenin!* addresses the complex issue of the 1989 fall of the Berlin Wall and the steps to German unification. It reflects the events via the fictive story of the East Berlin Kerner family. The film remembers ironically recent history and, with the disappearance of the GDR daily culture, also thematizes how past values and attitudes toward life are forgotten. The film attempts to stimulate the consideration of an alternative course of history. The societal developments put the protagonists in a host of self-discovery processes, which could stand prototypically for individual demographic groups in the GDR." See Bundeszentrale für politische Bildung, ed., *Good Bye, Lenin!* (Bonn: Bundeszentrale für politische Bildung, 2003), 8. See also Volcker Eckert, "Good bye, Ahnungslosigkeit: Kino als Geschichtsstunde," *Tagesspiegel*, 6 March 2003.

5. Constance Frey, "Die DDR ist längst Kult," *Tagesspiegel*, 5 June 2003; André Mielke, "Der Bundestag ist auch nur ein Mensch," *Die Welt*, 4 April 2003; Jan Thomsen, "Ein Kino-Besuch voller Missverständnisse," *Berliner Zeitung*, 3 April 2003; and "Betriebsausflug: Bundestag nimmt Abschied von Lenin," *Spiegel Online*, 3 April 2003, http://www.spiegel.de/kultur/gesellschaft/0,1518,243206,00.html.

6. See Jan Schulz-Ojala, "Beckers Bester," *Tagesspiegel*, 20 April 2003; Martina Kaden, "Good Bye, Lenin! Hello, Welterfolg!," *BZ*, 13 February 2003; Gunnar Deckar, "Ortswechsel. Zeitenwechsel. Weltenwechsel.," *Neues Deutschland*, 11 February 2003.

7. On the US reception, see "Lenin in Amerika," *Frankfurter Allgemeine Zeitung*, 18 March 2004, as well as Silke Mohr, "Good Bye, Lenin in Manhattan," *taz*, 4 March 2004. In Great Britain and in Ireland the film became the highest-grossing German film to date. See the untitled article in the *Frankfurter Allgemeine Sonntagszeitung*, 26 October 2003. The French reception became an almost diplomatic affair. Critics

extended backhanded compliments, speaking of "a German film that feels like an Italian comedy," or "a historical film, which the French are no longer capable of shooting." The *Frankfurter Allgemeine Zeitung* gushed that the film's reception could lead to a new chapter in the volatile German–French cultural relations. See J.M., "La victoire du capitalisme tenue secrète dans un îlot de Berlin-Est," *Le Monde*, 10 September 2003; Jürg Altwegg, "Gewinner: Good Bye, Lenin! in Frankreich," *Frankfurter Allgemeine Zeitung*, 15 September 2003; Anke Sterneborg, "Ein Jahr danach," *epd Film* 21(6) (2004): 52; and Hanns-Georg Rodek, "Danke, Lenin!," *Die Welt*, 21 February 2003.

8. For more on the issue of East–West historical ownership see, for example, Oliver Michalsky, "Da musste erst ein Wessi kommen?," *Die Welt*, 18 February 2003; Jan Schulz-Ojala, "Die große Illusion," *Tagesspiegel*, 9 February 2003; or Elmar Krekeler, "Nur im Falschen gibt es Wahres," *Die Welt*, 26 February 2003; Caroline M. Buck, "Eine Mutter-Sohn-Geschichte," *Neues Deutschland*, 13 February 2003; or Claudia Schwartz, "Die persönliche Biographie lenkt den Blick," *Neue Zürchner Zeitung*, 21 February 2003. For more on the Help e.V. lawsuit, see Helen Cafferty, "*Sonnenallee*: Taking Comedy Seriously in Unified Germany," in *Textual Reponses to German Unification*, eds. Carola Anne Costabile-Heming, Rachel J. Halverson, and Kristie A. Foell (Berlin: Walter de Gruyter, 2001), 253–71; here 255.

9. Jana Hensel, "Die DDR wird Spekulationsobjekt," *Die Welt am Sonntag*, 9 February 2003.

10. Christian Eger, *Mein kurzer Sommer der Ostalgie* (Dössel: Stekovics, 2004), 100 and 72. The Russian DJ and author Wladimir Kaminer mused that Western artists direct their attention to the GDR because West European capitalism is boring. See Wladimir Kaminer, "Good Bye, Lenin! Man sieht sich," *DW-WORLD.DE*, 12 February 2003, http://www.dw-world.de/dw/article/0,,777207,00.html.

11. Edgar Reitz, "Unabhängiger Film nach Holocaust?" in *Liebe zum Kino: Utopien und Gedanken zum Autorenfilm 1962-1983* (Cologne: Verlag KÖLN 78, 1984), 102; quoted in Anton Kaes, *From Hitler to Heimat* (Cambridge, MA: Harvard University Press, 1989), 184. See also Thomas Elsaesser, "Subject Positions, Speaking Positions: From *Holocaust, Our Hitler*, and *Heimat* to *Shoah* and *Schindler's List*," in *The Persistence of History: Cinema, Television and the Modern Event*, ed. Vivian Sobchack (New York: Routledge, 1996), 145–186.

12. See also Annette Leo, "Keine gemeinsame Erinnerung: Geschichtsbewusstsein in Ost und West," *Aus Politik und Geschichte* 40–41 (2003): 27–32.

13. Jens Bisky, "Zonensucht: Kritik der neuen Ostalgie," *Merkur* 58(2) (2004): 117–27; here 121. Nevertheless, Bisky sees *Good Bye, Lenin!* as another example of East German *Ostalgie*.

14. Marcus Jauer, "Wir lachen uns schlapp," *Süddeutsche Zeitung*, 30–31 August 2003.

15. For example: *Sonnenallee, Helden wie wir* (*Heroes Like Us*, 1999), *Der Zimmerspringbrunnen* (*The Room Fountain*, 2001), *Der Tunnel* (*The Tunnel*, 2001), *Berlin Is in Germany* (2001), *Wie Feuer und Flamme* (*Never Mind the Wall*, 2001), *Die Datsche* (*Home Truths*, 2002), *Drei Stern Rot* (*Three Star Red*, 2002), *Kleinruppin Forever* (2004), *NVA* (2005), and *Der rote Kakadu* (*The Red Cockatoo*, 2006).

16. See Anke Westphal, "Den Ossi an sich gab es nicht," *Berliner Zeitung*, 13 February 2003, as well as Nicole Dolif, "Lenin lässt die Kinokassen klingeln," *Die Welt*, 18 February 2003.

17. Jana Hensel, *Zonenkinder* (Reinbek bei Hamburg: Rowohlt, 2002). See, for other examples, Claudia Rusch, *Meine freie deutsche Jugend* (Frankfurt: Fischer, 2004); Wilhelm Solms, ed., *Begrenzt glücklich: Kindheit in der DDR* (Marburg: Hitzeroth, 2002); Michael Tetzlaff, *Ostblöckchen: Neues aus der Zone* (Frankfurt: Schöffling, 2004); or Abini Zöllner, *Schokoladenkind: meine Familie und andere Wunder* (Reinbek bei Hamburg: Rowohlt, 2003).

18. See Daphne Berdahl, "'(N)ostalgie' for the Present: Memory, Longing, and East German Things," *Ethnos* 64(2) (1999): 192–211; Thomas Ahbe, *Ostalgie: Zum Umgang mit der DDR-Vergangenheit in den 1990er Jahren* (Erfurt: Sömmerda, 2005), which also offers the pre-history leading up to the great *Ostalgie* wave of 2003; Paul Cooke, "Surfing for Eastern Difference: *Ostalgie*, Identity, and Cyberspace," *Seminar* 40(3) (2004): 207–20. See *The Economist*, 13 September 2003; Y. Euny Hong, "We'll Always Have East Berlin," *Boston Globe*, 7 September 2003; Richard Bernstein, "Warm, Fuzzy Feelings for East Germany's Gray Old Days," *New York Times*, 6 January 2004; Ben Aris, "How the GDR Became Cool," *The Guardian*, 24 July 2003; Laura Bly, "After the Fall," *USA Today*, 23 October 2009; as well as Anna Funder's book, *Stasiland* (London: Granta, 2003).
19. See Alexander Osang, "Zu Gast im Party-Staat," *Der Spiegel*, 8 September 2003, 212–22; here 213.
20. See Christiane Peitz, "Gefühlte Geschichte," *Tagesspiegel*, 2 February 2003.
21. Interview with Daniel Brühl on 3sat from 10 February 2003. One cinema-goer interviewed in Berlin observed, "I think you can tell from the laughs who comes from West Germany and who comes from East Germany." See Ole Meiners, "Der Plan ist übererfüllt," *Tagesspiegel*, 26 February 2003.
22. A number of GDR retrofilms which associate a nervous breakdown with the fall of the wall employ this perspective. In *Drei Stern Rot*, for example, the former NVA border guard Christian Blank plays a soldier like himself in an *Ostalgie* film set on the German–German border in 1987. Blank snaps when he thinks that his former commanding officer is among the actors, and undergoes psychoanalysis to work through his memories from the GDR. Although not afflicted with any diagnosable disease, Hinrich Lobek, the protagonist of *Der Zimmerspringbrunnen*, is an Easterner unable to cope with the new order. His self-pity and anti-social behavior cause his wife to abandon him. As we shall see in the next chapter, *Die Unberührbare* (*No Place to Go*, 2000) is the story of a Western Marxist for whom the fall of the wall creates an existential crisis. In these other films, the protagonist suffers a nervous breakdown in the wake of unification; each narrates its story from the perspective of "the patient."
23. See "Der Vorspann" in *Good Bye, Lenin!*, ed. Michael Töteberg (Berlin: Schwarzkopf & Schwarzkopf, 2003), 144–45.
24. Sarah Kozloff, *Invisible Storytellers: Voice-over Narration in American Fiction Film* (Berkeley: University of California Press, 1988), 53–54.
25. Film critics complained about the way in which these sequences become "number-revues" of German history. See Anke Westphal, "Was unterging, taucht nicht mehr auf," *Berliner Zeitung*, 8 February 2003, as well as H.G. Pflaum, "Der diskrete Charm der Ostalgie," *Süddeutsche Zeitung*, 13 February 2003.
26. This is a persistent trope in post-communist European films. Krzysztof Kieslowski's *La Double vie de Véronique* (*The Double Life of Veronique*, 1991) also features a scene in Poland in which a dismantled Lenin statue is hauled past the protagonist.
27. Both Wolfgang Becker and Florian Lukas address this in their DVD commentaries. Fans on internet chat sites often supposed Denis' *Matrix*-esque T-shirt was an anachronism that had slipped by continuity.
28. Robert Stam, *Reflexivity in Film and Literature: From Don Quixote to Jean-Luc Godard* (New York: Columbia University Press, 1985), 21.
29. See Svetlana Boym, *The Future of Nostalgia* (New York: Basic Books, 2001), 49.
30. Paul Cooke, "Performing 'Ostalgie': Leander Haußmann's *Sonnenallee*," *German Life and Letters* 56(2) (2003): 156–67.
31. See Anthony Enns, "The Politics of *Ostalgie*: Post-Socialist Nostalgia in Recent German Film," *Screen* 48(4) (2007): 475–91; here 478.
32. Seán Allan, "*Ostalgie*, Fantasy and the Normalization of East–West Relations in Post-Unification Comedy," in *German Cinema: Since Unification*, ed. David Clarke (London: Continuum, 2006), 105–26; here 123.

33. Allan, "Post-Unification Comedy," 124.
34. Allan, "Post-Unification Comedy," 122. Joseph F. Jozwiak and Elisabeth Mermann advance a similar argument, through a postcolonialist lens, in their essay "'The Wall in Our Minds?' Colonization, Integration, Nostalgia," *Journal of Popular Culture* 39(5) (2006): 780–95.
35. Stam, *Reflexivity in Film and Literature*, 13.
36. Nicholas Garnham, "TV Documentary and Ideology," *Screen Reader 1: Cinema/Ideology/Politics* (London: Society for Education in Film and Television, 1977), 55–61; here 61. See Peter Wollen, "Godard and Counter-Cinema: *Vent d'Est*," in *Narrative, Apparatus, Ideology*, ed. Philip Rosen (New York: Columbia University Press, 1986), 120–29.
37. Stam, *Reflexivity in Film and Literature*, 138. Further page numbers in this paragraph refer to this work.
38. From the "Making Of" DVD interview.
39. Christiane Peitz, "Gefühlte Geschichte," *Tagesspiegel*, 2 February 2003.
40. Jane Feuer, *The Hollywood Musical* (London: British Film Institute, 1982), 102–6, here 103. See also the discussion of the politics of self-reflexivity in Robert Stam, Robert Burgoyne, and Sandy Flitterman-Lewis, *New Vocabularies in Film Semiotics: Structuralism, Poststructuralism and Beyond* (London: Routledge, 1992), 201–3.
41. As Daniela Berghahn argues vis-à-vis *Sonnenallee* in her essay "East German Cinema after Unification," in *German Cinema: Since Unification*, ed. David Clarke (London: Continuum, 2006), 79–104; here 97.
42. Jennifer M. Kapczynski, "Negotiating Nostalgia: The GDR Past in *Berlin Is in Germany* and *Good Bye, Lenin!*," *The Germanic Review* 82(1) (2008): 78–100; here 86.
43. See Robert Burgoyne's excellent analysis of *Forrest Gump*, which has informed my understanding of the film, in *Film Nation* (Minneapolis: University of Minnesota Press, 1997), especially 114ff.
44. See, for example, the "Making Of" DVD interview.
45. Burgoyne, *Film Nation*, 109.
46. Burgoyne, *Film Nation*, 109–10.
47. Even thirteen years after unification, for example, only 1.4% of German marriages involved East–West couples. See "Westfrauen entdecken den Ostmann," *MDR.de*, 9 November 2004, http://www.mdr.de/umschau/1679747.html.
48. Elena Gorfinkel, "The Future of Anachronism: Todd Haynes and the Magnificient Andersons," in *Cinephilia: Movies, Love and Memory*, eds. Marijke de Valck and Malte Hagener (Amsterdam: Amsterdam University Press, 2005), 158.
49. See Thomas Elsaesser and Warren Buckland, *Studying Contemporary American Film* (London: Arnold, 2002), 246–47.
50. Evelyn Finger, "Die unsinkbare Republik," *Die Zeit*, 6 February 2003. Failure (Honecker) and triumph (Kohl) are depicted, in the critic's words, "in quite similarly foolish smugness."
51. See, for example, Sabine Hake's comments from 2002: "It may still be too early to expect any feature films about the political elites in the GDR, the power of the secret police, the work of political dissidents, and the role of artists and intellectuals." Sabine Hake, *German National Cinema*, (1st ed.), (London: Routledge, 2002), 189.
52. Reinhard Mohr, "Stasi ohne Spreewaldgurke," *Spiegel Online*, 15 March 2006, http://www.spiegel.de/kultur/kino/0,1518,406092,00.html. Higher-brow publications were similarly taken. See Evelyn Finger, "Die Bekehrung," *Die Zeit*, 23 March 2006.
53. For more on these films, see Leonie Naughton, *That Was the Wild East: Film Culture, Unification, and the "New" Germany* (Ann Arbor: University of Michigan Press, 2002), 207ff.
54. See the German Federal Film Board's market data at http://www.ffa.de.
55. Jaimey Fisher, "German Historical Film as Production Trend: European Heritage Cinema and Melodrama in *The Lives of Others*," in *The Collapse of the Conventional:*

German Film and Its Politics at the Turn of the Twenty-First Century, eds. Jaimey Fisher and Brad Prager (Detroit: Wayne State University Press, 2010), 186–215.

56. Matthew H. Bernstein lists a whole host of ironies in his "The Lives of Others," *Film Quarterly* 61(1) (2007): 30–36.

57. See Norman Friedman, "Forms of the Plot," in *The Theory of the Novel*, ed. Philip Stevick (New York: Macmillan, 1967), 145–66; here 162.

58. Robert McKee, *Story: Substance, Structure, Style, and the Principles of Screenwriting* (London: Methuen, 1999), 81.

59. McKee, *Story*, 126.

60. Daniela Berghahn, "Remembering the Stasi in a Fairy Tale of Redemption: Florian Henckel von Donnersmarck's *Das Leben der Anderen*," *Oxford German Studies* 38(3) (2009): 321–33; see especially 325. For David Bathrick's comments on the *Greuelmärchen*, see his article "Rescreening the 'Holocaust': The Children's Stories," *New German Critique* 80 (2000): 41–58.

61. Timothy Garton Ash, "The Stasi on Our Minds," *The New York Review of Books*, 31 May 2007, http://www.nybooks.com/articles/archives/2007/may/31/the-stasi-on-our-minds. Subsequent quotations refer to this article. Anna Funder was another vocal Anglophone critic. See her "Eyes without a Face," *Sight and Sound*, May 2007, 16–21.

62. Andreas Dresden, "Der falsche Kino-Osten," *Die Zeit*, 16 April 2009.

63. See, for example, Mary Beth Stein, "*Stasi* with a Human Face? Ambiguity in *Das Leben der Anderen*," *German Studies Review* 31(3) (2008): 567–79.

64. Sieland's betrayal and "sacrificial" death prompted critique in feminist readings. See, for example, Jennifer Creech, "A Few Good Men: Gender, Ideology, and Narrative Politics in *The Lives of Others* and *Good Bye, Lenin!*," *Women in German Yearbook: Feminist Studies in German Literature & Culture* 25 (2009): 100–26.

65. See, for example, Claudia Schwartz, "Die persönliche Biographie lenkt den Blick," *Neue Zürcher Zeitung*, 21 February 2003.

66. Elvis Mitchell, "*Good Bye, Lenin!* Restoring a Berlin Wall To Comfort Dear Old Mom," *New York Times*, 27 February 2004.

67. Tobias Kniebe, "Amelie und Anämie," *Süddeutsche Zeitung*, 3–4 May 2003.

68. Matthias Dell, "Sandmann, lieber Sandmann," *Freitag*, 28 February 2003. Indeed, these films must have both domestic and Europe-wide success (and, ideally, break into the North American and Asian markets). *Good Bye, Lenin!* became an advertisement for the German film industry and proof that German film is on top: this was, indeed, why X-Films invited members of the Bundestag to see the film in the middle of the debate on the new film subsidy regulations. See Jan Thomsen, "Ein Kino-Besuch voller Missverständnisse," *Berliner Zeitung*, 3 April 2003. In trade articles there existed a connection between *Good Bye, Lenin!* and a drive against resignation and pessimism in the industry. See Christina Nord, "Unbedingter Wille zum Selbstbewusstsein,"*taz*, 10 June 200; also Fritz Göttler, "Gutes Gefühl im Filmförderverein," *Süddeutsche Zeitung*, 4 April 2003.

69. Anthony Lane, "Guilty Parties: *The Lives of Others*," *The New Yorker*, 12 February 2007, http://www.newyorker.com/arts/critics/cinema/2007/02/12/070212crci_cinema_lane.

70. See Burgoyne, *Film Nation*, 108–9.

71. Nick Hodgin, "*Berlin Is in Germany* and *Good Bye, Lenin!* Taking Leave of the GDR?," *Debatte* 12(1) (2004): 25–45; here 44–45. Subsequent page numbers refer to this article.

72. Michael D. Richardson, "A World of Objects: Consumer Culture in Filmic Reconstructions of the GDR," in *The Collapse of the Conventional: German Film and Its Politics at the Turn of the Twenty-First Century*, eds. Jaimey Fisher and Brad Prager (Detroit: Wayne State University Press, 2010), 216–37; here 217.

73. Richardson, "A World of Objects," 217.

74. See, for example, Martin Blum, "Remaking the East German Past: *Ostalgie*, Identity, and Material Culture," *Journal of Popular Culture* 34(3) (2000): 229–53; here 241.

75. Richardson, "A World of Objects," 221–23.

76. See Patricia Hogwood, "Reconstructing Identity in Post-Communist Germany," *Journal of Communist Studies and Transition Politics* 16(4) (2000): 45–67; here 55.

77. Anna Saunders, "'Normalizing' the Past: East German Culture and *Ostalgie*," in *German Culture, Politics, and Literature into the Twenty-First Century*, eds. Stuart Taberner and Paul Cooke (Rochester, NY: Camden House, 2006), 89–103; here 102.

78. Matthias Stolz, "Ein Wiedersehen mit der DDR," *Frankfurter Allgemeine Zeitung*, 29 October 2001, discusses this. The quotation is from Petra Ahne and Felix Zimmermann, "Sozialismus auf 79 Quadratmetern," *Berliner Zeitung*, 7 February 2003. See also Marc Schweiger, "Die Ordnungsmacht des Alltags," *Die Welt am Sonntag*, 16 March 2003. According to this Western advertising executive, "the set designer has the toughest job." Holler was also interviewed in Ralph Geisenhanslüke, "Filmaufbau Ost," *Die Zeit*, 22 December 2003.

79. See Oliver Michalsky, "Da musste erst ein Wessi kommen?," *Die Welt*, 18 February 2003.

80. Homi K. Bhabha, "DissemiNation: Time, Narrative and the Margins of the Modern Nation," in *Nation and Narration*, ed. Homi K. Bhabha (London: Routledge, 1990), 297.

81. Paul Cooke argues that *Good Bye Lenin!* might be seen as "Westalgie," since, rather than an Eastern perspective, it reproduces the Western leftist "78er" generation's nostalgia in order to "lament the loss of much of the pre-*Wende* political agenda." See Paul Cooke, *Representing East Germany Since Unification: From Colonization to Nostalgia* (Oxford: Berg, 2005), 135. Roger F. Cook argues that the film works to make the GDR attractive to Westerners. See Roger F. Cook, "*Good Bye, Lenin!*: Free-Market Nostalgia for Socialist Consumerism," *Seminar* 43(2) (2007): 206–19.

82. Dieter Hoffmann-Axthelm, *Die dritte Stadt* (Frankfurt: Suhrkamp, 1993), 34.

Chapter 5

UNIFICATION, SPATIAL ANXIETY, AND THE RECUPERATION OF MATERIAL CULTURE
Die Unberührbare

Much of the critical discourse on postwall German historical cinema focuses on productions that take a reverent approach to authenticity, from *Aimée & Jaguar* (1999) and *Der Untergang* (*Downfall*, 2004) to *Good Bye, Lenin!* (2003) and *Das Leben der Anderen* (*The Lives of Others*, 2006). These films, which received much journalistic notice and scholarly regard, enjoyed relatively brisk box office both at home and abroad. Their aesthetics and ethics of historical representation and high production values—their very status as European "quality films"—made them viable for export abroad, and help to explain their popular success (within the circumscribed expectations of German filmmaking). Their aesthetic designs and their international distribution may also explain why the postwall historical cinema has most often been linked by Lutz Koepnick and the heritage critics to a conservative mise en scène, and criticized by reviewers Katja Nicodemus and Cristina Nord, and by scholars such as Jennifer Kapczynski, as attempts at naïve material authenticity.[1] There is a circularity to this discourse: certain films achieve recognition because of their careful attention to period detail (and the fact that they are exported at all); precisely these productions then become the archetypes for generalizations of the entire historical cinema. As a way to complicate this portrait of a cinema of blithe mimesis, this chapter examines closely a production that partakes of the past not only as a slick backdrop, but rather as a process of personal exploration and an investigation of cinema history.

Compared with recent German historical films that received careful journalistic and scholarly attention, Oskar Roehler's *Die Unberührbare* (*No Place to Go*, 2000), represents a marked exception to the mainstream rule. Its autobiographical narrative, stylized aesthetic, allegorical thrust, and overt references to contemporary cultural politics seem to have more in common with the endeavors of Rainer Werner Fassbinder or Helma Sanders-Brahms than with the contemporaneous *Sonnenallee* (*Sun Alley*, 1999) and *Aimée & Jaguar*. Like Hans-Christian Schmid,

Roehler (born in 1959) belongs to a small group of German directors looking critically and ambivalently to the generation of 1968; much more so than the director of *23* (1999), he offers an unconventional take on the present-day Federal Republic.

Roehler's output has partly revolved around stories of men who fail to negotiate stable family and romantic relationships.[2] Romantic dramadies with nervous protagonists have made up a good portion of his efforts, such as *Silvester Countdown* (1997) and *Gierig* (1999), the Freudian comedy *Suck My Dick* (2001), and the star-studded Michel Houellebecq adaptation *Elementarteilchen* (*Elementary Particles*, 2006). Film scholar Marco Abel summarizes these films' basic theme as "the (im)possibility of sustaining a (hetero-) sexual relationship in the age of postromance," that is, the context of an urban, post-1968, postfeminist skepticism toward the "traditional 'ideal' of lifelong, monogamous relationships."[3]

Abel attributes these films' attitude toward human relationships to the director's generation, the "78ers."[4] Historian Aleida Assmann describes this cohort as an "in-between generation" comprised of those born in the 1950s. Although this generation first celebrated the values of the 68ers, its "older siblings" or young parents, it then distanced itself from them in polemical fashion and took on "pragmatic or ideological ways of thinking."[5] This generation is particularly ambivalent, because its turn against the 68ers meant a turn against its earlier self; the social group was often the unthankful beneficiary of the 68ers' innovations: sexual revolution, the dismantling of the patriarchy, and the institution of new gender roles and lifestyles.[6] In turn, the 68ers have been most critical of the 78ers' rebellion; according to Abel, it is this complex relationship between the 68ers and 78ers that Roehler's cinema dramatizes so "obsessively."[7] The director's films "need to be understood as responding to a social transformation that configures the 78ers as merely a remnant."[8]

This characterization, for however much even Abel admits that it generalizes and subscribes to a romantic auteurism, implies a very personal reckoning with the past. Indeed, perhaps less acknowledged in assessments of Roehler is the role of history in his work. Beginning his film career as a screenwriter, Roehler co-wrote two scripts which satirized the ironies and absurdities of unification: Christoph Schlingensief's *Terror 2000 – Intensivstation Deutschland* (*Terror 2000*, 1992) and Niklaus Schilling's *Deutschfieber* (*German Fever*, 1992). Even Roehler's sometimes hyperactive directorial efforts about awkward sexual and social relationships provide a serious reckoning with history. *Der alte Affe Angst* (*Angst*, 2003) meditates, for instance, in a very personal way on the death of Roehler's father. *Agnes und seine Brüder* (*Agnes and His Brothers*, 2004) attends to another paternal figure, Fassbinder, in the way that it models the Agnes character quite directly on Erwin/Elvira from *In einem Jahr mit 13 Monden* (*In a Year of 13 Moons*, 1978). Yet another Fassbinder film, *Lola* (1981), inspires Roehler's 1950s romp *Lulu & Jimi* (2009), which depicts an interracial couple's romance in a tongue-in-cheek melodramatic form. His most recent project, *Jud Süß – Film ohne Gewissen* (*Jew Suss – Rise and Fall*, 2010), is a biopic of Ferdinand Marian, the star who played the title villain in Veit Harlan's *Jud Süß* (*Jew Suss*, 1940). Dramatizing the actor's life as a bargain for fame with a Mephistophelean Joseph Goebbels, the film chronicles Marian's initial resistance to play the role in the notorious anti-Semitic propaganda feature, the shooting and reception of the film, and Marian's subsequent descent into alcoholism. Reviews in the German and international press were scathing, castigating Moritz Bleibtreu for his mimetic performance of Goebbels, and taking Roehler to task for his dramaturgical inventions.[9] (Unlike in the historical record, for example, Marian's wife is depicted as partly Jewish, and it is implied that she died in the gas chambers.) Nevertheless, the film follows Roehler's previous efforts in its willingness to engage with national history in the realm of film history, entertaining the cultural power of cinema in the formation of social values. In Roehler's work, German history and cinema collide with autobiography and family. The director's tumultuous upbringing between the writer Gisela Elsner and the publisher Klaus Roehler—a prominent couple among leftist intellectual 68ers—reappears in curious formations throughout his oeuvre.[10] "History is the only source," according to Roehler, "from which you can create, as a collective and as an individual."[11]

Die Unberührbare juxtaposes the historic public events of November 1989 with a condensed rendering of Gisela Elsner's personal demise. The historical Elsner was born into the privilege of an upper-middle-class family in Nuremberg in 1937 and achieved a measure of literary fame for her 1964 debut novel, *Die Riesenzwerge* (*The Giant Dwarves*), a Kafkaesque satire on the gluttony of economic-miracle-era West Germany.[12] Subsequent efforts, such as *Das Berührungsverbot* (1970) and *Abseits* (1982) treated similar themes and examined the unbearable realities of life in Western capitalist society in grotesque detail. From 1964 on, Elsner's works had been published with Rowohlt, but after reports that her novels were selling only ten copies per year, she was dropped by the acclaimed publishing house.[13] Her brand of bitter social critique found little resonance in the 1980s and she fell into depression and paranoia, claiming in 1991 that she "hated writing": "a suicide attempt would at least generate publicity. But simply jump out of the window? From the fifth floor? I would get stuck on the gutter. And everybody would say: typical. She's never accomplished anything. A complete dilettante."[14] Elsner committed suicide by falling from the fifth floor of a Munich hospital on 13 May 1992.

Based loosely on these events, *Die Unberührbare* tracks a West German novelist named Hanna Flanders (played by Hannelore Elsner) from the fall of the Berlin Wall to her suicide in early 1990. Although Hanna was an officially sanctioned success in the GDR, her novels have become too Marxist for West German publishing houses. She senses, quite accurately, that the demise of real existing socialism bodes the end of her career as well. Desperate and broke, she gives up her Munich apartment and embarks on an odyssey through the two Germanys. She visits her son and a lover in Berlin, her parents in Nuremberg, and her ex-husband in Darmstadt before landing in a Munich clinic, where she plunges from a window. With a nightmarish mood sustained by a peculiarly nervous narrative, Roehler re-creates an apocalyptic, noirish Germany in autumn 1989.

In his insightful interpretation of *Die Unberührbare*, Johannes von Moltke situates the autobiographical discourses present in the film and its reception within the auteurist tradition of the New German Cinema.[15] According to von Moltke, Roehler's project revives what Thomas Elsaesser has called the "cinema of experience," which uses the "politically and cinematically authentic" idea of personal experience as an antidote to Hollywood's "politics of spectacle."[16] This argument sees Roehler's film as harking back to subjective and autobiographical historical representations such as *Deutschland, bleiche Mutter* (*Germany, Pale Mother*, 1980) or *Die Ehe der Maria Braun* (*The Marriage of Maria Braun*, 1979). These films, among others, "articulated (auto)biography, the narration of an individual's story, with German history."[17] Much in the vein of my argument about 23's biography of Karl Koch, von Moltke links *Die Unberührbare* to the New German "case studies" and in particular *Abschied von gestern* (*Yesterday Girl*, 1966), another black-and-white profile of a peripatetic woman caught between the landscapes of East and West Germany.

Similar to von Moltke, I see Roehler's project as largely in keeping with the New German mixtures of subjective autobiography and national history. This chapter, however, will approach *Die Unberührbare* through another part of this "historical imaginary": the tradition of what Elsaesser calls the "genealogy of elective affinities," the way in which the New German Cinema rewrote German history as film history.[18] In particular, this chapter proceeds by locating *Die Unberührbare* in terms of its appropriation of film noir and that form's tradition of social critique.

Classic film noir, as recent commentators have pointed out, dramatized post-World War II anxiety over contemporary urban and spatial transformation and the ensuing rips and tears in the American social fabric. James Naremore, for example, has shown how 1940s noir often served as a vehicle for leftist political engagement.[19] In particular, Edward Dimendberg has compellingly elaborated how the filmic spaces of this cycle enact the pathology and shape of the modern city.[20] Above all, noir remains preoccupied with "traumas of unrecoverable time and space, the inability to dwell comfortably either in the present or the past."[21] Contextualizing the cycle within 1940s and 1950s American urban philosophy and spatial practices, Dimendberg demonstrates how the often decrepit and derelict spaces featured in the productions are not merely representations of the American city (and especially New York and Los Angeles); they are critical interventions into debates about postwar urban space. In this way, for instance, the depictions of Penn Station and Times Square in *Killer's Kiss* (1955) function not merely as iconic city landmarks; rather, in the context of the rapid transformation of New York and the movement of many former residents to suburbs, they are nostalgic signposts of a city with declining centripetal spatial organization and practice.[22]

Die Unberührbare returns to the subtext of classic noir. Much like that form, the production attends to space and material culture and reinscribes both into the specific sociocultural environment of millennial Germany, another locus of great spatial and cultural transformation. Pursuing the film's appropriation of noir leads to a broader discussion of how the materiality of its cinematic intertext intervenes into contemporary intellectual debates and exemplifies a possibility of German historical cinema beyond discourses of "heritage" and "naïve authenticity."

Death by Framing

Hanna Flanders is in many ways reminiscent of a character from an American film noir. A comparison with Norma Desmond from Billy Wilder's *Sunset Boulevard* (1950) seems apt. Both women were stars in now anachronistic fields—Marxist *belles lettres* and silent film, respectively. Now in their fifties, however, they are past their prime. Still, each deems herself as important as ever and strives to complete her next great project, a work that clearly will never come to fruition. Hanna's paranoia and neurosis, and her excessive chain smoking, drinking, and drug use, are in keeping with the classic noir's psychogram of a dangerous and out-of-control woman.[23]

Nevertheless, to read *Die Unberührbare* as a film noir, at least in terms of its narrative, would prove fruitless; we find none of the cycle's staples: no detectives, femme fatales, or voice-over narrators. Indeed, there is not much narrative to speak of, for *Die Unberührbare* is above all a mood piece. With its limited flow of information, *Die Unberührbare*'s exemplifies Foster Hirsch's conception of European versions of the noir, which privilege "atmosphere, *Stimmung*, over narrative coherence."[24] *Die Unberührbare* returns to the essence of original noir, particularly in its expression of spatial anxiety. Roehler transmits this unease by updating aspects of the centrifugal film noir into a "framed" mise en scène.

Edward Dimendberg describes centrifugal film noir in reference to examples such as *Odds against Tomorrow* (1959), which depicts the "wide open spaces" of "a New York that conspicuously lacks a center"; in this production, recognizable landmarks are markedly absent. Centrifugal spaces include suburban settlements, industrial landscapes, shopping malls, and urban regions in decay because of renewal projects, suburban flight, or economic problems. In contrast, according to Dimendberg, centripetal film noir features frequent views through or into open windows and the continual attempts of characters to orient themselves within the city.[25]

Die Unberührbare's mise en scène might seem to recall centripetal American noir. There are, for example, frequent shots through and into windows. At the end of the first scene, the camera cranes down from the high-rise buildings beyond Hanna's Munich apartment to a long shot of Hanna, spatially trapped inside the square fish-bowl windows of her flat. Hanna's night in East Berlin public housing likewise concludes with a shot of the protagonist through a window. This composition recurs throughout the film.

Nevertheless, these are not the sorts of open windows that we find in American centripetal noir. They function neither to "establish the position of both spectators and characters," nor do they serve as the "pivot between interior and exterior space ... reinforcing its normally uncontested status as a neutral frame," as is the case with windows in *Black Angel* (1946) and *Port of New York* (1949).[26] The shots of Hanna through windows typically come at the end, not the beginning, of scenes. Roehler employs this composition in the tradition of Pasolini's *Teorema* (*Theorem*, 1968) and *Porcile* (*Pigpen*, 1969) or Fassbinder's *Angst essen Seele*

Figure 5.1: Windows and doors 1: Hanna in her chic Munich flat in *Die Unberührbare*. Image courtesy of Distant Dreams Filmproduktion.

Figure 5.2: Windows and doors 2: Hanna in an East Berlin pre-fabricated flat in *Die Unberührbare*. Image courtesy of Distant Dreams Filmproduktion.

auf (*Ali: Fear Eats the Soul*, 1974), in order to bring into relief the emotional condition of a character's felt social circumscription. The depiction of windows in these two centrifugal spaces (peripheral snob outpost and pre-fab council flat) recalls noirs such as *Street of Chance* (1942), where office glass windows convey the feeling of being under surveillance.[27] Filmed always from the outside in, the windows function as a subjective, centrifugal mediator of surveillance and anxiety. Its use here recalls Georg Simmel's discussion of the window in "Bridge and Door." Simmel ascribes to the door an "indifference of intention between entering and exiting," whereas the window is distinguished by a "teleological emotion … directed almost exclusively from inside to outside: it is there for looking out, not for looking in."[28] Although the character Hanna partakes of this "teleological emotion" that Simmel describes as taking place in architecture, the film spectator reverses this movement.

Television figures as another frame, a mediator for spatiotemporal proximity; this recalls the centrifugal noir, where communication networks and mass media substitute for recognizable visible landmarks.[29] The very first scene depicts Hanna threatening suicide on the phone with a mysterious man named Ronald (who only has a telephone and a television in his otherwise empty flat), over the jubilant cheers on television of Berliners crossing the now-porous Berlin Wall. As Hanna trembles and breaks down, a man cries in patriotic joy: "I was there to see the wall being built, and now I'm seeing it being torn down." Indeed, Roehler casts television as an ironic point of comparison to Hanna's state already in the first seconds of the film, where television audio is heard over the black credits. The first discernible language we hear is a reporter asking: "Where are you going to go to now?" An East

Figure 5.3: In *Die Unberührbare*, history is transmitted via television.
Image courtesy of Distant Dreams Filmproduktion.

German woman and man reply: "Well, first of all over to Charlottenburg [West Berlin]." The reporter follows up: "How did you find out that the border was open?" "On television!," the woman exclaims.

In contrast to the couple, Hanna lacks direction and destination, and cannot accept the events unfolding before her on the small screen. Television functions as an indicator that Hanna is out of step with public sentiment in Germany. Juxtaposing a personal story out of sync with a historic televisual moment, this sequence hinges on another irony legible to German viewers in 2000. They—as Hanna's stance anticipates—would have experienced the initial euphoria of November 1989 fade into a rancorous and messy affair.

The role of television recalls the figuration of mass communication in both Stanley Kubrick's late noir *Killer's Kiss*[30] as well as in several Fassbinder films, where it too offers a grand historical backdrop that is juxtaposed with ultra-personal narrative concerns.[31] Roehler explicitly quotes *In einem Jahr mit 13 Monden*, where a news story on Pinochet's sadism plays on television while Elvira, the doomed transsexual, sleeps. In a special column for *Die Zeit*, Roehler lauded Fassbinder's production as "the most impressive film of postwar German history," praising the director's rendering of the "anonymous spaces of which the horrible, fragmented universe of this film consists."[32]

Much in the way that Paul Virilio describes the screen replacing the public function of the city square, the events on television in *Die*

Unberührbare serve as a substitute for actually going to the city center.[33] After Hanna decides to pack up and leave for Berlin, Roehler lingers on a shot of a television in her now empty apartment. The broadcast shows the jubilant crowds at the Brandenburg Gate, images that will haunt Hanna for the rest of the film and reappear in the background of several key scenes. Hanna will never actually go to the Brandenburg Gate, the locus of urban and ideological tumult; she only experiences the city center via television. As the German title suggests, Hanna is "The Untouchable." Inflected as feminine in German, the name ironically connects Roehler's project to original American noir and alludes to Gisela Elsner's novel *Das Berührungsverbot* (The Prohibition of Contact).

The final sequence accentuates the framing motif and couples it with a centrifugal logic. Ronald visits Hanna at the clinic, entering a massive empty room that resembles a stage, replete with Doric columns and a frieze over the door. Roehler captures their existential conversation in four minutes of nearly 360° tracking shots that circle around the pair in alternately opposite directions, calling to mind Michael Ballhaus's trademark kinetic cinematographic flourishes in *Whity* (1971), *Martha* (1973), *Chinesisches Roulette* (*Chinese Roulette*, 1976), and his later American efforts such as *The Fabulous Baker Boys* (1989). By the conversation's end, the camera sweeps have slowed and the shot scale has changed from close-up to medium shot. This effect, of course, is centrifugal and is in keeping with the film's spatiality.

This logic also finds graphic illustration in architecture. Hanna ascends a very long flight of stairs and peers down onto the stage on which she has just performed, positioning herself as her own spectator. The vertiginous framed view of the staircase—rings of stairs that grow

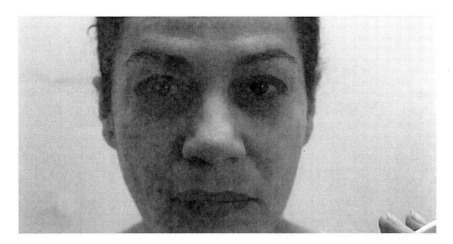

Figure 5.4: Hanna's final cigarette before the conclusion of *Die Unberührbare*. Image courtesy of Distant Dreams Filmproduktion.

Figure 5.5: Death by framing: *Die Unberührbare*. Image courtesy of
Distant Dreams Filmproduktion.

increasingly larger the closer they come to the camera—recalls the death
scene in *Mädchen in Uniform* (*Girls in Uniform*, 1931) and corresponds to
the centrifugal motion Hanna has just undergone to climb the steps.
Enclosed in a small bathroom stall, Hanna lights her last cigarette. The
camera approaches her face in extreme close-up, and for two seconds
Hanna looks directly into the camera before it zooms out again as she
takes another drag. Hanna exits the stall, opens the window, and falls
to the ground. For the first time, there is a shot of an open window from
the inside: Hanna's final performance is a death by framing.

A Peripheral Itinerary

Dimendberg diagnoses the fearfulness about the city center and its
changed status as key ingredients in noir's spatial anxiety.[34] If noir
tends to be employed in times of sociocultural insecurity over spatial
transformation and relations to the urban center, then millennial
Germany is a striking counterpart. In the 1990s, an "architecture
debate" began.[35] At stake was the difficult question of how to envision
and construct the unified Germany's new spaces.

There was often a hysterical tone to this debate, which persistently
transformed architectural and urban planning matters into ontological
questions of German identity. "In present-day Berlin," Svetlana Boym
wrote in 2001, "the discussion of architecture and urban planning is so
persistent that it seems to have become synonymous with the discussion
of Germanness and democratic transformation."[36] Symptomatic of this

discourse is a selection of book and article titles published at the turn of the millennium about contemporary Berlin's architecture and city planning: *Spaces of Uncertainty*; *In Search of a Lost City*; "Berlin: Self-Destruction and Recurrent Self-Fabrication"; "An Extreme Case of European Urban Crisis"; "Berlin: The Massacre of Ideas"; *No Place at This Point*; *Berlin: City Without Form*; *Capital of Repression*; "Aesthetics of Absence."[37] The general feeling was that Berlin—and by extension Germany—lacked a center. Even the Berlin Architectural Chamber's 1999 yearbook, a promotional publication meant to put a positive spin on the year's urban designs, featured an article by French guest architects who admitted to being "confused" due to Berlin's "lack of an old city core" and because it had no "clear division between 'center' and 'edge district.'"[38]

Die Unberührbare enacts this anxiety in the shape of the protagonist's itinerary. Hanna traverses the liminal spaces of the postwall, pre-unification Germanys, moving from Munich to West Berlin to East Berlin to Nuremberg to Darmstadt and back to Munich. In some ways this journey recalls Dimendberg's comments on the "walking cure," the practice of urban passage in film noir which functions to restore the character's "memory impressions that enter experience" and to organize city space into a coherent whole and thereby offer a "prophylactic encounter with endangered urban spaces."[39] Hanna certainly conceives of her journey as a chance to treat her fragile psyche. Rather than traveling through the urban center (as in centripetal films noir like *Street of Chance* [1942]), however, Hanna traverses the almost exclusively peripheral, centrifugal spaces of two countries by train and automobile. She walks over muddy fields, rather than city streets. The effect is anything but cohesive. It produces an entirely fragmentary picture of Germany in 1989.

If American noir characters "travel from the corruption of eastern cities to the unfulfilled promise of the western mirage,"[40] *Die Unberührbare* reroutes this geographic trajectory so that a woman seeks utopia in the crumbled ruins of the GDR, only to find the voids of empty promises. The film's domestic spaces are nearly uniformly empty and rendered in right-angled compositions. The emotional coldness of Hanna's parents' house, for instance, is a function of rectangular shapes and painterly frames that divide, delineate, and circumscribe the space. The interiors of other buildings, whether the East Berlin publishing house, a West Berlin hotel, or the Nuremberg train station, are eerie and desolate. Her ex-husband Bruno's Spartan flat, which betrays no signs of recent redecoration, is an empty castle in the Kristevean sense. Kristeva diagnoses architectural imaginaries ("an empty castle, haunted by unappealing ghosts—'powerless' outside, 'impossible' inside") in psychotic subjects who fortify themselves with self-made walls as defense mechanisms.[41] In this vein, Bruno's apartment is an anachronistic dwelling that translates visually a system of desire and way of seeing vacated by the toppling of the Berlin Wall: he still looks to the 1970s West German left-wing terrorist group RAF as a potential source of social renewal.

Only her son Viktor's cluttered apartment seems to imply a future. Hanna's son figures in the film as the only man actually able to come to terms with and even thrive in the new order: he and his wife make daily trips to East Berlin from their home in the western part of the city. Viktor's flat is no empty castle. In a baroque half-moon tracking shot partially obscured by a lamp in the foreground, the camera scans Viktor's study. Strewn books, empty Coca-Cola cans, a photograph of a topless woman, a German flag, a clunky proto-laptop where Viktor records his new writing ideas: the cluttered and excessive composition nonetheless appears somehow hopeful, especially in comparison to the barren spatial possibilities the film otherwise offers. Nevertheless, this figuration is highly ironic. Viktor—a stand-in for Roehler in any biographical reading—is played by Lars Rudolph, the meek German actor best known for playing retarded, traumatized, or perverse characters in films such as *Die totale Therapie* (*The Total Therapy*, 1996), *Die Siebtelbauern* (*The Inheritors*, 1998), and *Der Krieger und die Kaiserin* (*The Princess and the Warrior*, 2000). Rudolph's appearance as the savior of German masculinity in the face of the GDR's collapse sends a very mixed signal.

Hanna's itinerary provides a travelogue of the peripheral. Her parents live in suburban Nuremberg; Bruno drinks himself to death in Darmstadt, an unexceptional, quasi-suburb of Frankfurt; Berlin, Germany's "space of uncertainty," has a hole in its center. Hanna travels by anachronistic means, in a deserted first-class train wagon that Roehler captures as if he were trying to find a visual counterpart for Michel de Certeau's metaphor that train travel is incarceration:[42] Hanna is immobile, framed by portraits of Prussian aristocrats. After her arrival, she navigates the city with outdated maps, spending the night in the decidedly outmoded Hotel Excelsior peopled only by a gigolo and a bizarre porter.

However, Roehler's rendering of Berlin is not a series of *terrains vagues* and *non-lieux*.[43] Although the film's arguably most striking visuals depict Hanna hastening alone and hungover across empty fields, these "voids" are symbolically potent spaces. The nadir of Hanna's journey in East Berlin takes place in the northeastern suburbs of Hohenschönhausen and Marzahn. These areas had been envisioned by communist city planners in 1971 as a utopian cluster of high-rise apartment buildings and an antidote to an acute housing shortage. This dream turned into a nightmare as the poor construction quickly fell into disrepair. As a result, Marzahn became synonymous with the failure of socialism in practice. Herrmann Zschoche depicted the neighborhood as an architecture of doom and a symbol of government incompetence in his DEFA production, *Insel der Schwäne* (*The Island of Swans*, 1983), a film enthusiastically received by GDR audiences even as it was condemned by party organs. The story of a boy who moves from an idyllic village to the tough community features a panorama shot in which the children scramble to school among the dirty, half-finished housing blocks; it makes Marzahn look like a disaster area and prefigures Roehler's rendering of the muddy field. In the words of scholar Sabine Hake, Zschoche's film traces a "process of disillusionment through architectural metaphors indicating that the socialist homeland had become inhospitable and uninhabitable."[44]

In reality, the massive construction project at the edge of the city led to further decay of the city center. To this day still the largest industrially built residential area in Germany, encompassing 59,646 new units erected between 1977 and 1989, Marzahn was often described in the 1990s German architecture debate as an "anti-city" or "Germany's Brasilia."[45] Marzahn represents the failed utopianism of centrifugal spatial practice.

In spite of a general focus on peripheral topography, the cinematography lingers on one prominent Berlin landmark. Before leaving the city, Hanna calls from a phone booth in front of the Berlin Zoologischer Garten train station. However, even this potential point of orientation represents a former center about to be erased. Zoo station, once the heart of West Berlin, was abandoned around the turn of the millennium in favor of a new Central Station, located in the middle of unified Berlin.[46] The image of Zoo station thus stands as an emblem. Just as Zoo represents a city center being displaced to the periphery, so too is Hanna, once a celebrated literary figure, now marginalized. She is behind the times and out of fashion.

Sartorial Intertextuality

Paula Rabinowitz has written on how classic American noir achieves its identifying texture from material objects.[47] Her comments on noir's dialogue with US political history via consumer objects helps us better understand *Die Unberührbare*. Investigating the evolution of noir, Rabinowitz coins the term "noir sensibility" to describe how the form can and has been used as a historiography of exposing seedy American culture and politics (xi). In this vein, noir's "plot structure and visual iconography" can be helpful to understand "America's landscape and history" (14). Part of this noir sensibility attends to the fundamental semantics of this traditionally "B-movie" genre: pulp, trash, and detritus; for this reason, she inspects props, costumes, and set designs. Cigarette lighters, telephones, handbags, car windshields, doorways, and Venetian blinds, to cite some of Rabinowitz's examples, are essential elements of original noir's work (18; 171–92). Examining the black high-heeled pump typical of noir iconography in films such as *Double Indemnity* (1944), she points to the shoes' function as markers of "women's aggressive mobility in postwar urban spaces": they foreground and sexualize female legs, change her gait, and, by dint of the clacking sound they make on pavement, publicize her presence (174).

Die Unberührbare appropriates a version of noir sensibility by reclaiming fashion as an intertexually symbolic landscape for an uncanny film about artistic and intellectual homelessness. Sartorial allusions abound in the most unlikely places. Immediately after the shots of Hanna stumbling through an unkempt field in her extravagant clothing, she happens upon a fast-food joint housed in a trailer. The proprietor—in horn-rimmed glasses, black bowtie, pointed hat, and white uniform seemingly from the 1950s—appears to be muttering to himself as he wipes the table tops. In actuality he is reciting a Kafka poem:

Und die Menschen gehn in Kleidern	And the people take walks in clothes
schwankend auf dem Kies spazieren	shakily on the gravel
unter diesem großen Himmel,	under this large sky,
der von Hügeln in der Ferne	which spreads from hills
sich zu fernen Hügeln breitet.	in the distance to distant hills.

Kafka inserted these lines in his story, "Beschreibung eines Kampfes" (Description of a Struggle), years after he originally wrote them.[48] The poem seems to describe Hanna's struggle by narrating her stagger. In several scenes she stumbles, for instance, in suburban Berlin on the muddy field; her high heels slip into the cracks of cobblestone streets; the clacking of her shoes on the pavement, as in Rabinowitz's description of *Double Indemnity*, is prominent throughout. Furthermore, Kafka's verse explicitly evokes people "in clothes"—a tautology, one would think, for any description of city-dwellers going for a walk. Likewise, the story as a whole repeatedly returns to descriptions of clothes and dressing-up, just as Roehler foregrounds Hanna's sartorial show and makes it spectacular. The allusion is performative. The strange snack bar seems to be Hanna's subjective hallucination until a woman appears and invites Hanna to her house in an eerie monotone; the surreal spectacle exhibits a Kafkaesque uncanniness. Furthermore, the high-rises and vacant fields also recall similarly desolate compositions in Orson Welles' Kafka adaptation, *Le Procès* (*The Trial*, 1962), which was filmed among socialist apartment blocks in Zagreb.

Fashion, according to Elizabeth Wilson, may be regarded as "one means by which the fragmentary self is glued together into the semblance of a unified identity."[49] This idea underpins Hanna's public transformations. *Die Unberührbare* devotes considerable attention to scenes in which the nervous, strung-out protagonist reappears newly dressed and made-up, with her wig once again on her head and a fresh cigarette in her hand. Hanna's performance is a temporal make-over that seeks to reclaim her success of the 1960s by perpetually refashioning herself in her former image. At one point, Hanna admits to Bruno that it is only because she has been wearing "the same make-up for 30 years" that she can be distinguished. This idea informs another fashionable intertext. At his apartment Bruno and Hanna dance wildly to the song "Devil in Disguise." Sartorial deception and masquerade serve as metaphors for Hanna's anachronistic ideology: it is a routine, dogmatic security that she clings to even after it is long out of style. In attempting to retain her past appearance, she tries to elude the effects of time. Fittingly, the song is a bad cover version, a knock-off of a song that Elvis Presley made famous.

Press photos and publicity stills featured an iconic image: actress Hannelore Elsner as Hanna Flanders, adorned with a bushy black wig, heavy black eye shadow, an ostentatious coat, and a cigarette. Hanna's wig provides a special point of irritation throughout the film. She fiddles with it and informs the gigolo she sleeps with that her hair is fake. The wig calls attention to itself above all in the scene at Bruno's apartment. Bruno chides her for wearing "that silly thing" and begs her to get rid of it: does she also have sex in the wig and would she perhaps take it off for Lenin? For Hanna, appearing without the wig is the "ultimate nakedness": "I look ugly without [the wig]. I look like the woman from *Naked Kiss*."

The dialogue refers to the notorious opening sequence of the Sam Fuller feature, where prostitute Kelly (Constance Towers) beats her drunken pimp, who cheated her out of seventy-five dollars. In the

Figure 5.6: Hanna traversing a muddy field in her wig and Dior coat à la Veronika Voss. Image courtesy of Distant Dreams Filmproduktion.

scuffle the pimp pulls off Kelly's wig to reveal her completely bald head; he had drugged her and shaved her head because she had incited his top six call girls to walk off the job. The subsequent credits sequence has Kelly looking directly into the camera as if it were a mirror, carefully re-applying the wig and tousling her fake hair.

The Naked Kiss (1964) is a curious reference. Like *Die Unberührbare*, Fuller's film is about how hard it is to maintain a disguise. Kelly retreats from the world of prostitution to Grantville, a small town where she works as a nurse in the hospital's orthopedics ward. A detective (and former client) threatens to blow her cover and destroy her new life. Her fiancé, industrialist-philanthropist and town namesake Grant, also has a secret: he is a pedophile. Even if Hanna wishes to avoid looking like "the woman from *Naked Kiss*" by donning the wig, she still fancies herself to be someone like Kelly: a woman who, misunderstood by a community, ends up in jail after she catches her future husband molesting a child and kills him. She is framed (in its meanings of "unfairly accused" and literally circumscribed in the mise en scène within bars) by men and an intolerant society.

The Naked Kiss is a key example in Rabinowitz's argument about noir and material culture; she examines Kelly's shoes and leather handbag as symbolic objects.[50] In the opening scene Kelly beats her pimp with her black patent leather purse, standing over him in her stilettos. She does the same thing to the local madam and eventually to Grant (using a Bakelite telephone receiver). Transforming her "work" uniform (prostitute's heels) into a weapon against her exploiters, according to Rabinowitz's reading, Kelly is able to put fashion and household objects to extraordinary use despite countervailing social forces.[51]

The clear difference between the stories lies in their endings. Although Kelly is vindicated, in a vivid tableau she is dramatically confronted by the townspeople's stares. She skips town, presumably to start afresh once again. The anonymous geographical quality of Fuller's film allows this. "Grantville" is purposely constructed as Anywhere, USA. In *Die Unberührbare*, even though Ronald encourages Hanna to leave town and start anew, in the end there is nowhere left for her to go. Hanna does not suffer from the life-threatening problems that befall Kelly. Her imprisonment and persecution is imaginary, or at best metaphorical. The difference is marked sartorially: when Kelly's pimp rips off her wig, her head is revealed as bald; under Hanna's wig is a full head of hair. While Kelly has suffered the loss of something real (her hair), Hanna laments the loss of something imagined: her utopian projection of the GDR and her previous celebrity and sense of importance.

Like the wig, Hanna's coat remains conspicuous throughout the film. After her initial desperate phone call to Ronald, Hanna calls her publisher and tells him, "I don't know my way around here anymore." The film then cuts to Munich's most fashionable shopping district.

Hanna buys the flamboyant coat from the house of Dior directly before her tour of East Germany, where the couturier design immediately stands out among GDR burghers still clad in drab and ill-fitting socialist ware. Upon her desperate final return to Munich, she uses the coat as a makeshift blanket when she sleeps on the floor of her barren apartment before attempting to return it for half-price. The Dior coat, in keeping with Stella Bruzzi's argument, is iconic: it represents a spectacular intervention that interferes with the scenes in which it appears, a couturier design that disrupts the narrative by creating an authorial statement by the designer for the viewer.[52] The retro black-and-white coat both mimics and stands out within Roehler's black-and-white aesthetic, which itself is an anachronism. And just as Hanna's purchase is conspicuous consumption in Thorstein Veblen's sense[53]—a visual reminder of her wealth, to be flaunted in the very space of poverty to which she will journey—the garment design is the viewer's aide-mémoire of *Die Sehnsucht der Veronika Voss* (*Veronika Voss*, 1982) and Fassbinder. It is a replica of the robe that Veronika Voss wears in her death scene at the end of that film.

There are many thematic parallels between *Die Unberührbare* and *Veronika Voss* as well as strong similarities between their respective protagonists. Drawing heavily on *Sunset Boulevard*, Fassbinder's film is set in Munich in the 1950s and illustrates the last days of a washed-up and drug-addled German actress with a high-contrast black-and-white noir aesthetic. The narrative follows the perspective of a sports reporter who becomes obsessed with the actress. He tries, in vain, to save Veronika from a doctor who profits from her addiction.

As compelling as these similarities are—and there are many more[54]—I would like to focus on the appearance of the robe in *Veronika Voss*. At the very end of the story Veronika goes into a tailspin. The doctor locks her in a room with a lethal amount of morphine. In the last few minutes of the film, the narrative unwinds into a dizzying flurry of disconnected scenes. Veronika sings her last performance with her old film friends and ex-husband amid long, drawn-out tracking shots: it is her "farewell party." Fassbinder cuts between the party and Veronika waking up; the robe makes its first appearance on the end of her bed. As the compositions at the fest become increasingly stylized into tableaux and the acting stiffens, it is uncertain which scenes are flashbacks, which are "real," and which might be the hallucinations of a dying drug addict. In Veronika's locked room, deafening church bells drone over the radio sounds of a Latin mass and then Tennessee Ernie Ford's "16 Pounds." She dons the robe and looks into the mirror; realizing that the door is locked from the outside, she falls to the floor. Aware that there is no escape, she makes up her face and peacefully swallows the deadly final dose.

Die Unberührbare replays the closing scene from *Veronika Voss* with studious and conscious care. Wrapped in Veronika's death gown, Hanna's tour of Germany is a long "farewell party." Like the appropriation of Hanna's coat out of Veronika Voss' robe, Roehler fashions his film out of Fassbinder's excessive epilogue, out of its nightmare narrative logic and spatial entrapment. When Hanna buys the coat and the store clerk tells Hanna the coat "looks as though it was made for [her]," the sartorial merges with cinephilia. *Die Unberührbare* heralds the return of film history as clothing.

Up to this point I have outlined narrative, formal, and stylistic parallels contained in these sartorial intertexts. But it is curious to note whose works Roehler quotes. An archive of exile and homelessness begins to emerge in these figures. Citing Billy Wilder implicates his exile story and the exodus of other German-speaking Jews who left Europe and revitalized Hollywood. Fassbinder, controversial in Germany even as he was hailed as a genius by French and Anglo-American film critics, had a remarkably difficult relationship with his homeland: he once famously claimed he would rather be a streetsweeper in Mexico than a director in Germany.[55] Sam Fuller was forced for financial reasons to live for twenty years in France, where he was praised as the greatest living American director in *Cahiers du Cinéma*, at the same time that he could not get a job directing a B-movie in Hollywood.[56] Orson Welles was driven from the United States and made to wander around Europe from project to project.[57] A "German" writer in Prague, Kafka was a dislocated foreigner in his own land.[58] The pattern should be familiar to any viewer of *Die Unberührbare*, the story of a woman from West Germany who can find no publisher in her homeland, even while she was a celebrity in the GDR.

Moreover, the references to Billy Wilder, Orson Welles, and Sam Fuller are allusions to noir directors *par excellance*.[59] There has been much written on how film noir, both in its narratives and as a function of works made by displaced people, is a form of filmmaking inextricably connected to discourses of exile, homelessness, displacement, and dislocation. Some commentators have attempted to locate its origins in Weimar expressionism; since many German-speaking émigrés such as Robert Siodmak, Fritz Lang, and Peter Lorre were key players in noir classics, and because noir is associated with the stories of seedy immorality, canted angles, high-key lighting, and shadowy aesthetic also typical of some prominent 1920s productions, these interlocutors see the cycle as the continuation of "German" style within Hollywood narratives. Paul Schrader's influential "Notes on Film Noir," which sees film noir as a marriage of 1930s Warner Bros. gangster pictures, French poetic realism, and German expressionism has been paradigmatic for many later commentators.[60] In this vein, Barbara Steinbauer-Grötsch has compared the common aesthetic emphases and iconographical motifs between the two cycles, and reads film noir as an allegory of the "nightmare" of emigration and exile.[61] This line of argument has often implied that Hollywood noir is a German cinema in exile or an indication of what 1930s and 1940s domestic production might have been, had Hitler not come to power; the obsessive attention to discourses of the pre-World War II diaspora of German and Austrian directors in the German-language secondary literature on the noir is symptomatic. An article by Christian Cargnelli that points to how emigrants like Peter Lorre thematized their own exile status in the narratives of their noirs is exemplary of the nostalgic, "German-ed" perspective on the noir in some German-language scholarship.[62]

The characterization of noir as "German expressionism in Hollywood" has been challenged by Thomas Elsaesser, who argues that the simplified historical trajectory, of Berlin to Hollywood, conflates two traditions of filmmaking that are themselves partly imaginary and reduces noir scholarship to little more than tracing iconographic echoes and filmmakers' itinerant biographies.[63] Gerd Gemünden and Anton Kaes have questioned the "nightmare" model of accounting for the Weimar-era exodus to Hollywood. Moving away from a purely biographical focus to a more "dynamic scenario of intercultural tension and negotiation," they propose to explore exile as a "productive encounter and active engagement with a new culture" and as an opportunity for "self-examination and social critique."[64] Disputing the history that noir style was imported by visionary Germans, Marc Vernet has shown how the stylistic techniques and narrative conventions associated with the cycle are to be found in American films well before the émigrés arrived.[65]

Real or imaginary, however, the stubborn belief that there is a connection between German cinema and noir, a critically constructed special relationship, makes it a potent trope with retrospective value. Tim Bergfelder has demonstrated the influence of American noir on postwar German film culture, pointing to how "classical noir tropes featured and were reinterpreted in German productions of the 1940s and 1950s" and identifying German productions that "performed a similar *function* to that which classical noir offered its American audiences."[66] Seen through Dimendberg's critical discourses on noir, the "rubble film" *Die Mörder sind unter uns* (*The Murderers Are Among Us*, 1946) can be productively seen as negotiating topographical and gender anxieties of postwar West Germany; referring to productions such as *Das Mädchen Rosemarie* (*The Girl Rosemarie*, 1958) and *Der Rest ist Schweigen* (*The Rest Is Silence*, 1959), Bergfelder notes how postwar features sometimes "employed a noir visual style to represent new urban developments and interior design as metaphors for the shallowness of West Germany's economic miracle and its attendant consumerist ethics."[67] Bergfelder moves beyond the usual Berlin to

Hollywood teleology and points usefully to the bilateral itineraries of noir filmmakers, coining the term "noir trajectory" to refer to the fate of many German filmmakers who went into foreign exile and returned home in the attempt to continue their careers, only to find themselves lost in "detours and dead ends."[68]

Die Unberührbare can be positioned in a longer genealogy of postwar German noir and not merely because of its aesthetic or because of its negotiation of historically specific spatial instability. It alludes to particular films and filmmakers whose work and lives are intimately linked to discourses of exile, dislocation, and noir itself. This strategy recalls the appropriations of noir in postwar German art cinema. Writing about the role of noir in the New German Cinema, Paul Cooke has suggested that *Veronika Voss*, for example, uses the template of Wilder's *Sunset Boulevard* in order to deal with National Socialism.[69] By evoking Wilder and his émigré story, Fassbinder "produces an emotional connection to this forbidden period in the spectator, reinstating it into the historical consciousness of his generation."[70]

The films of Wim Wenders, in particular *Der amerikanische Freund* (*The American Friend*, 1977) and *Hammett* (1982), also self-reflexively meditate on film history via noir. The former, a loose adaptation of Patricia Highsmith's novel *Ripley's Game*, features Bruno Ganz as Jonathan Zimmerman, a frame maker who learns he may have a terminal illness and, in a bargain to receive potentially life-saving treatment, becomes embroiled in the criminal activities of the American gangster Ripley (played by Dennis Hopper). In Cooke's reading, the film's appropriation of noir is, like in the Fassbinder example, meant to comment on the function of America and American culture in Europe.[71] It sets up an initial opposition between the authentic European and the inauthentic American, only to blur these boundaries; ultimately, the production conveys a "tension between the repulsion and attraction towards Hollywood."[72] In this vein, *Die Unberührbare*'s intertextuality parallels Wim Wenders' European (neo-)noir about displacement and homelessness; in *Der amerikanische Freund*, noir idols Sam Fuller and Nicholas Ray appear as actors. Like in the above examples, noir functions as a sensibility that allows access to a displaced history and film history via the shorthand of material culture. Read through its costume, *Die Unberührbare* proves *unheimlich*; uncanny and "unhomely," it rewrites a history of personal loss and public transformation with the materiality of film history.

Ostalgie Re-dressed

Hanna's coat and wig exceed the demands of realism and narrative comprehensibility, and explicitly link the film to resonant historical discourses. This serious treatment of material culture contrasts with another contemporaneous cycle of films looking back to the Eastern past, namely the *Ostalgie* film.

David Bathrick has argued that the GDR's ideology of progress was based on a critique of modernity in both its avant-garde and mass cultural forms, the only alternative to which was a rejuvenated national culture.[73] And yet during the lifespan of the GDR, the national culture project was always undermined by the vision of Western mass culture and consumerism. Curiously then, it is the surface signs and symptoms of the GDR's national culture that *Ostalgie* most fondly recalls: the uniforms, the circumscribed choices for consumption, the stars of thinly veiled propaganda films. One is reminded of Henri Lefebvre's observation that countries undergoing rapid development destroy spaces. It is only toward the end of this period of accelerated growth that they discover how such spaces might be pressed into the service of cultural consumption and "what had been annihilated in the earlier frenzy of growth now becomes an object of adoration."[74] Lefebvre's statements were often borne out around the turn of the millennium in Germany, when the hangover of unification was producing peculiarly twisted retrospections.

In *Ostalgie* films such as *Sonnenallee* (1999) or *Good Bye, Lenin!* (2003), as we have seen in the preceding chapter, surface manifestations are normalized. They are used as props for comic relief and to establish a sense of cultural authenticity, but are then immediately forgotten. In contrast, the coat, the wig, and the sartorial in general in *Die Unberührbare* are always foregrounded. Visually, they appear ridiculous, campy, and ostentatious. They are also somewhat contradictory in that they connect Hanna to a rebellious, Cassandra-like figure (Kelly from *Naked Kiss*) and to a delusional conformist (Veronika Voss). Indeed, they are "spectacular interventions," particularly for the cineliterate viewer who can read the film history inscribed into them.

Die Unberührbare's sartorial intertext corresponds to its representation of space. Its meaning derives from the creative appropriation of void, similar to the scenes of Berlin's northeastern suburbs. By locating serious intertextual references and grappling with film history in the very sites where *Ostalgie* films fetishize and indulge in pastiche, *Die Unberührbare* recuperates sartorial and material culture, and gestures toward Henri Lefebvre's more synthetic approach. Lefebvre's theory not only analyzes the tyrannies that have been imposed on "everyday life," but also recognizes sustenance, clothing, furniture, homes, neighborhoods, and environments as arenas of freedom, creativity, and, potentially, social critique.[75]

Lefebvre's attitude toward the quotidian develops out of a critique of the foundations of Western philosophy, which, since its Greek origins, has posited a number of human activities deemed to be worthwhile— art, theology, the imaginary, the pursuit of truth, philosophy itself—at the expense of all others. This binary, according to Lefebvre, has meant that the everyday has always been defined negatively: that which displaces or prevents higher thinking, spirituality, and all other kinds of transcendence.[76] The pessimistic attitude toward the everyday has meant that it has been overlooked as an avenue of intellectual inquiry; paradoxically, the "concept of everydayness reveal[s] the extraordinary in the ordinary."[77]

Beyond this general recuperation of material culture, Lefebvre is concerned with the "triumph of homogeneity" in city planning;[78] referring to the architectural theories that envisioned the high-rise blocks in Marzahn and Hohenschönhausen, Lefebvre writes that in spite of some good intentions, modernist city planning reduces the everyday to a "chemically pure state" which isolates and dissociates bodies and spirits, and destroys their "basic spontaneity."[79] Indeed, ideological interests—including both free-market capitalism and real-existing socialism—have exploited the realm of material culture; the planning of urban space is increasingly the object of political struggle. Central to this struggle is the issue of the center and periphery; Lefebvre criticizes the centrifugal displacement of living space to the periphery and the concomitant centralization of commercial consumption.[80]

Nevertheless, material culture remains a fundamental locus of revolutionary potential;[81] this is the essential link to history and historical analysis. Although the everyday is associated with repetition, mass production, and boredom, it contains the potential for the transformation of the modern world: "everyday life emerges as a critique, a critique of the superior activities in question and what they produce: *ideologies*."[82] In other words: precisely because of material culture's marginalization at the expense of belief systems and ideologies, it becomes an ideal vehicle with which to overturn them. Lefebvre is not advocating a celebration of the quotidian nor the perpetuation of the binary that defines it; nevertheless, "the true critique of everyday life" must entail "a *rehabilitation of everyday life*."[83]

Die Unberührbare's synthetic appropriation of urban space and material culture contributes to a complex intervention into the historiography of unification. In *Good Bye, Lenin!*, the victims of unification, such as the unemployed neighbor Ganske and the former school director Klapprath, are sent up as drunks and eccentrics. They are minor, undynamic characters without avenues for identification; their social problems provide opportunities for laughter and situation comedy, rather than ideas for reflection. Roehler's film also features a character whose addictions and psychological maladies can be attributed partly to the trauma of impending unification; its sympathy with her dilemma is ambivalent at best. Even though it suggests that Hanna's reaction to unification is exaggerated and hypocritical, however, it entertains alternative subject positions as serious possibilities. Rather than *Good*

Bye, Lenin!'s retrospective coming-of-age story, by which unification was always inevitable, *Die Unberührbare* acknowledges the larger and more complex discourses from 1989 and 1990, and registers the nervousness with which many West German intellectuals responded to the fall of the wall. In those days, some commentators spoke out passionately on the subject. Günter Grass pleaded in the *New York Times* against unification and for a type of confederation that would allow the GDR to pursue a "third way" socialism; Jürgen Habermas ridiculed the idea of a nation that would unite behind the D-Mark.[84] However, there were many, particularly those on the left, who remained reticent about the implosion of the GDR. Commenting in *Die Zeit*, the author Friedrich Christian Delius argued that Western leftists should overcome their trauma at the loss of real-existing socialism and instead embrace current events as a "liberation"; "Relieved of the pressure of the reality of a fraudulent socialism … The end of having their minds made up for them, of false authorities and fronts, the demystification of concepts, what an opportunity!"[85] Conservative publisher Joachim Fest interpreted leftists' confusion as a sign of an inability to face reality, since "most of them reserved their enthusiasm for imaginary paradises, untouched by the misery of the people next door."[86]

Regardless of whether Fest's comments about all progressive West German intellectuals are exaggerated, they certainly speak to the case of Hanna (as well as her model, Gisela Elsner). Based on absolute oppositions of communism and capitalism and the two German states, the critical position from which many West German leftist intellectuals had spoken suddenly vanished, to be replaced by "manic denial" and "melancholia."[87] In an interview with a reporter directly after she has purchased the Dior coat, Hanna claims she wants "truth" as opposed to consumerism. Hanna scathingly attacks the East Germans pouring over the borders and into West German department stores and shopping malls:

> It makes me sick to see these "unity" people. It nauseates me how they rummage through the underwear, how they grab. Now, suddenly, I see the depressing reality, that they're fighting for Mon Chéri cherry pralines. And so they can stuff Western tampons, Coca-Cola bottles, and bananas into their cunts. They're not fighting for truth the way Lenin meant.

The speaking position on offer in *Die Unberührbare* dismantles the rigid binary between "truth" and material culture. It suggests that Hanna's loss is imaginary; after all, Hanna experiences a special form of *Ostalgie*: she wishes for the continued existence of the GDR precisely because she never knew it as a real space. Nevertheless, it clearly depicts the existential effects of even imaginary losses. Even with a hint of irony, the chronicle of one misguided writer's demise gives serious voice to a spectrum of more utopian versions of history.[88]

As such, *Die Unberührbare* speaks from a critical perspective between the fronts of Kohl and Fest on the one side and, on the other side, the dogmatic leftists who collapsed under a lazy delusion of utopian socialism. In this context it is useful to consider how this middle path might resound with the insights of Andreas Huyssen, who in his intervention into the debate of German nationhood argued that "both the new nationalists and the antinationalists are heavily mortgaged to the politics of the past."[89] The former "reproduce delusions of national grandeur—Germany as the central European power in Bismarckian terms or worse"; the latter "remain tied nostalgically" to the "postfascist exceptionalism of the old Federal republic, thus representing what George Orwell in 1945 called 'negative nationalism.'"[90]

Die Unberührbare's re-appropriation of the material, its refusal to subscribe to the classic opposition between "truth" and the everyday, criticizes the circumscribed political positioning that Hanna represents but also complicates the reactionary nostalgia typical of *Das Wunder von Bern* (*The Miracle of Bern*, 2003) and, to a large extent, *Good Bye, Lenin!* It attempts to create an alternative vision—and feel—of history. Coming to terms with twentieth-century German history, according to Roehler, need "not be left up to the Schlöndorffs and the other politically correct."[91] By introducing a critical path between Hanna's dogmatic entrapment and the commodity fetishism of German–German history in the *Ostalgie* films, *Die Unberührbare* provides one possible place for postwall German historical cinema to go.

Notes

1. See Lutz Koepnick, "Reframing the Past: Heritage Cinema and Holocaust in the 1990s," *New German Critique* 87 (2002): 47–82; Katja Nicodemus, "Unsere kleine Traumfabrik," *Die Zeit*, 28 August 2003; Cristina Nord, "Die neue Naivität," *taz*, 20 October 2008; Jennifer M. Kapczynski, "Imitation of Life: The Aesthetics of Agfacolor in Recent Historical Cinema," in *The Collapse of the Conventional: German Film and Its Politics at the Turn of the Twenty-First Century*, eds. Jaimey Fisher and Brad Prager (Detroit: Wayne State University Press, 2010), 39–62.
2. See Matthias Altenburg, "Silvester Countdown – Der schönste Sexfilm aller Zeiten," in *Szenenwechsel: Momentaufnahmen des jungen deutschen Films*, ed. Michael Töteberg (Reinbek bei Hamburg: Rowohlt, 1999), 140–44; Marco Abel, "Failing to Connect: Itineraries of Desire in Oskar Roehler's Postromance Films," *New German Critique* 109 (2010): 75–98.
3. Abel, "Failing to Connect," 77.
4. Abel, "Failing to Connect," 79.
5. Aleida Assmann, *Geschichte im Gedächtnis: Von der individuellen Erfahrung zur öffentlichen Inszenierung* (Munich: Beck, 2007), 63.
6. Assmann, *Geschichte im Gedächtnis*, 64.
7. Abel, "Failing to Connect," 79.
8. Abel, "Failing to Connect," 79.

9. See for example, Tobias Kniebe, "Erfolgsgetrieben und naiv," *Süddeutsche Zeitung* http://www.sueddeutsche.de/kultur/jud-suess-film-ohne-gewissen-erfolgsgetrieben-und-naiv-1.168161.
10. For more on Gisela Elsner and Klaus Roehler's celebrity and Oskar Roehler's tragicomic coming-of-age, see Rebecca Casati, "Oskar Roehler über Familie," *Süddeutsche Zeitung*, 17–18 January 2009.
11. Quoted in Tilman Krause, "Geschichte ist die einzige Quelle," *Die Welt*, 6 May 2000.
12. See her obituary: "Gisela Elsner," *Der Spiegel*, 25 May 1992, 248.
13. "Schriftstellerleben verramscht," *Der Spiegel*, 15 June 1992, 216.
14. Quoted in her obituary, "Gisela Elsner," *Der Spiegel*, 25 May 1992, 248
15. Johannes von Moltke, "*Terrains Vagues*: Landscapes of Unification in Oskar Roehler's *No Place to Go*," in *The Collapse of the Conventional: German Film and Its Politics at the Turn of the Twenty-First Century*, eds. Jaimey Fisher and Brad Prager (Detroit: Wayne State University Press, 2010), 157–85; here 163.
16. Thomas Elsaesser, "The New German Cinema's Historical Imaginary," in *Framing the Past: The Historiography of German Cinema and Television*, eds. Bruce A. Murray and Christopher J. Wickham (Carbondale: Southern Illinois University Press, 1992), 303. See also Thomas Elsaesser, *New German Cinema: A History*, 151ff.
17. von Moltke, "*Terrains Vagues*," 164.
18. Elsaesser, "The New German Cinema's Historical Imaginary," 287–88.
19. James Naremore, *More than Night: Film Noir in its Contexts* (Berkeley: University of California Press, 1998), 104.
20. Edward Dimendberg, *Film Noir and the Spaces of Modernity* (Cambridge, MA: Harvard University Press, 2004).
21. Dimendberg, *Film Noir and the Spaces of Modernity*, 1.
22. Dimendberg, *Film Noir and the Spaces of Modernity*, 136ff.
23. See Paul Coates, *The Gorgon's Gaze* (Cambridge: Cambridge University Press, 1991), 173–76.
24. Foster Hirsch, *Detours and Lost Highways: A Map of the Neo-Noir* (New York: Limelight, 1999), 101. Reviews and articles on the film typically fill in narrative gaps with extratextual biographical details. The film's darkness and utter lack of narrative transparency led to much confusion and annoyance in the popular reception of the film. Some Anglo-American critics complained that the film was "too German": "Whilst *Die Unberuehrbare* [sic] has received the greatest plaudits, quite frankly it would have been better as a twenty-minute short. It is what people expect of German film: black and white, slow, lacking in plot and depressing: all of which are to my mind old-fashioned and predictable—yet another film about a disorientated, boozy, old writer, who has lost her ideology and her publishing deal." See Elke de Wit, "Panel Games: *Neue deutsche Filme* at the Berlin Film Festival," *Central European Review* 3(10) (2001), http://www.ce-review.org/01/10/kinoeye10_dewit.html.
25. Dimendberg, *Film Noir and the Spaces of Modernity*, 175–76.
26. Dimendberg, *Film Noir and the Spaces of Modernity*, 176, 105.
27. Dimendberg, *Film Noir and the Spaces of Modernity*, 126.
28. Georg Simmel, "Bridge and Door," trans. Mark Ritter, *Theory, Culture and Society* 11 (1994): 5–10.
29. Dimendberg, *Film Noir and the Spaces of Modernity*, 178.
30. In Kubrick's film, Vinnie watches the television broadcast of the boxing match rather than actually attending it (Dimendberg, *Film Noir and the Spaces of Modernity*, 139).
31. Anton Kaes discusses the role of radio in *Die Ehe der Maria Braun* (*The Marriage of Maria Braun*, 1979) in *From Hitler to Heimat: The Return of History as Film* (Cambridge, MA: Harvard University Press, 1989). See also my discussion in Chapter 3.
32. Oskar Roehler, "Schöne Seelen," *Die Zeit*, 2 June 2005.
33. Paul Virilio, "The Overexposed City," in *Lost Dimension*, trans. Daniel Moshenberg (New York: Semiotext(e), 1991), 9–27.

34. Dimendberg, *Film Noir and the Spaces of Modernity*, 109.
35. See *Einfach schwierig: eine deutsche Architekturdebatte*, ed. Gert Kähler (Braunschweig: Vieweg, 1995).
36. Svetlana Boym, *The Future of Nostalgia* (New York: Basic Books, 2001), 80.
37. See Kenny Cupers and Markus Miessen, *Spaces of Uncertainty* (Wuppertal: Müller + Busmann, 2002); Gerwin Zohlen, *Auf der Suche nach der verlorenen Stadt: Berliner Architektur am Ende des 20. Jahrhunderts* (Berlin: Nicolai, 2002); Ian Buruma, "Die kapitale Schnauze: Berlin – Selbstzerstörung und wiederkehrende Selbsterzeugung," *Lettre International* 43 (1998): 36–39; Dieter Hoffmann-Axthelm, "An Extreme Case of European Urban Crisis," *Lotus* 80 (1994): 37–49; Rem Koolhaas, "Massakrierte Ideen," *Frankfurter Allgemeine Zeitung*, 16 October 1991; Daniel Libeskind, *Kein Ort an dieser Stelle – Schriften zur Architektur, Visionen für Berlin, Dresden und Basel* (Dresden: Verlag der Kunst, 1995); Philipp Oswalt, *Berlin: Stadt ohne Form* (Munich: Prestel, 2000); Uwe Rada, *Hauptstadt der Verdrängung – Berliner Zukunft zwischen Kiez und Metropole* (Berlin: Schwarze Risse, 1997); Richard Shusterman, "Ästhetik der Abwesenheit: Der Wert der Leere, Pragmatische Überlegungen zu Berlin," *Lettre International* 43 (1998): 30–35.
38. Dorothée Kohler and Boris Grésillon, "Berlin aus französicher Sicht," in *Architektur in Berlin: Jahrbuch 1999*, ed. Architektenkammer Berlin (Hamburg: Junius, 1999), 10.
39. Dimendberg, *Film Noir and the Spaces of Modernity*, 129 and 121.
40. Kelly Oliver and Benigno Trigo, *Noir Anxiety* (Minneapolis: University of Minnesota Press, 2003), 229.
41. Julia Kristeva, *Powers of Horror*, trans. Leon Roudiez (New York: Columbia University Press, 1982), 48–49.
42. Michel de Certeau, *The Practice of Everyday Life*, trans. Steven Rendall (Berkeley: University of California Press, 1984), 112–15.
43. See Ignasi Solà-Morales Rubió, "Terrain Vague," in *Anyplace*, ed. Cynthia Davidson (New York: Anyone, 1995), 118–23. Although Solà-Morales Rubió specifically mentions "post-Stalinist" Alexanderplatz as an example of the *terrain vague* (123), he is also insistent that these spaces are not purely negative, in contrast to the futureless spaces Roehler captures: "Void, absence, yet also promise, the space of the possible, of expectation" (120). See also Marc Augé, *Non-Places: Introduction to an Anthropology of Supermodernity*, trans. John Howe (London: Verso, 1995).
44. Sabine Hake, *German National Cinema*, 2nd rev. ed. (London: Routledge, 2008), 149.
45. See Günter Peters, "Zur Baugeschichte – Drei Gründerzeiten," and Wolfgang Kil, "Dilemma der Moderne, aufgestoßene Tür," in *Marzahn*, ed. Gerrit Engel (Cologne: König, 1999), 15–17 and 21–22, respectively.
46. Berlin mayor Klaus Wowereit introduced numerous policies to try to revive the now struggling "City-West" neighborhood around the Zoo station. A sign of the times, Parker Brothers announced on 16 October 2006 that in that year's "Monopoly Heute 2006" the Bahnhof Zoo would no longer appear on the game board.
47. See Paula Rabinowitz, *Black & White & Noir: America's Pulp Modernism* (New York: Columbia University Press, 2002). Further references to this work in this paragraph are cited in the text.
48. Franz Kafka, *Sämtliche Erzählungen* (Frankfurt: Fischer, 1987), 197–232.
49. Elizabeth Wilson, *Adorned in Dreams: Fashion and Modernity* (London: Virago, 1985), 12.
50. Rabinowitz, *Black & White & Noir*, 175.
51. Rabinowitz, *Black & White & Noir*, 192.
52. Stella Bruzzi, *Undressing Cinema: Clothing and Identity in the Movies* (London: Routledge, 1997), xv.
53. Thorstein Veblen, *The Theory of the Leisure Class: An Economic Study of Institutions* (New York: Mentor, 1899).

54. Paul Cooke outlines many of these in his article "Whatever Happened to Veronika Voss? Rehabilitating the '68ers' and the Problem of *Westalgie* in Oskar Roehler's *Die Unberührbare* (2000)," *German Studies Review* 27(1) (2004): 33–43.

55. Rainer Werner Fassbinder, "I'd Rather Be a Streetsweeper in Mexico than a Filmmaker in Germany," in *The Anarchy of the Imagination: Interviews, Essays, Notes*, ed. Michael Töteberg and Leo A. Lensing, trans. Krishna Winston (Baltimore: Johns Hopkins University Press, 1992), 139–43.

56. See Lisa Dombrowski, *The Films of Sam Fuller: If You Die, I'll Kill You!* (Middletown, CT: Wesleyan University Press, 2008), esp. 196.

57. See Bert Rebhandl, *Orson Welles: Genie im Labyrinth* (Vienna: Zsolnay, 2005).

58. See Gilles Deleuze and Félix Guattari, *Kafka: Toward a Minor Literature*, trans. Dana Polan (Minneapolis: University of Minnesota Press, 1986).

59. For more on Wilder, exile, and noir, see Gerd Gemünden, *A Foreign Affair: Billy Wilder's American Films* (New York: Berghahn, 2008).

60. Paul Schrader, "Notes on Film Noir," in *The Film Noir Reader*, eds. Alain Silver and James Ursini (Pompton Plains, NJ: Limelight, 1996), 53–63. Despite later appropriations of his essay, Schrader does warn of the risk of "over-emphasizing the German influence in Hollywood" (55).

61. Barbara Steinbauer-Grötsch, *Die lange Nacht der Schatten: Film noir und Filmexil* (Berlin: Bertz, 1997).

62. See Christian Cargnelli, "New York is not Sopron. Exilantenschicksale im Film noir," in *Schatten. Exil. Europäische Emigranten im Film noir*, eds. Christian Cargnelli and Michael Omasta (Vienna: PVS, 1997), 55–87.

63. See Thomas Elsaesser, "A German Ancestry to Film Noir?," *Iris* 21 (1996): 129–44; Thomas Elsaesser, *Weimar Cinema and After: Germany's Historical Imaginary* (London: Routledge, 2000), 420–43.

64. See Gerd Gemünden and Anton Kaes, "Introduction," *New German Critique* 89 (2003): 3–8; here 1–2. See also Gemünden, *A Foreign Affair*).

65. Marc Vernet, "Film Noir on the Edge of Doom," in *Shades of Noir*, ed. Joan Copjec (London: Verso, 1993), 1–31. Lutz Koepnick also criticizes the easy linking of German expressionism and Hollywood noir in his *The Dark Mirror: German Cinema between Hitler and Hollywood* (Berkeley: University of California Press, 2002), 164–200.

66. Tim Bergfelder, "German Cinema and Film Noir," in *European Film Noir*, ed. Andrew Spicer (Manchester: Manchester University Press, 2007), 138–63; here 140–41.

67. Bergfelder, "German Cinema and Film Noir," 155.

68. Bergfelder, "German Cinema and Film Noir," 156.

69. Paul Cooke, "German Neo-Noir," in *European Film Noir*, ed. Andrew Spicer (Manchester: Manchester University Press, 2007), 164–84; here 169–70.

70. Cooke, "German Neo-Noir," 170.

71. Cooke, "German Neo-Noir," 170–71.

72. Cooke, "German Neo-Noir," 171.

73. David Bathrick, *The Powers of Speech: The Politics of Culture in the GDR* (Lincoln: University of Nebraska Press, 1995).

74. See Henri Lefebvre, *The Production of Space*, trans. Donald Nicholson-Smith (Oxford: Blackwell, 1991), 360–63.

75. See Henri Lefebvre, *Everyday Life in the Modern World*, trans. Sacha Rabinovitch (New Brunswick: Transaction, 1984), esp. 21.

76. Henri Lefebvre, *Critique of Everyday Life*, vol. I, trans. John Moore (London: Verso, 1991), 86.

77. Henri Lefebvre, "The Everyday and Everydayness," trans. Christine Levich, *Yale French Studies* 73 (1987): 7–11; here 9.

78. Lefebvre, *The Production of Space*, 337.

79. Henri Lefebvre, *Critique of Everyday Life*, vol. II, trans. John Moore (London: Verso, 2002), 78.
80. Henri Lefebvre, *Writings on Cities*, trans. and ed. Eleonore Kofman and Elizabeth Lebas (Oxford: Blackwell, 1996), 169.
81. Lefebvre, *Everyday Life in the Modern World*, 73.
82. Lefebvre, *Critique of Everyday Life*, vol. I, 87.
83. Henri Lefebvre, *Critique of Everyday Life*, vol. I, 127. Emphasis in original.
84. Günter Grass, "Don't Reunify Germany," in *When the Wall Came Down: Reactions to German Unification*, eds. Harold James and Marla Stone (New York: Routledge, 1992), 57–59; Jürgen Habermas, "Yet Again: German Identity—A Unified Nation of Angry DM-Burghers?," in *When the Wall Came Down*, eds. Harold James and Marla Stone (New York: Routledge, 1992), 86–102.
85. Friedrich Christian Delius, "The West Is Getting Wilder. Intellectuals and the German Question: The Claims are Being Staked Out," in *When the Wall Came Down*, eds. Harold James and Marla Stone (New York: Routledge, 1992), 71–76; here 75.
86. Joachim Fest, "The Silence of the Clerks," in *When the Wall Came Down*, eds. Harold James and Marla Stone (New York: Routledge, 1992), 52–56; here 53.
87. Helmut Dubiel, "Linke Trauerarbeit," *Merkur* 496 (1990): 482–91.
88. In interviews, for instance on the e-m-s DVD, Roehler said he hoped the irony of his approach to Hanna's lost utopia is apparent to spectators.
89. Andreas Huyssen, "Nation, Race, and Immigration: German Identities after Unification," in *The Power of Intellectuals in Contemporary German*, ed. Michael Geyer (Chicago: University of Chicago Press, 2001), 317.
90. Huyssen, "Nation, Race, and Immigration," 317.
91. Quoted in Tilman Krause, "Geschichte ist die einzige Quelle," *Die Welt*, 6 May 2000.

Chapter 6

THE FUTURE OF THE GERMAN PAST

Jaimey Fisher and Brad Prager, the editors of the collection *The Collapse of the Conventional: German Film and Its Politics at the Turn of the Twenty-First Century*, note how "German cinema at the turn of the century can best be approached as a politically charged polyvocal arena."[1] Although they acknowledge their own "nostalgia for the political cinema of the late 1960s and the 1970s" and conceive of the collected essays as being concerned primarily with "the films' politics—their orientation toward Germany's divided past, their working out of wartime guilt, and their willingness to challenge audiences with formal innovation," the editors reject the tendency to erect binary, mutually exclusive categories.[2] They admit the convenience of dividing recent German productions into "bad ideological films and good cultural-critical films," and yet they conclude that "this dichotomy is as unsatisfying as it is false."[3] On this point I agree with Fisher and Prager. Rather than an "either/or" of history vs. "reality," contemporary German cinema accommodates a whole host of forms, styles, genres, and attitudes; the preceding case studies have demonstrated how recent historical films partake of complex constellations of history via film history.

There is little doubt that history will continue to constitute a major source for German films. Less clear is whether it might appear more in stylized visions of young artists or as lucrative exports of ambitious producers like Nico Hofmann or the late Bernd Eichinger.[4] By way of conclusion, I would like to return once again to the postwall historical cinema and review the ways in which its regard of the past differs from the historiographical attitudes of the acclaimed 1970s New German Cinema. In so doing, however, I also want to blur the stark boundaries that German film historians have often erected between the attitude toward history in the 1970s productions and those on offer in the postwall German historical cinema.

For the angry young men and women associated with the New German Cinema, the prospect was clear: the cinema of their fathers and grandfathers was illegitimate. The films emanating from Goebbels' Ministry of Propaganda constituted an illusionist fantasy that either extolled or veiled racism and militarism; the conformist Adenauer-era films represented a continuation of this strategy. In response, young directors offered an auteurist counter-cinema and experimented with personal and autobiographical subjects, narrative intransitivity, estrangement effects, aperture, and unpleasure. The New German Cinema's historical films, both provocative and outspoken, sought to unmask the continuities between the National Socialist state and the postwar regime. Their interpretation of national history underlined the support of a mass public for the Nazis, the lack of any serious resistance to fascism, and the longer traditions of German anti-Semitism: in sum, they espoused the critical historiography of a generation raised on tales of German suffering.[5]

Postwall historical films widen their focus beyond National Socialism and its continuities. Unification and its discontents, the value of the East German past, and the generation of 1968's legacy have emerged as significant preoccupations of cultural memory and national redefinition. Moreover, themes such as 1970s left-wing terrorism and the 1980s West German ecological movement have become historical arenas in which German films rehearse contemporary anxieties about Islamic violence or the threat of climate change. In these diversified historiographical approaches, the fronts have become vague and the speaking positions more intricate. The postwall historical cinema is, like the New German Cinema, a subset of German domestic output, but today's much larger national film industry is defined by genre, production, and exhibition, rather than determined by a political-, auteurist-, or criticism-led approach.[6] It defies the binaries so important to the identity of the New German Cinema and to the understanding of German national cinema as a whole hitherto, such as auteur vs. metteurenscène, or radical vs. conservative. Even those recent historical films that might be said to replicate conservative or reactionary speaking positions—for example, *Good Bye, Lenin!* (2003), *Das Wunder von Bern* (*The Miracle of Bern*, 2003), or *Der Untergang* (*Downfall*, 2004)—often encode their discourses in complex and reflexive forms. The epithets "whores in historicism's bordello" or "German Heritage Films" offer little help in comprehending the variety and sophistication of these productions.

Indeed, surveying the domestic landscape since 1999, the historiographic approaches of German films have become more varied. Generational conflict, perhaps the most ubiquitous theme of the New German Cinema, still prevails, but has become ambiguous and ambivalent in its postwall formulations. Looking at the films under closest scrutiny in this book—*Das Wunder von Bern, Baader* (2002), *23* (1999), *Good Bye, Lenin!*, and *Die Unberührbare* (*No Place to Go*, 2000)—is revealing. Four of the five consider the past in the figure of or through the perspective of a boy or young man. The films feature idealists and dreamers, characters who live out of step with their times and are disappointed with or deformed by the course of German history; Christiane Kerner in *Good Bye, Lenin!*, Hanna in *Die Unberührbare*, *Das Wunder von Bern*'s Richard Lubanski, and *Baader*'s Horst Herold struggle to meet the challenges of the present. Nevertheless, the respective films' attitudes toward the possibility of incorporating or reintegrating these anachronistic figures is hardly uniform. Much like Elena Gorfinkel's analysis of retro-sensibilities in *Boogie Nights* (1997) and *Far From Heaven* (2002), the German historical films under scrutiny "are *about* anachronism as much as they *use* it."[7] The postwall historical cinema similarly uses "allusion to bridge the gap between past and present through the act of reworking and restaging film history."[8]

Well-known Oedipal patterns still function in the postwall historical cinema, but with a twist: for instance, in *23*, in which Karl Koch fights in Brokdorf against "the crap of [his father's] generation," the 68ers, without necessarily sympathizing with the enemy (the Nazi generation) of this enemy. These dilemmas—unlike the elders' clearly defined friend-or-foe rhetoric—characterize the children of the New German Cinema's generation of "fatherless sons." The softer subjunctive of "I don't know what I would have done, were I alive back then" has replaced the 68ers' demand "What did you do between 1933 and 1945?" Perhaps the persistence of Oedipal patterns is unsurprising. After all, as Thomas Elsaesser argues, cinephilia functions on an "oedipal time," which he defines as "the kind of temporal succession that joins and separates paternity and generational repetition in difference."[9] One of "cinephilia's original charateristics" is "a gesture towards cinema framed by nostalgia and other retroactive temporalities."[10]

The new historical films arise in an era of new confidence in German national identity and history. The attitude toward the past in the Federal Republic, according to historian Nobert Frei, has changed from a "battle over memory" to a "culture of memory."[11] As the World War II generation fades away and its children and grandchildren have assumed charge of government, universities, schools, and the media, Frei argues, the politics of national history has become "chic."[12] A "normal patriotism" emerged during and following the 2006 soccer World Cup: suddenly, it has become much more acceptable for a German to hang the national flag without being considered to harbour neo-Nazi sentiments. These are characteristics of a nation whose citizens have now in the majority experienced the war not as a memory, but through the prisms of school lessons and TV-movies.

The postwall historical films are products of a new attitude toward national history in general and a confident domestic industry in specific. To be sure, the nation's broadsheets still perennially bemoan lackluster domestic market share and predict dire paths for the national cinema. These functional prescriptions notwithstanding, the belief that Germany should be producing a popular cinema—whether by itself or alongside aesthetically sophisticated filmmaking—has become more or less conventional wisdom. Changes in subsidy and tax laws, and the interventions of regional funding bodies such as the Medienboard Berlin-Brandenburg and the Filmstiftung NRW have allowed for bigger budgets in domestic pictures, ambitious international co-productions, and heavy German investment in Hollywood.[13] The German Film Prize, once adjudicated by a panel that included politicians and the clergy, now awards the "Lola" according to the votes of a German Film Academy along the lines of the American Academy of Motion Pictures Arts and Sciences. Moritz Bleibtreu, Daniel Brühl, Martina Gedeck, Nina Hoss, Diane Krüger, Alexandra Maria Lara, Matthias Schweighöfer: a star system has emerged in Germany, with recognizable faces transitioning from theater, television, domestic feature films, and international productions.[14] Under the leadership of Dieter Kosslick, the Berlin International Film Festival has solidified its reputation as part of the most important European festivals alongside Cannes and Venice, and introduced a new level of glamour in its selections. In the capital's Potsdamer Platz, the art-house Kino Arsenal, the library of the Deutsche Kinemathek, and a refurbished Filmmuseum, which includes a permanent exhibition on the history of the national cinema, preserve the national film legacy. The success of *Nirgendwo in Afrika* (*Nowhere in Africa*, 2001) and *Das Leben der Anderen* (*The Lives of Others*, 2006) at the Academy Awards and the almost annual short-listing of a German (historical) production for the Best Foreign Language Film category have further promoted the national cinema abroad.

Although the new prominence of German historical productions might be partly explained by a specific German desire for an emotional experience of the past or by a mass cultural phenomenon, these concepts are not sufficient. We must also attend to the real material changes in the production of films in Germany since the days of the New German Cinema. Those art films were shielded from much market pressure and owed their existence to governmental and quasi-governmental financing. The start-up capital from the Kuratorium Junger Deutscher Film launched the careers of Kluge and Herzog, among others; the Filmförderungsanstalt enabled the makers of certain productions (those deemed of "quality" by the federal censors) to be granted funding for their next project, even if these films attained a very modest gross. Directors received commissions from regional television stations, ad hoc partnerships that were formalized by the Television Framework Agreement from 1974. This funding structure was based on the official political position, espoused by the contemporary ruling coalitions, that cinema is a cultural form on par with opera, classical music, and the fine arts.[15]

Today, domestic producers face what commentators describe as the most elaborate funding system in Europe, or, simply, a "funding jungle."[16] The model—which relies increasingly on private investment, pre-selling broadcast and DVD rights, or monetary stimulus from film festivals—services a sector understood to be more of a commercial enterprise than primarily, (as perhaps was the case under the governments of Willy Brandt and Helmut Schmidt), as an expressive art. Federal and regional funding subsidies still do exist. In addition to the federal Filmförderungsanstalt, which continues to play a major role, local funding bodies—such as the Filmfernsehfonds Bayern, Filmförderung Hamburg, and Medienboard Berlin-Brandenburg— help to co-finance productions.

Nevertheless, even the "public" bodies have changed. The Filmförderungsanstalt has become more professionalized as an industrial, rather than cultural, force. The central committee's members from outside the industry (for example, representatives of the Catholic and Protestant Church) were removed in a 1999 reform. Artistic concerns that enabled producers of sophisticated, but poorly attended features to achieve funding have not been lost altogether, but the metrics used (festival invitations, award nominations) presuppose some level of commercial viability.[17] Furthermore, although the *Länder*-based organizations may have a stake in promoting film art, they certainly have other, competing interests. As registered limited-liability corporations, many include private television stations as minority partners. (For example, although Bavaria has a 51 percent stake in the Filmfernsehfonds Bayern, so do private channels RTL [4 percent] and Pro Sieben/SAT1 [6 percent].)[18] These boards, which often require a part of the film to be shot locally, instrumentalize their subsidies as a way to create jobs in depressed areas and to advertise for local tourism.

In the years 2004–2006, the average German film to appear in theaters was funded by the federal government (26 percent), one or more regional subsidy bodies (27 percent), and private capital (17 percent)—with the remaining portion supplied by television stations (public or private) or through the sale of distribution rights.[19] Of course, this assumes a production funded only by public institutions or private corporations domiciled in Germany, a scenario which has become an increasing rarity; co-productions, which rely also on foreign investments or EU support from programs such as MEDIA, continue to flourish. Alternative collective funding structures, such as New German Cinema-generation Filmverlag der Autoren are not unknown, but have become much more pragmatic. Examples include Stefan Arndt, Wolfgang Becker, Dani Levy, and Tom Tykwer, the founders of X-Films, which maintains intimate connections to Warner Bros.[20] As the Federal Republic's official position toward film has embraced entertainment, recent governments have provided tax incentives in order to stimulate investment in production. These regulations were so unique and generous that they produced unintended consequences.

Hollywood studios set up sham German ownership of ventures in order to reap, in the Tinseltown idiom, "stupid German money."[21]

In the context of these industrial realities, some unique to Germany and many others part of international trends, we need to be prepared to see the proliferation of German historical films not only as a reflection of some vague Zeitgeist. History—and uniquely and especially German history—sells. (Zombies, vampires, and Nazis, any commercial movie producer can testify, are sure-fire hits with mass audiences.)[22] Unlike comedies, German historical films fare well on the export market. In turn, further projects attract foreign investment, which thus allows for bigger budgets, longer shoots, better costumes, and more glamorous stars.[23] In a market analysis for SPIO (the umbrella lobby organization for the German motion picture industry), "Where Does the Material for the German Dream Factory Come From?," the historical film is revealed to be the domestic industry's most profitable genre between 1997 and 2006.[24] Even though the study's author uses a very restricted definition of the genre that includes only films based on "important historical events" or "historically relevant protagonists," and thus excludes hits such as *Sonnenallee, Good Bye, Lenin!*, and *Nirgendwo in Afrika*, the genre accounts for €17.6 million average revenue per film—by far outranking the next most profitable source material for films: TV show adaptations (€10.9 million) and comic book adaptations (€9.4 million).[25] Canny producers, directors, and screenwriters take up historical projects in order to profit from what industry insiders have referred to as the "Adolf-Bonus":[26] this is the advantage that German productions about national history enjoy with Academy voters, specifically, and in Hollywood and international markets, in general. A cynic might claim that the national past has become yet another product for Germany, one of the world's largest exporters, to sell.

Indeed, a savvy, professionalized, historically aware group of filmmakers is at work in the country. Some have received their training abroad or have been educated at an expanded array of domestic film schools. Along with the now venerable film academies of the first generation such as the dffb Berlin, the HFF Munich, and the HFF Konrad Wolf Potsdam-Babelsberg, a number of other institutions train industry practitioners, including the Hamburg Media School, the Internationale Filmschule (ifs) Cologne, the KHM Cologne, the HDM Stuttgart, and the Filmakademie Baden-Württemberg in Ludwigsburg. To be sure, this training concentrates more on business activity than was the case in the early graduating classes of Harun Farocki or Wim Wenders. It responds to the reality that a graduate today is more likely to produce a SAT1 made-for-TV movie, edit a commercial, or design the set of a music video, than have final cut on an art film. At the same time, these up-and-coming filmmakers—and the German populace in general—have a much easier access to film history. Since the mid-1990s, the increasing ubiquity of movies on cable television and the availability of restored films on video, DVD, and new media have made possible a more direct and encompassing confrontation with film history.[27] As Jenna Ng argues, the "unique thrust of contemporary cinephilia is its fluency of transcultural film literacy, one manifestation of which lies in today's plethora of cross-cultural filmic intertextuality, born from a diversity of film culture experiences afforded primarily by home video, cable networks and most recently the internet and DVD."[28] Although this is surely a global phenomenon (Amazon, Ebay, Netflix, Lovefilm, imdb. com, and so on), it is especially fostered by certain media conditions in the Federal Republic of Germany. Compared with Britain, Italy, Sweden, and other European countries, public television in Germany offers an exceptional program of both art films and international genre pictures. The federalistic partnership of ARD, ZDF, the German–Austrian–Swiss channel 3sat, the French–German cultural partnership arte, and the regional channels (WDR, BR, NDR, RBB, MDR, HR, and SWR), present the viewer with a rich array of older and more recent quality films. These offerings suggest a higher potential for cine-literacy among public-television viewers and the domestic industry.

Waves of Seeing

In a variety of generic and commercial forms, rather than exclusively in auteurist shapes, German cinema is assuming "ownership" for the past. This change in national film culture is being mourned, debated, criticized, and celebrated. The conventional way to account for the shift in cinematic retrospection between the heyday of Fassbinder, Syberberg, Sanders-Brahms, and Reitz to the years of Wortmann, Becker, Roehler, and Vilsmaier pits one epoch against another. Depending on tastes and politics, the commentators criticize the new productions as reactionary, naïve, and apolitical, or laud them as popular and successful. This has also been the traditional way to react to the proposition of Germany as a "normal" or "confident" nation: to take an ideologically charged position. The conservative camp cries "about time!," while leftist commentators speak of lost chances and a frightening return to nationalist sentiment. On the whole, where one stands on the new history wave reflects one's side in the cultural battle over 1968.[29]

It has been one task of this book to reveal why, although individual productions may deserve castigation or praise, blanket judgments ignore the new pluralization of memory that has developed, and simply reproduce the New German Cinema's historiographical paradigm. The films discussed in this study work alternately with, against, through, and/or across a variety of styles, genres, and traditions, employing a diversity of attitudes toward previous interpretations of the past. Germany's postwall historical cinema is above all a site of contestation and debate, where a multi-polar refashioning of national identity is taking place.

The assessment of recent German historical productions occasions a chance to reappraise the New German Cinema and its legacy. In what way, for example, did the New German Cinema's regard of the past actually signify a flight from history? Although the filmmakers may have been influenced in theory by pedagogical Brechtianism, one wonders what this distanciation achieved in the practice of consumption. Even ignoring the films' meager attendance figures, we might consider whether the aesthetic formalism produced an irreparable rift between the work and the spectator. Furthermore, there is an argument to be made that the rejection of the poisoned national film language and the deeds or non-resistance of the parents cast the postwar generation as victims without responsibility for their own actions. Imagining the Adenauer era as a laboratory of evil conveniently excused the young generation for any of its own faults. It behooves us to ask in which ways the New German Cinema actually anticipated the postwall historical films. Through media performances and provocative subject matter, Fassbinder and his contemporaries profited from foreign responses to the dark reaches of national history. Did their arthouse commodities not also exploit some kind of "Adolf-Bonus"? *Hitler – Ein Film aus Deutschland* (*Our Hitler*, 1977), *Deutschland, bleiche Mutter* (*Germany, Pale Mother*, 1980), *Heimat* (1984): the most celebrated examples of the late New German Cinema more than gesture toward the "reactionary" revisionism (Germans as victims of the Nazis, the Allies, or a cruel course of history) that critics today so detest in the postwall productions.[30]

In this way, we should not caricature these "waves" as opposing swings of some historical pendulum, but rather also be willing to see them in a continuum. Branding the postwall historical cinema as diametrically antithetical to the New German Cinema would merely replicate the 68ers' own Zero Hour myth. For—*pace* the New German polemics against "Grandpa's Cinema"—in fact, old personalities, structures, and practices persisted. Rather than appearing out of a vacuum, the filmmakers looked to France, found inspiration in Italian cinema, and had an ambivalent regard of Hollywood and American culture. In the same way, some of the New German Cinema's energies persist today. Productions with similar aesthetics, politics, and state-subsidized funding models—yes, even many filmmakers from back then still continue to play an important role in the domestic scene. Harun Farocki, Wim Wenders, and Volker Schlöndorff persist on the festival circuit and as teachers at the German film academies. Christian Petzold and the Berlin School, Oskar Roehler, Romauld Karmaker,

Michael Klier: these figures take more than a little inspiration from the old guard. The example of *Deutschland 09—13 kurze Filme zur Lage der Nation* (*Germany 09: 13 Short Films About the State of the Nation*, 2009), an omnibus project in the spirit of *Deutschland im Herbst* (*Germany in Autumn*, 1978), points to a domestic cinema which is certainly not uniformly radical, but remains neither apolitical nor ignorant of its heritage. To be sure, many of these figures encounter difficulties in securing funding or disseminating their projects, and most are less prominent in journalistic and academic circles than in the 1970s. Nevertheless, just as the postwall historical attitudes depart in focus, attitude, and purpose from the New German retrospection, they are also unthinkable without that tradition.

The course of this national film history might help us think about what happens to film movements after they no longer receive attention on magazine covers, at festivals, and from movie reviewers. Waves— whether Italian neo-realism, French nouvelle vague, New German Cinema, or Dogme95—are always defined by some quotient of filmmakers' productions and critics' constructions. After the publicity subsides and scholarly interest wanes, strands of these tendencies remain, perhaps submerged. Layers of past waves and ways of seeing commingle with new forms.

It is in this spirit that we cannot accept *Good Bye, Lenin!* as an index of postwall cinema's relationship to history in the way that *Abschied von gestern* (*Yesterday Girl*, 1966)—literally "Leave-taking from yesterday"—has been considered as a programmatic title of the Young German Film. It is tempting to think of Becker's film as a declared farewell from the past and, especially, from the postwar discourses of ideological and political divisions in the geography of the German nation. Nevertheless, as we have seen, such films enact a complex and channeled historiography: most bid a departure from a certain historiography, but neither from national history nor from film history.

In closing, I return to the final sentence of Anton Kaes's prescient film history, *From Hitler to Heimat*. "As the Hitler era slowly passes from the realm of experience and personal memory into the realm of images," Kaes asked in 1989, "will it also become a mere movie myth?"[31] Today I can answer Kaes in the affirmative, but argue that this development is not as dire as it must have seemed a quarter-century ago. Even attempts to foreclose the past prevent it from vanishing.

Notes

1. Jaimey Fisher and Brad Prager, "Introduction," in *The Collapse of the Conventional: German Film and Its Politics at the Turn of the Twenty-First Century*, eds. Jaimey Fisher and Brad Prager (Detroit: Wayne State University Press, 2010), 32.

2. Fisher and Prager, "Introduction," 5, 10.
3. Fisher and Prager, "Introduction," 11.
4. See Maxim Leo, "Hofmanns Erzählungen," *Frankfurter Rundschau*, 1 November 2011, 20–21.
5. Robert Moeller, *War Stories: The Search for a Usable Past in the Federal Republic of Germany* (Berkeley: University of California Press, 2001), 175.
6. Andrew Higson distinguishes between economic, text-based, generic, exhibition-led, and criticism-led approaches to national cinema in his "The Concept of National Cinema," *Screen* 30(4) (1989): 36–46.
7. Elena Gorfinkel, "The Future of Anachronism: Todd Haynes and the Magnificient Andersons," in *Cinephilia: Movies, Love and Memory*, eds. Marijke de Valck and Malte Hagener (Amsterdam: Amsterdam University Press, 2005), 155.
8. Gorfinkel, "The Future of Anachronism," 155.
9. Thomas Elsaesser, "Cinephilia or the Uses of Disenchantment," in *Cinephilia: Movies, Love and Memory*, eds. Marijke de Valck and Malte Hagener (Amsterdam: Amsterdam University Press, 2005), 31.
10. Elsaesser, "Cinephilia or the Uses of Disenchantment," 27.
11. Norbert Frei, *1945 und wir: Das dritte Reich im Bewußtsein der Deutschen*, rev. ed. (Munich: dtv, 2009), 41.
12. Frei, *1945 und wir*, 19.
13. See Randall Halle, *German Film after Germany: Toward a Transnational Aesthetic* (Urbana: University of Illinois Press, 2008).
14. See, for the beginnings of this process, Heiko R. Blum and Katharina Blum, *Gesichter des neuen deutschen Films* (Munich: Heyne, 1999), as well as Malte Hagener, "German Stars of the 1990s," in *The German Cinema Book*, eds. Tim Bergfelder, Erica Carter, and Deniz Göktürk (London: British Film Institute, 2002), 98–105.
15. See Thomas Elsaesser, *New German Cinema: A History* (London: British Film Institute, 1989), 22, 33, and 28.
16. See Halle, *German Film after Germany*, 23 and Oliver Castendyk, *Die deutsche Filmförderung: Eine Evaluation* (Konstanz: UVK, 2008), 63.
17. See Castendyk, *Die deutsche Filmförderung*, 45.
18. See the *FFF Jahresrückblick 2009*, http://www.fff-bayern.de/index.php?id=47.
19. See Castendyk, *Die deutsche Filmförderung*, 62–63.
20. See Halle, *German Film after Germany*, 56–57.
21. See, for instance, Edward Jay Epstein, *The Hollywood Economist: The Hidden Financial Reality behind the Movies* (Brooklyn, NY: Melville House, 2010), 104–6.
22. Interview with Hollywood producer Benjamin Forkner, Los Angeles, 18 March 2010.
23. Cf. Bernd Eichinger's comments about the financial liquidity needed to produce an epic historical film in Germany in Hellmuth Karasek and Christiane Peitz, "Eine kräftige Prise Hollywood," *Der Tagesspiegel*, 14 June 2002.
24. Wilfried Berauer, "Quellenanalyse deutscher Film 1997–2006: Woher kommt der Stoff der deutschen Traumfabrik?," *SPIO, Abteilung für Statistik*, 2 November 2007, 1–4: http://www.spio.de/media_content/777.pdf.
25. Wilfried Berauer, "Quellenanalyse deutscher Film 1997–2006," 1–2.
26. See Hanns-Georg Rodek, "Das Leben der Anderen geht ins Oscar-Rennen," *Die Welt*, 23 January 2007. For a report on Hollywood's perennial recourse to Nazism, see Bernard-Henri Lévy, "Hollywood's Nazi Revisionism," trans. Janet Lizop, *Wall Street Journal*, 6–7 March 2010.
27. See, for instance, David Bordwell, *The Way Hollywood Tells It: Story and Style in Modern Movies* (Berkeley: University of California Press, 2006), especially 25; Barbara Klinger, "The Contemporary Cinephile: Film Collecting in the Post-Video Era," in *Hollywood Spectatorship: Changing Perceptions of Cinema Audiences*, eds. Melvyn Stokes and Richard Maltby (London: British Film Institute, 2001), 132–51; or Laura Mulvey, *Death 24x a Second: Stillness and the Moving Image* (London: Reaktion, 2006).

28. Jenna Ng, "Love in the Time of Transcultural Fusion: Cinephila, Homage and *Kill Bill*," in *Cinephilia: Movies, Love and Memory*, eds. Marijke de Valck and Malte Hagener (Amsterdam: Amsterdam University Press, 2005), 67.

29. See, for instance, Heimo Schwilk and Ulrich Schacht, eds., *Die selbstbewußte Nation*, 3rd rev. ed. (Frankfurt: Ullstein, 1995) or Stuart Parks, *Understanding Contemporary Germany* (London: Routledge, 1997), 198ff. For more on the *Kulturkampf* over 1968, see Gunter Hofmann, "Kulturkampf gegen die Kulturrevolutionäre," *Die Zeit*, 1 January 1993; and Wolfgang Kraushaar, *Achtundsechzig: eine Bilanz* (Berlin: Propyläen, 2008), especially 42ff.

30. Eric Rentschler makes a similar point about the New German Cinema's victimhood in "Remembering Not to Forget: A Retrospective Reading of Kluge's *Brutality in Stone*," *New German Critique* 49 (1990): 38. He outlines the foreign contribution to the success of the New German Cinema in "American Friends and New German Cinema: Patterns of Reception," *New German Critique* 24–25 (1981–1982): 7–35.

31. Anton Kaes, *From Hitler to Heimat: The Return of History as Film* (Cambridge, MA: Harvard University Press, 1989), 198.

SELECT BIBLIOGRAPHY

"23." *Blickpunkt Film* 30–31 (1998): 32.

1954. Süddeutsche Zeitung WM-Bibliothek. Munich: Süddeutsche Zeitung, 2005.

Abel, Marco. "Failing to Connect: Itinerations of Desire in Oskar Roehler's Postromance Films." *New German Critique* 109 (2010): 75–98.

Ahbe, Thomas. *Ostalgie: Zum Umgang mit der DDR-Vergangenheit in den 1990er Jahren*. Erfurt: Sömmerda, 2005.

Ahne, Petra, and Felix Zimmermann. "Sozialismus auf 79 Quadratmetern." *Berliner Zeitung*, 7 February 2003.

Allan, Seán. "*Ostalgie*, Fantasy and the Normalization of East–West Relations in Post-Unification Comedy." In *German Cinema: Since Unification*. Ed. David Clarke. London: Continuum, 2006. Pp. 105–26.

Altenburg, Matthias. "Silvester Countdown – Der schönste Sexfilm aller Zeiten." In *Szenenwechsel: Momentaufnahmen des jungen deutschen Films*. Ed. Michael Töteberg. Reinbek bei Hamburg: Rowohlt, 1999. Pp. 140–44.

Althen, Michael. "Systemsieg." *Frankfurter Allgemeine Zeitung*, 10 June 2003.

———. "Die Wahrheit liegt auf dem Platz." *Frankfurter Allgemeine Zeitung*, 15 October 2003.

Altman, Rick. *Film/Genre*. London: British Film Institute, 1999.

Altwegg, Jürg. "Gewinner: Good Bye, Lenin! in Frankreich." *Frankfurter Allgemeine Zeitung*, 15 September 2003.

Aris, Ben. "How the GDR Became Cool." *The Guardian*, 24 July 2003.

Ash, Timothy Garton. "The Stasi in Our Minds." *The New York Review of Books*, 31 May 2007.

Assmann, Aleida. *Geschichte im Gedächtnis: Von der individuellen Erfahrung zur öffentlichen Inszenierung*. Munich: Beck, 2007.

Augé, Marc. *Non-Places: Introduction to an Anthropology of Supermodernity*. Trans. John Howe. London: Verso, 1995.

Aust, Stefan. *Der Baader Meinhof Komplex*. Rev. ed. Munich: Goldmann, 1998.

Baer, Hester. *Dismantling the Dream Factory: Gender, German Cinema, and the Postwar Quest for a New Film Language*. New York: Berghahn, 2009.

Balio, Tino. *The American Film Industry*. Madison: University of Wisconsin Press, 1976.

———. "Hollywood Production Trends in the Era of Globalisation." In *Genre and Contemporary Hollywood*. Ed. Steve Neale. London: British Film Institute, 2002. Pp. 165–84.

Bathrick, David. *The Powers of Speech: The Politics of Culture in the GDR*. Lincoln: University of Nebraska Press, 1995.

———. "Rescreening the 'Holocaust': The Children's Stories." *New German Critique* 80 (2000): 41–58.

Baumgarten, Oliver. "Child in Time. Verfolgungswahn statt Verfolgungsjagd: *23*." *Schnitt* 13 (1999): 23–23 [*sic*].

———."Mythos als Lektion." *Schnitt.de*, http://www.schnitt.de/202, 1161,1.

"Betriebsausflug: Bundestag nimmt Abschied von Lenin." *Spiegel Online*, 3 April 2003. http://www.spiegel.de/kultur/gesellschaft/0,1518,243206,00.html.

Beier, Lars-Olav. "Der Traum vom großen Kick." *Der Spiegel*, 14 July 2003.

———, and Wieland Wagner. "Das deutsche Kinowunder." *Der Spiegel*, 11 July 2005.

Berauer, Wilfried Berauer. "Quellenanalyse deutscher Film 1997–2006: Woher kommt der Stoff der deutschen Traumfabrik?" *SPIO, Abteilung für Statistik*, 2 November 2007. http://www.spio.de/media_content/777.pdf.

Berdahl, Daphne. "'(N)ostalgie' for the Present: Memory, Longing, and East German Things." *Ethnos* 64(2) (1999): 192–211.

Berg, Ulrich von. "Raritäten: *Das große Spiel*, der beste aller Fußballfilme." *Steadycam* 23 (1992): 12–21.

Bergfelder, Tim. "German Cinema and Film Noir." In *European Film Noir*. Ed. Andrew Spicer. Manchester: Manchester University Press, 2007. Pp. 138–63.

———. "Shadowlands: The Memory of the *Ostgebiete* in Contemporary German Film and Television." In *Screening the War: Perspectives on German Suffering*. Eds. Paul Cooke and Marc Silberman. Rochester, NY: Camden House, 2010. Pp. 123–44.

Berghahn, Daniela. "East German Cinema after Unification." In *German Cinema: Since Unification*. Ed. David Clarke. London: Continuum, 2006. Pp. 79–104.

———. *Hollywood behind the Wall: The Cinema of East Germany*. Manchester: Manchester University Press, 2005.

————. "Remembering the Stasi in a Fairy Tale of Redemption: Florian Henckel von Donnersmarck's *Das Leben der Anderen*." *Oxford German Studies* 38(3) (2009): 321–33.

Bernstein, Matthew H. "The Lives of Others." *Film Quarterly* 61(1) (2007): 30–36.

Bernstein, Richard. "Germany's Grief and Glory, Wrapped Up in a Soccer Ball." *New York Times*, 10 November 2003.

————. "Warm, Fuzzy Feelings for East Germany's Gray Old Days." *New York Times*, 6 January 2004.

Beyer, Tom, and Benjamin Heßler. "In der Schwebe." *Schnitt* 8 (1997): 18.

Bhabha, Homi K. "DissemiNation: Time, Narrative and the Margins of the Modern Nation." In *Nation and Narration*. Ed. Homi K. Bhabha. London: Routledge, 1990. Pp. 291–322.

Bisky, Jens. "Zonensucht: Kritik der neuen Ostalgie." *Merkur* 58(2) (2004): 117–27.

Blickle, Peter. *Heimat: A Critical Theory of the German Idea of Homeland*. Rochester: Camden House, 2002.

Blum, Heiko R., and Katharina Blum. *Gesichter des neuen deutschen Films*. Munich: Heyne, 2002.

Blum, Martin. "Remaking the East German Past: *Ostalgie*, Identity, and Material Culture." *Journal of Popular Culture* 34(3) (2000): 229–53.

Blumenberg, Hans-Christoph. "Der italienische Western – ein Fazit nach sechs Jahren." In *Um sie weht der Hauch des Todes: Der Italowestern – die Geschichte eines Genres*. 2nd rev. ed. Ed. Studienkreis Film. Bochum: Schnitt, 1999. Pp. 7–13.

Bly, Laura. "After the Fall." *USA Today*, 23 October 2009.

Bock, Hans-Michael and Tim Bergfelder, eds. *The Concise CineGraph: Encyclopaedia of German Cinema*. Oxford: Berghahn, 2009.

Bordwell, David. *Making Meaning: Inference and Rhetoric in the Interpretation of Cinema*. Cambridge, MA: Harvard University Press, 1989.

————. *The Way Hollywood Tells It: Story and Style in Modern Movies*. Berkeley: University of California Press, 2006.

Boym, Svetlana. *The Future of Nostalgia*. New York: Basic Books, 2001.

Brandlmeier, Thomas. "Von Hitler zu Adenauer." In *Zwischen gestern und morgen: Westdeutscher Nachkriegsfilm 1945–1961*. Eds. Hilmar Hoffmann and Walter Schobert. Frankfurt: Deutsches Filmmuseum, 1989. Pp. 32–59.

Braun, Rainer. "Dem Hacker auf der Spur." *Märkische Allgemeine*, 14 January 1999.

Brinkbäume, Klaus. "Der Chef und sein Boss." *Der Spiegel*, 6 October 2003.

Bruzzi, Stella. *Undressing Cinema: Clothing and Identity in the Movies*. London: Routledge, 1997.

Buck, Caroline M. "Eine Mutter-Sohn-Geschichte." *Neues Deutschland*, 13 February 2003.

Bühler, Philipp. "Geheimziffer 23, Quersumme 5," *taz*, 14 January 1999.

———. "Keine Ahnung von Computern." *taz*, 14 January 1999.

Bundeszentrale für politische Bildung. *Good Bye, Lenin!* Bonn: Bundeszentrale für politische Bildung, 2003.

Burgoyne, Robert. *Film Nation*. Minneapolis: University of Minnesota Press, 1997.

———. *The Hollywood Historical Film*. Malden, MA: Blackwell, 2008.

Buruma, Ian. "Die kapitale Schnauze: Berlin – Selbstzerstörung und wiederkehrende Selbsterzeugung." *Lettre International* 43 (1998): 36–39.

Buß, Christian. "Unter den Trümmern der Popkultur: Jugend im deutschen Film," *filmportal.de*, http://www.filmportal.de/df/5d/Artikel,,,,,,,,EF9D885C6CAB0403E03053D50B376B9F,,,,,,,,,,,,,,,,,,,,,·html.

Cafferty, Helen. "*Sonnenallee*: Taking Comedy Seriously in Unified Germany." In *Textual Reponses to German Unification*. Eds. Carola Anne Costabile-Heming, Rachel J. Halverson, and Kristie A. Foell. Berlin: Walter de Gruyter, 2001. Pp. 253–71.

Cammann, Alexander, Jens Hacke, and Stephan Schlak. "Geschichtsgefühl." *Ästhetik und Kommunikation* 122–23 (2003): 12–13.

Cargnelli, Christian, and Michael Omasta, eds. *Schatten. Exil. Europäische Emigranten im Film noir*. Vienna: PVS, 1997.

Carroll, Noël. "The Future of Allusion: Hollywood in the Seventies (and Beyond)." *October* 20 (1982): 51–81.

Carter, Erica. *How German Is She? Postwar German Reconstruction and the Consuming Woman*. Ann Arbor: University of Michigan Press, 1997.

———. "Sweeping Up the Past: Gender and History in the Post-War German 'Rubble Film.'" In *Heroines Without Heroines: Reconstructing Female and National Identities in European Cinema, 1945–1951*. Ed. Ulrike Sieglohr. London: Cassell, 2000. Pp. 91–110.

Casati, Rebecca. "Oskar Roehler über Familie." *Süddeutsche Zeitung*, 17–18 January 2009.

Castendyk, Oliver. *Die deutsche Filmförderung: Eine Evaluation*. Konstanz: UVK, 2008.

Certeau, Michel de. *The Practice of Everyday Life*. Translated by Steven Rendall. Berkeley: University of California Press, 1984.

Chion, Michel. *Audio-Vision: Sound on Screen*. Trans. and ed. Claudia Gorbman. New York: Columbia University Press, 1994.

———. *The Voice in Cinema*. Trans. and ed. Claudia Gorbman. New York: Columbia University Press, 1999.

Chun, Wendy Hui Kyong. *Control and Freedom: Power and Paranoia in the Age of Fiber Optics*. Cambridge, MA: MIT Press, 2006.

Clarke, David, ed. *German Cinema: Since Unification*. London: Continuum, 2006.

Coates, Paul. *The Gorgon's Gaze: German Cinema, Expressionism, and the Image of Horror*. Cambridge: Cambridge University Press, 1991.

Cook, Roger F. "*Die fetten Jahre sind vorbei*: Edukating the Post-Left Generation." In *The Collapse of the Conventional: German Film and Its Politics at the Turn of the Twenty-First Century*. Eds. Jaimey Fisher and Brad Prager. Detroit: Wayne State University Press, 2010. Pp. 309–32.

———. "*Good Bye, Lenin!*: Free-Market Nostalgia for Socialist Consumerism." *Seminar* 43(2) (2007): 206–19.

Cooke, Paul. "German Neo-Noir." In *European Film Noir*. Ed. Andrew Spicer. Manchester: Manchester University Press, 2007. Pp. 164–84.

———. "Performing 'Ostalgie': Leander Haußmann's *Sonnenallee*," *German Life and Letters* 56(2) (2003): 156–67.

———. *Representing East Germany since Unification: From Colonization to Nostalgia*. Oxford: Berg, 2005.

———. "Surfing for Eastern Difference: *Ostalgie*, Identity, and Cyberspace." *Seminar* 40(3) (2004): 207–20.

———. "Whatever Happened to Veronika Voss? Rehabilitating the '68ers' and the Problem of *Westalgie* in Oskar Roehler's *Die Unberührbare* (2000)." *German Studies Review* 27(1) (2004): 33–43.

———, and Chris Homewood, eds. *New Directions in German Cinema*. Basingstoke: I.B. Tauris, 2011.

———, and Marc Silberman, eds. *Screening the War: Perspectives on German Suffering*. Rochester, NY: Camden House, 2010.

Creech, Jennifer. "A Few Good Men: Gender, Ideology, and Narrative Politics in *The Lives of Others* and *Good Bye, Lenin!*" *Women in German Yearbook: Feminist Studies in German Literature & Culture* 25 (2009): 100–126.

Cupers, Kenny, and Markus Miessen. *Spaces of Uncertainty*. Wuppertal: Müller + Busmann, 2002.

Custen, George F. *Bio/Pics: How Hollywood Constructed Public History*. New Brunswick, NJ: Rutgers University Press, 1992.

Dalle Vacche, Angela. *Cinema and Painting: How Art Is Used in Film*. London: Athlone, 1996.

Deckar, Gunnar. "Ortswechsel. Zeitenwechsel. Weltenwechsel." *Neues Deutschland*, 11 February 2003.

Dehnhardt, Sebastian. *Das Wunder von Bern: Die wahre Geschichte*. Munich: Heyne, 2004.

Deleuze, Gilles, and Félix Guattari. *Kafka: Toward a Minor Literature*. Trans. Dana Polan. Minneapolis: University of Minnesota Press, 1986.

Delius, Friedrich Christian. *Der Sonntag an dem ich Weltmeister wurde*. Reinbek bei Hamburg: Rowohlt, 1994.

———. "The West Is Getting Wilder. Intellectuals and the German Question: The Claims Are Being Staked Out." In *When the Wall Came*

Down: Reactions to German Unification. Eds. Harold James and Marla Stone. New York: Routledge, 1992. Pp. 71–76.

Dell, Matthias. "Sandmann, lieber Sandmann." *Freitag*, 28 February 2003.

De Valck, Marijke, and Malte Hagener. "Down with Cinephilia? Long Live Cinephilia? And Other Videosyncratic Pleasures." *Cinephilia: Movies, Love and Memory*. Eds. Marijke de Valck and Malte Hagener. Amsterdam: Amsterdam University Press, 2005. Pp. 11–24.

De Wit, Elke. "Panel Games: *Neue deutsche Filme* at the Berlin Film Festival." *Central European Review* 3(10) (2001). http://www.ce-review.org/01/10/kinoeye10_dewit.html.

Dimendberg, Ed. *Film Noir and the Spaces of Modernity*. Cambridge, MA: Harvard University Press, 2004.

Distelmeyer, Jan. "Baader: Christopher Roths Terroristen-Biographie scheitert an ihren Vorgaben." *epd Film* 19(10) (October 2002): 44.

Dockhorn, Katharina. "Am Computer bin ich Laie." *Neues Deutschland*, 14 January 1999.

Dolif, Nicole. "Lenin lässt die Kinokassen klingeln." *Die Welt*, 18 February 2003.

Dombrowski, Lisa. *The Films of Sam Fuller: If You Die, I'll Kill You!* Middletown, CT: Wesleyan University Press, 2008.

Dresden, Andreas. "Der falsche Kino-Osten." *Die Zeit*, 16 April 2009.

Dubiel, Helmut. "Linke Truerarbeit." *Merkur* 496 (1990): 482–91.

Eckert, Volcker. "Good bye, Ahnungslosigkeit: Kino als Geschichtsstunde." *Tagesspiegel*, 6 March 2003.

Eger, Christian. *Mein kurzer Sommer der Ostalgie*. Dössel: Stekovics, 2004.

Eggers, Erik. *Die Stimme von Bern: Das Leben von Herbert Zimmermann, Reporterlegende bei der WM 1954*. Augsburg: Wißner, 2004.

Eisenhauer, Bertram. "Jugend forscht für die Weltverschwörung." *Frankfurter Allgemeine Zeitung*, 20 January 1999.

Elsaesser, Thomas. "Cinephilia or the Uses of Disenchantment." In *Cinephilia: Movies, Love and Memory*. Eds. Marijke de Valck and Malte Hagener. Amsterdam: Amsterdam University Press, 2005. Pp. 27–43.

———. *Fassbinder's Germany: History, Identity, Subject*. Amsterdam: Amsterdam University Press, 1996.

———. "From Censorship to Over-Exposure: The Red Army Fraction, *Germany in Autumn* and *Death Game*." In *I limiti della rappresentazione/ The Bounds of Representation*. Eds. Leonardo Quaresima, Alessandra Raengo, and Laura Vichi. Udine: Forum, 2000. Pp. 289–308.

———. "A German Ancestry to Film Noir?" *Iris* 21 (1996): 129–44.

———. *New German Cinema: A History*. London: British Film Institute, 1989.

———. "The New German Cinema's Historical Imaginary." In *Framing the Past: The Historiography of German Cinema and Television*. Eds.

Bruce A. Murray and Christopher J. Wickham. Carbondale: Southern Illinois University Press, 1992. Pp. 280–307.

———. "Subject Positions, Speaking Positions: From *Holocaust, Our Hitler*, and *Heimat* to *Shoah* and *Schindler's List*." In *The Persistence of History: Cinema, Television, and the Modern Event*. Ed. Vivian Sobchack. New York: Routledge, 1996. Pp. 145–86.

———. *Terror und Trauma: Zur Gewalt des Vergangenen in der BRD*. Berlin: Kadmos, 2006.

———. *Weimar Cinema and After: Germany's Historical Imaginary*. London: Routledge, 2000.

———, and Warren Buckland. *Studying Contemporary American Film*. London: Arnold, 2002.

Engel, Gerrit, ed. *Marzahn*. Cologne: Walther König Buchhandlung, 1999.

Enns, Anthony. "The Politics of *Ostalgie*: Post-Socialist Nostalgia in Recent German Film." *Screen* 48(4) (2007): 475–91.

Ensslin, Felix. "Die doppelte Verdrängung." *Die Zeit*, 22 March 2007.

Epstein, Edward Jay. *The Hollywood Economist: The Hidden Financial Reality behind the Movies*. Brooklyn, NY: Melville House, 2010.

Eue, Ralph. "Alles Feeling!" *Tagesspiegel*, 17 October 2002.

Fassbinder, Rainer Werner. "I'd Rather Be a Streetsweeper in Mexico than a Filmmaker in Germany." In *The Anarchy of the Imagination: Interviews, Essays, Notes*. Eds. Michael Töteberg and Leo A. Lensing. Trans. Krishna Winston. Baltimore: Johns Hopkins University Press, 1992. Pp. 139–43.

Fehrenbach, Heide. *Cinema in Democratizing Germany: Reconstructing National Identity after Hitler*. Chapel Hill: University of North Carolina Press, 1995.

Fest, Joachim. "The Silence of the Clerks." In *When the Wall Came Down: Reactions to German Unification*. Eds. Harold James and Marla Stone. New York: Routledge, 1992. Pp. 52–56.

Festenberg, Nikolaus von. "Der beseelte Mann." *Der Spiegel*, 28 September 2003.

———. "Kinder haften für ihre Eltern." *Der Spiegel*, 24 March 2003.

Feuer, Jane. *The Hollywood Musical*. London: British Film Institute, 1982.

Finger, Evelyn. "Die Bekehrung." *Die Zeit*, 23 March 2006.

———. "Die unsinkbare Republik." *Die Zeit*, 6 February 2003.

Fisher, Jaimey. "Deleuze in a Ruinous Context: German Rubble-Film and Italian Neorealism." *Iris* 23 (1997): 53–74.

———. *Disciplining Germany: Youth, Reeducation, and Reconstruction after the Second World War*. Detroit: Wayne State University Press, 2007.

———. "German Historical Film as Production Trend: European Heritage Cinema and Melodrama in *The Lives of Others*." In *The Collapse of the Conventional: German Film and Its Politics at the Turn of the Twenty-First Century*. Eds. Jaimey Fisher and Brad Prager. Detroit: Wayne State University Press, 2010. Pp. 186–215.

————, and Brad Prager, eds. *The Collapse of the Conventional: German Film and its Politics at the Turn of the Twenty-First Century*. Detroit: Wayne State University Press, 2010.

Frei, Norbert. *1945 und wir: Das dritte Reich im Bewußtsein der Deutschen*. 2nd rev. ed. Munich: dtv, 2009.

Freud, Sigmund. *Zur Psychopathologie des Alltagslebens*. Frankfurt: Fischer, 1987.

Frey, Constance. "Die DDR ist längst Kult." *Tagesspiegel*, 5 June 2003.

Frey, Mattias. "No(ir) Place to Go: Spatial Anxiety and Sartorial Intertextuality in *Die Unberührbare*." *Cinema Journal* 45(4) (2006): 64–80.

Friedman, Norman. "Forms of the Plot." In *The Theory of the Novel*. Ed. Philip Stevick. New York: Macmillan, 1967. Pp. 145–66.

Friedrich, Jörg. *Der Brand: Deutschland im Bombenkrieg 1940-1945*. Munich: Propyläen, 2002.

————. *Brandstätten: Der Anblick des Bombenkrieges*. Munich: Propyläen, 2003.

Fukuyama, Francis. *The End of History and the Last Man*. New York: Free Press, 1992.

Funder, Anna. "Eyes Without a Face." *Sight and Sound*, May 2007.

————. *Stasiland: True Stories from Behind the Berlin Wall*. London: Granta, 2003.

Galli, Matteo. "Paralleoli Bioi: Andres Veiel, *Black Box BRD* (2001)." In *Da Caligari a Good Bye, Lenin! Storia e cinema in Germania*. Ed. Matteo Galli. Florence: Le Lettere, 2004. Pp. 539–57.

Gansera, Rainer. "Bewusst, wie ein Projektil." *Süddeutsche Zeitung*, 17 October 2002.

Garnham, Nicholas. "TV Documentary and Ideology." In *Screen Reader 1: Cinema/Ideology/Politics*. Ed. Society for Education in Film and Television. London: Society for Education in Film and Television, 1977. Pp. 55–61.

Geisenhanslüke, Ralph. "Filmaufbau Ost." *Die Zeit*, 22 December 2003.

Geisler, Michael E. "The Disposal of Memory: Fascism and the Holocaust." In *Framing the Past: The Historiography of German Cinema and Television*. Eds. Bruce A. Murray and Christopher J. Wickham. Carbondale: Southern Illinois University Press, 1992. Pp. 220–60.

Gemünden, Gerd. *Framed Visions: Popular Culture, Americanization, and the Contemporary German and Austrian Imagination*. Ann Arbor: University of Michigan Press, 1998.

————. *A Foreign Affair: Billy Wilder's American Films*. New York: Berghahn, 2008.

————, and Anton Kaes. "Introduction." *New German Critique* 89 (2003): 3–8.

Genette, Gérard. *Palimpsestes: La Littérature au Second Degré*. Paris: Seuil, 1982.

Gilbey, Ryan. "Killing to Be Cool." *New Statesman*, 17 November 2008.

"Gisela Elsner." *Der Spiegel*, 25 May 1992, 248.

Glowna, Vadim. *Der Geschichtenerzähler: Erinnerungen*. Berlin: Ullstein, 2006.

Göttler, Fritz. "Gutes Gefühl im Filmförderverein." *Süddeutsche Zeitung*, 4 April 2003.

―――. "Hallo, Helmut!" *Süddeutsche Zeitung*, 16 October 2003.

Goodnow, Katherine J. *Kristeva in Focus: From Theory to Film Analysis*. New York: Berghahn, 2010.

Goodwin, James. *Akira Kurasowa and Intertextual Cinema*. Baltimore, MD: Johns Hopkins University Press, 1994.

Gorfinkel, Elena. "The Future of Anachronism: Todd Haynes and the Magnificient Andersons." In *Cinephilia: Movies, Love and Memory*. Eds. Marijke de Valck and Malte Hagener. Amsterdam: Amsterdam University Press, 2005. Pp. 153–67.

Grass, Günter. "Don't Reunify Germany." In *When the Wall Came Down: Reactions to German Unification*. Eds. Harold James and Marla Stone. New York: Routledge, 1992. Pp. 57–59.

Greffath, Bettina. *Gesellschaftsbilder der Nachkriegszeit: Deutsche Spielfilme 1945–1949*. Pfaffenweiler: Centaurus, 1995.

Haase, Christine. "Ready For His Close-Up? On the Success and Failure of Representing Hitler in *Der Untergang/The Downfall* (2004)." *Studies in European Cinema* 3(3) (2007): 189–99.

Haasis, Bernd. "Eine vertane Chance: Die Lüge vom deutschen Desperado." *Stuttgarter Nachrichten*, 17 October 2002.

Habermas, Jürgen. "Yet Again: German Identity—A Unified Nation of Angry DM-Burghers?" In *When the Wall Came Down: Reactions to German Unification*. Eds. Harold James and Marla Stone. New York: Routledge, 1992. Pp. 86–102.

Hagener, Malte. "German Stars of the 1990s." In *The German Cinema Book*. Eds. Tim Bergfelder, Erica Carter, and Deniz Göktürk. London: British Film Institute, 2002. Pp. 98–106.

Hake, Sabine. *German National Cinema*. London: Routledge, 2002.

―――. *German National Cinema*. 2nd rev. ed. London: Routledge, 2008.

―――. "Historisierung der NS-Vergangenheit: *Der Untergang* (2004) zwischen Historienfilm und Eventkino." In *NachBilder des Holocaust*. Eds. Inge Stephan and Alexandra Tacke. Cologne: Böhlau, 2007. Pp. 188–218.

Halle, Randall. *German Film after Germany: Toward a Transnational Aesthetic*. Urbana: University of Illinois Press, 2008.

―――. "Happy Ends to Crises of Heterosexual Desire: Toward a Social Psychology of Recent German Comedies." *Camera Obscura* 15(2) (2000): 1–39.

Hanich, Julian. "Die DDR soll leben." *Tagesspiegel*, 28 October 2001.

Hansen, Miriam. "Cooperative Auteur Cinema and Oppositional Public Sphere: Alexander Kluge's Contribution to *Germany in Autumn*." *New German Critique* 24–25 (1981–1982): 36–56.

Haskell, Molly. *From Reverence to Rape: The Treatment of Women in the Movies*. 2nd rev. ed. Chicago: University of Chicago Press, 1987.

Hauser, Dorothea. *Baader und Herold: Beschreibung eines Kampfes*. Frankfurt: Fischer, 1998.

———, and Andreas Schroth. "'Das Thema ist erledigt': Romuald Karmakar, Christian Petzold und Andres Veiel zum Politischen im deutschen Film." *Ästhetik und Kommunikation* 117 (2002): 44–60.

Hensel, Jana. "Die DDR wird Spekulationsobjekt." *Die Welt am Sonntag*, 9 February 2003.

———. *Zonenkinder*. Reinbek bei Hamburg: Rowohlt, 2002.

Hermes, Manfred. "Der Ort ist eine Hauptfigur." *taz*, 31 July 2003.

Herzog, Dagmar. "'Pleasure, Sex and Politics Belong Together': Post-Holocaust Memory and the Sexual Revolution in West Germany." *Critical Inquiry* 24(2) (1998): 393–444.

———. *Sex after Fascism: Memory and Morality in Twentieth-Century Germany*. Princeton, NJ: Princeton University Press, 2005.

Hickethier, Knut. *Geschichte des deutschen Fernsehens*. Stuttgart: Metzler, 1998.

Higson, Andrew. "The Concept of National Cinema." *Screen* 30(4) (1989): 36–46.

Hirsch, Foster. *Detours and Lost Highways: A Map of the Neo-Noir*. New York: Limelight, 1999.

Hockenos, Paul. "Hindsight turns German Militants into T-shirt Icons." *Christian Science Monitor*, 31 October 2002.

Hodgin, Nick. "*Berlin Is in Germany* and *Good Bye, Lenin!* Taking Leave of the GDR?" *Debatte* 12(1) (2004): 25–45.

Hoerschelmann, Olaf. "'*Memoria Dextera Est*': Film and Public Memory in Postwar Germany." *Cinema Journal* 40(2) (2001): 78–97.

Hoffmann-Axthelm, Dieter. *Die dritte Stadt*. Frankfurt: Suhrkamp, 1993.

———. "An Extreme Case of European Urban Crisis." *Lotus* 80 (1994): 37–49.

Hofmann, Gunter. "Kulturkampf gegen die Kulturrevolutionäre." *Die Zeit*, 1 January 1993.

Hogwood, Patricia. "Reconstructing Identity in Post-Communist Germany." *Journal of Communist Studies and Transition Politics* 16(4) (2000): 45–67.

Homann, Peter. "Aber nicht andere nur, auch uns töten wir." *Der Spiegel*, 21 October 2002.

———. "Volksgericht im Wüstensand." *Der Spiegel*, 19 May 1997.

Homewood, Chris. "Challenging the Taboo: the Memory of West Germany's Terrorist Past in Andres Veiel's *Black Box BRD* (2001)." *New Cinemas* 5(2) (2007): 115–26.

———. "Making Invisible Memory Visible: Communicative Memory and Taboo in Andres Veiel's *Black Box BRD*." In *Baader-Meinhof Returns: History and Cultural Memory of German Left-Wing Terrorism.* Eds. Gerrit-Jan Berendse and Ingo Cornils. Amsterdam: Rodopi, 2008. Pp. 231–49.

———. "The Return of 'Undead' History: The West German Terrorist as Vampire and the Problem of 'Normalizing' the Past in Margarethe von Trotta's *Die bleierne Zeit* (1981) and Christian Petzold's *Die innere Sicherheit* (2001)." In *German Culture, Politics and Literature into the Twenty-First Century: Beyond Normalization.* Eds. Stuart Taberner and Paul Cooke. Rochester: Camden House, 2006. Pp. 121–35.

———. "Von Trotta's *The German Sisters* and Petzold's *The State I Am In*: Discursive Boundaries in the Films of the New German Cinema to the Present Day." *Studies in European Cinema* 2(2) (2005): 93–102.

Hong, Y. Euny. "We'll Always Have East Berlin." *Boston Globe*, 7 September 2003.

Huyssen, Andreas. "Nation, Race, and Immigration: German Identities after Unification." In *The Power of Intellectuals in Contemporary German.* Ed. Michael Geyer. Chicago: University of Chicago Press, 2001. Pp. 314–34.

Iordanova, Dina. "East of Eden." *Sight and Sound*, August 2003.

James, Caryn. "These Are Works of Art, Not Children's Schoolbooks." *New York Times*, 21 May 1995.

Jameson, Fredric. "Postmodernism, or the Cultural Logic of Late Capitalism." *New Left Review* 1(146) (1984): 53–92.

Jauer, Marcus. "Wir lachen uns schlapp." *Süddeutsche Zeitung*, 30–31 August 2003.

Joannou, Mary and Steve McIntyre, "Lust for Lives: Report from a Conference on the Biopic." *Screen* 24(4–5) (1983): 145–49.

Jozwiak, Josepf F., and Elisabeth Mermann. "'The Wall in Our Minds?' Colonization, Integration, Nostalgia." *Journal of Popular Culture* 39(5) (2006): 780–95.

Jung, Barbara, and Holger Stark. "Als die Hacker ihre Unschuld verloren." *taz*, 6 February 1999.

Kaden, Martina. "Good Bye, Lenin! Hello, Welterfolg!" *BZ*, 13 February 2003.

Kaes, Anton. *From Hitler to Heimat: The Return of History as Film.* Cambridge, MA: Harvard University Press, 1989.

Kafka, Franz. *Sämtliche Erzählungen*. Frankfurt: Fischer, 1987.

Kähler, Gert, ed. *Einfach schwierig: eine deutsche Architekturdebatte.* Braunschweig: Vieweg, 1995.

Kaminer, Wladimir. "Good Bye, Lenin! Man sieht sich." *DW-WORLD.DE*, 12 February 2003. http://www.dw-world.de/dw/article/0,,777207,00.html.

Kapczynski, Jennifer M. "Imitation of Life: The Aesthetics of Agfacolor in Recent Historical Cinema." In *The Collapse of the Conventional: German Film and Its Politics at the Turn of the Twenty-First Century*. Eds. Jaimey Fisher and Brad Prager. Detroit: Wayne State University Press, 2010. Pp. 39–62.

———. "Negotiating Nostalgia: The GDR Past in *Berlin Is in Germany* and *Good Bye, Lenin!*" *The Germanic Review* 82(1) (2007): 78–100.

———. "Newer German Cinema: From Nostalgia to Nowhere." *The Germanic Review* 82(1) (2007): 3–6.

Karasek, Hellmuth, and Christiane Peitz. "Eine kräftige Prise Hollywood." *Der Tagesspiegel*, 14 June 2002.

Keathley, Christian. *Cinephilia and History, or the Wind in the Trees*. Bloomington: Indiana University Press, 2006.

Kil, Wolfgang. "Dilemma der Moderne, aufgestoßene Tür." In *Marzahn*. Ed. Gerrit Engel. Cologne: König, 1999. Pp. 21–22.

Kilzer, Annette. "Auf der Highschool ist die Hölle los." *Schnitt* 16 (1999): 20–21.

Kline, Jefferson T. *Screening the Text: Intertextuality in French New Wave Cinema*. Baltimore: Johns Hopkins University Press, 1992.

Klingenmaier, Thomas. "Das Mosaik der Welt." *Stuttgarter Zeitung*, 13 January 1999.

Klinger, Barbara. "The Contemporary Cinephile: Film Collecting in the Post-Video Era." In *Hollywood Spectatorship: Changing Perceptions of Cinema Audiences*. Eds. Melvyn Stokes and Richard Maltby. London: British Film Institute, 2001. Pp. 132–51.

Kniebe, Tobias. "Amelie und Anämie," *Süddeutsche Zeitung*, 3–4 May 2003.

———. "Erfolgsgetrieben und naiv," *Süddeutsche Zeitung*, 13 August 2009. http://www.sueddeutsche.de/kultur/jud-suess-film-ohne-gewissen-erfolgsgetrieben-und-naiv-1.168161

———. "Hannover kann sehr kalt sein." *Süddeutsche Zeitung*, 14 January 1999.

Knoben, Martina. "Das Kapital sind die Darsteller: Zum Stand der Dinge im aktuellen deutschen Kino." *epd film* 20(4) (April 2003): 22–25.

Koepnick, Lutz. "Amerika gibts überhaupt nicht: Notes on the German Heritage Film." In *German Pop Culture: How American Is It?* Ed. Agnes Müller. Ann Arbor: University of Michigan Press, 2004. Pp. 191–208.

———. *The Dark Mirror: German Cinema between Hitler and Hollywood*. Berkeley: University of California Press, 2002.

———. "Public Viewing: Soccer Patriotism and Post-Cinema." In *The Collapse of the Conventional: The German Film and its Politics at the*

Turn of the Twenty-First Century. Eds. Jaimer Fisher and Brad Prager. Detroit: Wayne State University Press, 2010. Pp. 63–80.

———. "Reframing the Past: Heritage Cinema and Holocaust in the 1990s." *New German Critique* 87 (2002): 47–82.

Kohler, Dorothée, and Boris Grésillon. "Berlin aus französicher Sicht." In *Architektur in Berlin: Jahrbuch 1999.* Ed. Architektenkammer Berlin. Hamburg: Junius, 1999. Pp. 10–13.

Koolhaas, Rem. "Massakrierte Ideen." *Frankfurter Allgemeine Zeitung*, 16 October 1991.

Kopp, Kristin. "Exterritorialized Heritage in Caroline Link's *Nigendwo in Afrika.*" *New German Critique* 87 (2002): 106–32.

Körte, Peter, and Nils Minkmar. "Das Wesentliche am Terrorismus ist die Inszenierung." *Frankfurter Allgemeine Zeitung*, 17 October 2002.

Kozloff, Sarah. *Invisible Storytellers: Voice-over Narration in American Fiction Film.* Berkeley: University of California Press, 1988.

Kraus, Petra, et al., eds. *Deutschland im Herbst: Terrorismus im Film.* Munich: Münchner Filmzentrum, 1997.

Krause, Tilman. "Geschichte ist die einzige Quelle." *Die Welt*, 6 May 2000.

Kraushaar, Wolfgang. *Achtundsechzig: eine Bilanz.* Berlin: Propyläen, 2008.

Krekeler, Elmar. "Nur im Falschen gibt es Wahres." *Die Welt*, 26 February 2003.

Kriest, Ulrich. "Der Fernsehfilm *Brandstifter.*" In *Inside Lemke: Ein Klaus Lemke Lesebuch.* Ed. Brigitte Werneburg. Cologne: Schnitt, 2006. Pp. 104–19.

Kristeva, Julia. *Desire in Language: A Semiotic Approach to Literature and Art.* Ed. Leon S. Roudiez. Trans. Thomas Gora, Alice Jardine, and Leon S. Roudiez. New York: Columbia University Press, 1980.

———. *Powers of Horror.* Trans. Leon Roudiez. New York: Columbia University Press, 1982.

Kundnani, Hans. *Utopia or Auschwitz: Germany's 1968 Generation and the Holocaust.* London: Hurst, 2009.

Landgraeber, Wolfgang. "Das Thema 'Terrorismus' in deutschen Spielfilmen 1975–1985." In *Deutschland im Herbst: Terrorismus im Film.* Eds. Petra Kraus et al. Munich: Münchner Filmzentrum,1997. Pp. 11–21.

Landsberg, Alison. *Prosthetic Memory: The Transformation of American Remembrance in the Age of Mass Culture.* New York: Columbia University Press, 2004.

Landy, Marcia. *Cinematic Uses of the Past.* Minneapolis: University of Minnesota Press, 1996.

———. *The Historical Film: History and Memory in Media.* London: Athlone, 2001.

Lane, Anthony. "Guilty Parties: *The Lives of Others.*" *The New Yorker*, 12 February 2007.

Lefebvre, Henri. *Critique of Everyday Life*. 3 vols. Trans. John Moore. London: Verso, 1991.

———. "The Everyday and Everydayness." Trans. Christine Levich. *Yale French Studies* 73 (1987): 7–11.

———. *Everyday Life in the Modern World*. Trans. Sacha Rabinovitch. New Brunswick: Transaction, 1984.

———. *The Production of Space*. Trans. Donald Nicholson-Smith. Oxford: Blackwell Publishers, 1991.

———. *Writings on Cities*. Trans. and ed. Eleonore Kofman and Elizabeth Lebas. Oxford: Blackwell, 1996.

"Lenin in Amerika." *Frankfurter Allgemeine Zeitung*, 18 March 2004.

Leo, Annette. "Keine gemeinsame Erinnerung: Geschichtsbewusstsein in Ost und West." *Aus Politik und Geschichte* 40–41 (2003): 27–32.

Leo, Maxim. "Hofmanns Erzählungen." *Frankfurter Rundschau*, 1 November 2011.

Lequeret, Elisabeth. "Printemps allemande." *Cahiers du Cinéma*, February 2006.

Lettenewitsch, Natalie, and Nadine-Carina Mang. "Helden und Gespenster: Die RAF untot auf der Leinwand." *Ästhetik & Kommunikation* 117 (2002): 29–34.

Lévy, Bernard-Henri. "Hollywood's Nazi Revisionism." Trans. Janet Lizop. *Wall Street Journal*, 6–7 March 2010.

Leyenberg, Hans-Joachim. "Im Sonderzug zurück nach Bern." *Frankfurter Allgemeine Zeitung*, 16 October 2003.

Libeskind, Daniel. *Kein Ort an dieser Stelle – Schriften zur Architektur, Visionen für Berlin, Dresden und Basel*. Dresden: Verlag der Kunst, 1995.

Liebs, Holger. "Die Söhne Stammheims." *Süddeutsche Zeitung*, 17 October 2002.

Link, Oliver. "Das Spiel ist niemals aus." *Der Stern*, 29 September 2003.

Lury, Celia. *Prosthetic Culture: Photography, Memory and Identity*. London: Routledge, 1998.

Mailer, Norman. "Footfalls in the Crypt." *Vanity Fair*, February 1992.

Manovich, Lev. *The Language of New Media*. Cambridge, MA: MIT Press, 2001.

Martenstein, Harald. "Die Rückkehr der Killer-Tomaten." *Tagesspiegel*, 16 February 2002.

McKee, Robert. *Story: Substance, Structure, Style and the Principles of Screenwriting*. London: Methuen, 1999.

Meiners, Ole. "Der Plan ist übererfüllt." *Tagesspiegel*, 26 February 2003.

Melley, Timothy. *Empire of Conspiracy: The Culture of Paranoia in Postwar America*. Ithaca, NY: Cornell University Press, 2000.

Meza, Ed. "World Cup Boosts Teuton Soccer Pic." *Variety*, 28 June 2002.

Michalsky, Oliver. "Da musste erst ein Wessi kommen?" *Die Welt*, 18 February 2003.

Mielke, André. "Der Bundestag ist auch nur ein Mensch." *Die Welt*, 4 April 2003.

Miller, Robert Milton. *Star Myths: Show-Business Biographies on Film*. Metuchen, NJ: Scarecrow, 1983.

Mitchell, Elvis. "*Good Bye, Lenin!* Restoring a Berlin Wall to Comfort Dear Old Mom." *New York Times*, 27 February 2004.

Mitscherlich, Alexander, and Margarete Mitscherlich. *The Inability to Mourn: Principles of Collective Behavior*. Trans. Beverly R. Placzek. New York: Grove Press, 1975.

Mlodinow, Leonard. *The Drunkard's Walk: How Randomness Rules Our Lives*. New York: Pantheon, 2008.

Moeller, Robert. *War Stories: The Search for a Usable Past in the Federal Republic of Germany*. Berkeley: University of California Press, 2001.

Mohr, Reinhard. "Die Prada-Meinhof-Bande." *Der Spiegel*, 25 February 2002.

———. "Stasi ohne Spreewaldgurke." *Spiegel Online*, 15 March 2006. http://www.spiegel.de/kultur/kino/0,1518,406092,00.html.

Mohr, Silke. "Good Bye, Lenin in Manhattan." *taz*, 4 March 2004.

Moltke, Johannes von. *No Place Like Home: Locations of Heimat in German Cinema*. Berkeley: University of California Press, 2005.

———. "*Terrains Vagues*: Landscapes of Unification in Oskar Roehler's *No Place to Go*." In *The Collapse of the Conventional: German Film and Its Politics at the Turn of the Twenty-First Century*. Eds. Jaimey Fisher and Brad Prager. Detroit: Wayne State University Press, 2010. Pp. 157–85.

Muller, Adam. "Notes toward a Theory of Nostalgia: Childhood and the Evocation of the Past in Two European 'Heritage' Films." *New Literary History* 37(4) (2006): 739–60.

Mulvey, Laura. *Death 24x a Second: Stillness and the Moving Image*. London: Reaktion, 2006.

Naremore, James. *More Than Night: Film Noir in its Contexts*. Berkeley: University of California Press, 1998.

Naughton, Leonie. *That was the Wild East: Film Culture, Unification, and the "New" Germany*. Ann Arbor: University of Michigan Press, 2002.

Naziri, Gérard. *Paranoia im amerikanischen Kino: Die 70er Jahre und die Folgen*. Sankt Augustin: Gardez!, 2003.

Ng, Jenna. "Love in the Time of Transcultural Fusion: Cinephilia, Homage and *Kill Bill*." In *Cinephilia: Movies, Love and Memory*. Eds. Marijke de Valck and Malte Hagener. Amsterdam: Amsterdam University Press, 2005. Pp. 65–79.

Nicodemus, Katja. "Film der neunziger Jahre. Neues Sein und altes Bewußtsein." In *Geschichte des deutschen Films*. 2nd rev. ed. Eds. Wolfgang Jacobsen, Anton Kaes, and Hans Helmut Prinzler. Weimar: Metzler, 2004. Pp. 319–56.

————. "Unsere kleine Traumfabrik." *Die Zeit*, 28 August 2003.

Niven, Bill, ed. *Germans as Victims: Remembering the Past in Contemporary Germany*. Houndmills: Palgrave Macmillan, 2006.

Nord, Cristina. "Beinahe kaberettistisch." *taz*, 18 October 2002.

————. "Die neue Naivität." *taz*, 20 October 2008.

————. "Unbedingter Wille zum Selbstbewusstsein." *taz*, 10 June 2003.

Oliver, Kelly, and Benigno Trigo. *Noir Anxiety*. Minneapolis: University of Minnesota Press, 2003.

Osang, Alexander. "Zu Gast im Party-Staat." *Der Spiegel*, 8 September 2003.

Oswalt, Phillipp. *Berlin: Stadt ohne Form*. Munich: Prestel, 2000.

Palfreyman, Rachel. "The Fourth Generation: Legacies of Violence as Quest for Identity in Post-Unification Terrorism Films." In *German Cinema: Since Unification*. Ed. David Clarke. London: Continuum, 2006. Pp. 11–42.

Parks, Stuart. *Understanding Contemporary Germany*. London: Routledge, 1997.

Pavlovic, Milan. "Ein Wunder, das noch immer Wunden heilt." *Süddeutsche Zeitung*, 6 October 2003.

Pedersen, Henrik. "RAF auf der Bühne. Inszenierung und Selbstinszenierung der deutschen Terroristen." *Trans* 9 (March 2001). http://www.inst.at/trans/9Nr/pedersen9.htm.

Peitz, Christiane. "Gefühlte Geschichte." *Tagesspiegel*, 2 February 2003.

————. "Karl und wie er die Welt sah." *Die Zeit*, 14 January 1999.

Pelzer, Jürgen. "'The Facts behind the Guilt'? Background and Implicit Intentions in *Downfall*." *German Politics and Society* 25(1) (2007): 90–101.

Peters, Günter. "Zur Baugeschichte – Drei Gründerzeiten." In *Marzahn*. Ed. Gerrit Engel. Cologne: König, 1999. Pp. 15–17.

Pflaum, H.G. "Der diskrete Charm der Ostalgie." *Süddeutsche Zeitung*, 13 February 2003.

Pipes, Daniel. *Conspiracy: How the Paranoid Style Flourishes and Where It Comes From*. New York: Free Press, 1997.

Platen, Heide. "'Baader war ein rührender Verlierer.'" *taz*, 15 February 2002.

Pleyer, Peter. *Deutscher Nachkriegsfilm 1946–1948*. Münster: Fahle, 1965.

Polan, Dana. *Power and Paranoia: History, Narrative, and the Narrative Cinema, 1940–1950*. New York: Columbia University Press, 1986.

Pratt, Ray. *Projecting Paranoia: Conspiratorial Visions in American Film*. Lawrence: University Press of Kansas, 2001.

Preece, Julian. "Between Identification and Documentation, 'Autofiction' and 'Biopic': The Lives of the *RAF*." *German Life and Letters* 56(4) (2003): 363–76.

Proll, Astrid, ed. *Hans und Grete: Bilder der RAF 1967–1977*. Berlin: Aufbau, 2004.

Rabinowitz, Paula. *Black & White & Noir: America's Pulp Modernism.* New York: Columbia University Press, 2002.

Rada, Uwe. *Hauptstadt der Verdrängung – Berliner Zukunft zwischen Kiez und Metropole.* Berlin: Schwarze Risse, 1997.

Rebhandl, Bert. *Orson Welles: Genie im Labyrinth.* Vienna: Zsolnay, 2005.

Reicher, Isabella. "Es muss auf die Fresse geben." *Der Standard,* 3 December 2002.

Reinecke, Stefan. "Einsamkeitshelden unter sich." *taz,* 18 October 2002.

———. "Keine Stille nach dem Schuss: Terrorismus im deutschen Film." *Filmportal.de,* http://www.filmportal.de/df/7e/Artikel,,,,,, ,FC5331E6248E2C3EE03053D50B376058,,,,,,,,,,,,,,,,,,,,,.html.

———. "Verrückte Märchen, Gespenster aus der Vergangenheit: 25 Jahre Deutscher Herbst und das Kino." *epd Film* 19(10) (2002): 18–23.

"Rein zufällig," *Frankfurter Rundschau,* 29 October 2002.

Rentschler, Eric. "American Friends and New German Cinema: Patterns of Reception." *New German Critique* 24–25 (1981–1982): 7–35.

———. "From New German Cinema to the Post-Wall Cinema of Consensus." In *Cinema and Nation.* Eds. Mette Hjort and Scott MacKenzie. London: Routledge, 2000. Pp. 260–77.

———, ed. *German Film and Literature: Adaptations and Transformations.* New York: Methuen, 1986.

———. *The Ministry of Illusion: Nazi Cinema and Its Afterlife.* Cambridge, MA: Harvard University Press, 1996.

———. "Remembering Not to Forget: A Retrospective Reading of Kluge's *Brutality on Stone.*" *New German Critique* 49 (1990): 23–41.

Richardson, Michael D. "A World of Objects: Consumer Culture in Filmic Reconstructions of the GDR." In *The Collapse of the Conventional: German Film and Its Politics at the Turn of the Twenty-First Century.* Eds. Jaimey Fisher and Brad Prager. Detroit: Wayne State University Press, 2010. Pp. 216–23.

Rodek, Hanns-Georg. "Danke, Lenin!" *Die Welt,* 21 February 2003.

———. "Das Leben der Anderen geht ins Oscar-Rennen." *Die Welt,* 23 January 2007.

———. "Verfilmt den RAF-Terroristen Baader als Popstar: Christopher Roth." *Die Welt,* 18 October 2002.

Roehler, Oskar. "Schöne Seelen." *Die Zeit,* 2 June 2005.

Roth, Christopher. "Der Stil des Terrorismus." *Süddeutsche Zeitung,* 17 March 2001.

Roth, Wolfgang. "Das stille Einverständnis mit dem Terror." *Süddeutsche Zeitung,* 5–6 April 2007.

Ruoff, Alexander. "Die Renaissance des Historismus in der Populärkultur: Über den Kinofilm *Der Untergang.*" In *Filmriss: Studien über Der Untergang.* Ed. Willi Bischof. Münster: Unrast, 2005. Pp. 69–78.

Rusch, Claudia. *Meine freie deutsche Jugend.* Frankfurt: Fischer, 2004.

Rutschky, Michael. *Erfahrungshunger: Ein Essay über die siebziger Jahre.* Frankfurt: Fischer, 1982.

Sabatini, Arthur J. "Terrorismus und Performance." *Kunstforum International* 117 (1992): 147–51.

Saunders, Anna. "'Normalizing' the Past: East German Culture and Ostalgie." In *German Culture, Politics, and Literature into the Twenty-First Century.* Eds. Stuart Taberner and Paul Cooke. Rochester, NY: Camden House, 2006. Pp. 89–103.

Sayre, Nora. "Winning the Weepstakes: The Problems of American Sports Movies." In *Film Genre: Theory and Criticism.* Ed. Barry K. Grant. Metuchen, NJ: Scarecrow, 1977. Pp. 182–94.

Schirmer, Lothar. *Das Wunder in Bildern. Bern 1954. Deutschland – Ungarn 3:2. 73 Reportagephotographien vom Endspiel.* Munich: Schirmer/Mosel, 2004.

Schmitz, Helmut. "The Birth of the Collective from the Spirit of Empathy: From the 'Historians' Dispute' to German Suffering." In *Germans as Victims: Remembering the Past in Contemporary Germany.* Ed. Bill Niven. Houndmills: Palgrave Macmillan, 2006. Pp. 93–108.

Schrader, Paul. "Notes on Film Noir." In *The Film Noir Reader.* Eds. Alain Silver and James Ursini. Pompton Plains, NJ: Limelight, 1996. Pp. 53–63.

"Schriftstellerleben verramscht." *Der Spiegel,* 15 June 1992, 216.

Schulz-Ojala, Jan. "Beckers Bester." *Tagesspiegel,* 20 April 2003.

———. "Die große Illusion." *Tagesspiegel,* 9 February 2003.

———. "Kleinbürger, überlebensgroß." *Tagesspiegel,* 17 October 2002.

———. "Wir Wunderkinder." *Tagesspiegel,* 14 January 1999.

Schulze, Gerhard. *Die Erlebnisgesellschaft: Kultursoziologie der Gegenwart.* Frankfurt: Campus, 1992.

Schwartz, Claudia. "Die persönliche Biographie lenkt den Blick." *Neue Zürchner Zeitung,* 21 February 2003.

Schweiger, Marc. "Die Ordnungsmacht des Alltags." *Die Welt am Sonntag,* 16 March 2003.

Schweizerhof, Barbara. "Überblendung." *Freitag,* 18 October 2002.

Schwilk, Heimo, and Ulrich Schacht, eds. *Die selbstbewußte Nation: "Anschwellender Bocksgesang" und weitere Beiträge zu einer deutschen Debatte.* 3rd rev. ed. Frankfurt: Ullstein, 1995.

Sedgwick, Eve. *Between Men: English Literature and Male Homosocial Desire.* New York: Columbia University Press, 1985.

Seibel, Alexandra, and Christian Höller. "Was tun…? Inszenierungsformen des Politischen im aktuellen Spielfilm." *Kolik. film* 3 (2005): 6–14.

Sennhauser, Michael. "Hacken in der Eiszeit." *Neue Zürcher Zeitung,* 29 January 1999.

Shandley, Robert R. *Rubble Films: German Cinema in the Shadows of the Third Reich.* Philadelphia: Temple University Press, 2001.

Shea, Robert, and Robert Anton Wilson. *The Illuminatus! Trilogy.* London: Raven, 1998.

Shusterman, Richard. "Ästhetik der Abwesenheit: Der Wert der Leere, Pragmatische Überlegungen zu Berlin." *Lettre International* 43 (1998): 30–35.

Sieglohr, Ulrike. "Hildegard Knef: From Rubble Woman to Fallen Woman." In *Heroines without Heroines: Reconstructing Female and National Identities in European Cinema, 1945–1951.* Ed. Ulrike Sieglohr. London: Cassell, 2000. Pp. 113–27.

Siemes, Christof. *Das Wunder von Bern.* Cologne: Kiepenhauer & Witsch, 2003.

Silberman, Marc. "European Cinema in the 90s: Whither Germany?" In *Schreiben nach der Wende. Ein Jahrzehnt deutscher Literatur 1989–1999.* Eds. Gerhard Fischer and David Roberts. Tübingen: Stauffenberg, 2001. Pp. 317–30.

Simmel, Georg. "Bridge and Door." Trans. Mark Ritter. *Theory, Culture and Society* 11 (1994): 5–10.

Sklar, Robert. "The Baader Meinhof Complex." *Cineaste* 34(4) (2009): 42–44.

Sobchack, Vivian. " … Baseball in the Post-American Cinema, or Life in the Minor Leagues." In *Out of Bounds: Sports, Media, and the Politics of Identity.* Eds. Aaron Baker and Todd Boyd. Bloomington: Indiana University Press, 1997. Pp. 175–97.

———. "Introduction: History Happens." In *The Persistence of History: Cinema, Television, and the Modern Event.* Ed. Vivian Sobchack. New York: Routledge, 1996. Pp. 1–16.

Solà-Morales Rubió, Ignasi. "Terrain Vague." In *Anyplace.* Ed. Cynthia Davidson. New York: Anyone, 1995. Pp. 118–23.

Solms, Wilhelm, ed. *Begrenzt glücklich: Kindheit in der DDR.* Marburg: Hitzeroth, 2002.

Stam, Robert. *Reflexivity in Film and Literature: From Don Quixote to Jean-Luc Godard.* New York: Columbia University Press, 1985.

———, Robert Burgoyne, and Sandy Flitterman-Lewis. *New Vocabularies in Film Semiotics: Structuralism, Poststructuralism and Beyond.* London: Routledge, 1992.

Staud, Toralf. "Ossis sind Türken." *Die Zeit,* 2 October 2003.

Stein, Mary Beth. "*Stasi* with a Human Face? Ambiguity in *Das Leben der Anderen.*" *German Studies Review* 31(3) (2008): 567–79.

Steiner, Frederik. *Stepping Out. Von der Filmhochschule zum Spielfilm. Junge Regisseure erzählen.* Marburg: Schüren, 2003.

Sterneborg, Anke. "Ein Jahr danach," *epd Film* 21(6) (2004): 52.

Stolz, Matthias. "Ein Wiedersehen mit der DDR." *Frankfurter Allgemeine Zeitung,* 29 October 2001.

Strunz, Dieter. "Der Tod des Hacker-Königs." *Berliner Morgenpost,* 14 January 1999.

Taylor, Henry M. *Rolle des Lebens: Die Filmbiographie als narratives System.* Marburg: Schüren, 2002.

Tetzlaff, Michael. *Ostblöckchen: Neues aus der Zone.* Frankfurt: Schöffling, 2004.

Thomsen, Jan. "Ein Kino-Besuch voller Missverständnisse." *Berliner Zeitung,* 3 April 2003.

Töteberg, Michael, ed. *Good Bye, Lenin!* Berlin: Schwarzkopf & Schwarzkopf, 2003.

―――, ed. *Szenenwechsel. Momentanaufnahmen des jungen deutschen Films.* Reinbek bei Hamburg: Rowohlt, 1999.

Tschiedert, Markus. "Bitte einmal ohrfeigen." *Hamburger Abendblatt,* 13 February 2003.

Ulrich, Franz, and Dominik Slappnig. "Hast 'ne Idee? Gespräch mit Wolfgang Becker." *Zoom: Zeitschrift für Film,* September 1993.

Veblen, Thorstein. *The Theory of the Leisure Class: An Economic Study in the Evolution of Institutions.* New York: Mentor, 1899.

Vernet, Marc. "Film Noir on the Edge of Doom." In *Shades of Noir.* Ed. Joan Copjec. London: Verso, 1993. Pp. 1–31.

Vidler, Anthony. "The Architecture of the Uncanny: The Unhomely Houses of the Romantic Sublime." *Assemblage* 3 (1987): 6–29.

Vincendeau, Ginette, ed. *Film/Literature/Heritage: A Sight and Sound Reader.* London: British Film Institute, 2001.

―――. *Jean-Pierre Melville: An American in Paris.* London: British Film Institute, 2003.

Virilio, Paul. "The Overexposed City." In *Lost Dimension.* Trans. Daniel Moshenberg. New York: Semiotext(e), 1991. Pp. 9–27.

―――. *War and Cinema. The Logistics of Perception.* Trans. Patrick Camiller. London: Verso, 1989.

Walter, Fritz. *Der Chef – Sepp Herberger.* Munich: Copress, 1964.

―――. *3:2: Das Spiel ist aus! Deutschland ist Weltmeister!* Munich: Copress, 2004.

Wedel, Mathias. *Einheitsfrust.* Berlin: Rowohlt, 1994.

Werber, Niels. "Die Prada-Meinhof-Bande." *Literaturen* 12 (2001): 28–31.

Werneburg, Brigitte, ed. *Inside Lemke: Ein Klaus Lemke Lesebuch.* Cologne: Schnitt, 2006.

"Westfrauen entdecken den Ostmann." *MDR.de,* 9 November 2004. http://www.mdr.de/umschau/1679747.html.

Westphal, Anke. "Den Ossi an sich gab es nicht." *Berliner Zeitung,* 13 February 2003.

―――. "Was unterging, taucht nicht mehr auf."*Berliner Zeitung,* 8 February 2003.

White, Hayden. "The Modernist Event." In *The Persistence of History: Cinema, Television, and the Modern Event.* Ed. Vivian Sobchack. New York: Routledge, 1996. Pp. 17–38.

Willeman, Paul. "Through a Glass Darkly: Cinephilia Reconsidered." In *Looks and Frictions: Essays in Cultural Studies and Film Theory*. London: British Film Institute, 1994. Pp. 223–57.

Williams, Linda. "Film Bodies: Gender, Genre, and Excess." *Film Quarterly* 44(4) (1991): 2–13.

Wilson, Elizabeth. *Adorned in Dreams: Fashion and Modernity*. London: Virago, 1985.

Wollen, Peter. "Godard and Counter-Cinema: *Vent d'Est*." In *Narrative, Apparatus, Ideology*. Ed. Philip Rosen. New York: Columbia University Press, 1986. Pp. 120–29.

Worthmann, Merten. "Ich bin schuld an Tschernobyl." *Berliner Zeitung*, 14 January 1999.

Zohlen, Gerwin. *Auf der Suche nach der verlorenen Stadt: Berliner Architektur am Ende des 20. Jahrhunderts*. Berlin: Nicolai, 2002.

Zöllner, Abini. *Schokoladenkind: meine Familie und andere Wunder*. Reinbek bei Hamburg: Rowohlt, 2003.

INDEX